Praise for *Love and Literacy*

"If you believe—as I do—that understanding literature is not a destination but rather a lifelong journey, this book will resonate deeply. Along with practical protocols for supporting young readers on the path to comprehension, the authors offer a model curriculum that 'whispers what the world is and what it might become.' Pedagogy by readers for readers."

—Carol Jago is a longtime English teacher and past president of the National Council of Teachers of English. She is the author of many books for teachers including *The Book in Question: Why and How Reading Is in Crisis*.

"What's not to love? A resource for encouraging students to engage in productive conversations about texts? This highly readable and practical guide shows you how to make this a reality in your classroom."

—Douglas Fisher & Nancy Frey, San Diego State University

"*Love and Literacy* gives teachers accessible, practical guidance they may be hard-pressed to find elsewhere. The authors explain how educators can ensure students have the background knowledge they need to understand complex literature without simultaneously depriving them of the opportunity for 'productive struggle'—one of the trickiest of all pedagogical balancing acts."

—Natalie Wexler, author of *The Knowledge Gap: The Hidden Cause of America's Broken Education System—and How to Fix It*, and coauthor of *The Writing Revolution: A Guide to Advancing Thinking Through Writing in All Subjects and Grades*

"One of the most powerful reminders in *Love and Literacy* is 'Text is claim: the heart of any writing is the statement it makes.' Bambrick-Santoyo and Chiger begin by speaking persuasively of the claims that teachers and schools make by simply choosing one text over another, arguing that we must try to be inclusive and wide-ranging in designing our literacy curriculum so that all voices may be heard. They then examine teaching practices, to help us think about how we might encourage readers to examine the claims they find in the texts they read, so that they might become the more responsible citizens our democracy so desperately needs."

—Robert E. Probst, Professor Emeritus of English Education, Georgia State University

"This book is about many things, but centrally it's about operationalizing the latest cognitive science to promote active and informed teaching, at the point of learner need and struggle, to help learners grow as readers of literature. This text is a gift that will help you to consciously use many powerful tools of guided inquiry to get more done, and to do it with more efficiency, engagement, and joy."

—Jeffrey D. Wilhelm, Distinguished Professor of
Literacy at Boise State University,
Author of *Planning Powerful Instruction*

"I could not put down this book once I started reading it. This book gives a road map to school leaders and teachers on how to ignite the love of reading for *all* students. It makes the invisible work of teaching reading into actionable and visible strategies. For too long, it has seemed like a mystery on how to create lifelong readers—this book provides the answers."

—Celeste Douglas, Community Superintendent,
District 18, Brooklyn, New York

"For teachers who want to get their students to love reading, this book has the solution. *Love and Literacy* teaches you literacy learning strategies, gives you space to reflect on your practice, and coaches you with written and visual examples. It truly expands and diversifies your thinking about how to approach literacy instruction. If you are preparing secondary English teachers, this book should be on your syllabus."

—Ayanna Taylor, Clinical Assistant Professor of English Education,
NYU Steinhardt

"If people 'fall in love with what they know how to do,' then educators will fall deeply in love with reading instruction once armed with the strategies in *Love and Literacy*. I have long been a fan of Paul's work because of his keen ability to demystify what works in schools by making successful strategies accessible to all of us. Together with literacy expert Steve Chiger, they have managed to pull back the wizard's curtain of reading instruction and show us that, in fact, we can teach reading to secondary students if we just learn, name, and practice the right moves."

—Jenn David-Lang, Editor, THE MAIN IDEA

"This book is a love story. It's about the love of literature and literacy to be sure but even more it's about loving our students as learners. It's about recognizing their potential and being committed to doing all that we can to help them realize it. But it does more than provide a powerful call about how things could be. It is filled with ideas about how to make it so."

—Michael W. Smith, Professor, Department of Teaching & Learning, College of Education and Human Development, Temple University

"In our best English classrooms, the flywheels of love and literacy seem to spin effortlessly. In this book, the writers break down incrementally the steps educators can take to set those wheels in motion. The aim is clear: that all our children understand themselves and the world more keenly through the diverse literature they study and the rigour with which they study it. And more: that for them, literacy becomes 'a way of happening, a mouth.'"

—Mark Gregory, Regional Director, Ark Schools, UK

"Students come to love the texts they read when they have had a meaningful interaction with significant ideas. The authors of *Love and Literacy* challenge educators to create those meaningful interactions through an examination of their own core beliefs about pedagogy and literature."

—Allan A. De Fina, PhD, Professor of Literacy Education and former Dean of the College of Education, New Jersey City University

"Bambrick-Santoyo partners with Stephen Chiger to do what he does best: create a compelling vision of instructional excellence (complete with videos!) and deliver the practical tools to bring it to life. *Love and Literacy* is a must read for any secondary educator who is committed to building a literacy program grounded in research, relevance, and—most importantly—love."

—Leah Peters, Vice President of Academics, DSST Public Schools

"Bambrick-Santoyo's work has truly impacted my leadership. The work of school transformation is messy and tough to manipulate, but books like *Love and Literacy* give clear, actionable steps that I can use immediately. The vision of what is possible in reading is most compelling and for that I'm most grateful."

—Anetra Cheatham, Chief Innovation Officer, Beaumont ISD

"*Love & Literacy* is a jam-packed toolbox of instructional moves and models that is not just about tricks to get students to read and understand a text. It's a practical guide to reshape the academic culture within your literacy classroom in ways that transform students into lasting, lifelong lovers of literature with a reverence for the power of the words of others and their own voice."

—Michael Bateman, Instructional Leader (Denver, CO)

LOVE & LITERACY

A Practical Guide for Grades 5–12 to
Finding the Magic in Literature

LOVE & LITERACY

A Practical Guide for Grades 5–12 to Finding the Magic in Literature

Paul Bambrick-Santoyo
Stephen Chiger

JB JOSSEY-BASS™
A Wiley Brand

Jossey-Bass
A Wiley Imprint
111 River St, Hoboken, NJ 07030
www.josseybass.com

Jossey-Bass books and products are available through most bookstores. To contact Jossey-Bass directly, call our Customer Care Department within the U.S. at 800 -956 -7739, outside the U.S. at +1 317 572 3986, or fax +1 317 572 4002.

Wiley also publishes its books in a variety of electronic formats and by print-on-demand. Some material included with standard print versions of this book may not be included in e-books or in print-on-demand. If this book refers to media such as a CD or DVD that is not included in the version you purchased, you may download this material at http://booksupport.wiley.com. For more information about Wiley products, visit www.wiley.com.

Library of Congress Cataloging-in-Publication Data is Available:
ISBN 978-111-9751-656 (Paperback)
ISBN 978-111-9751-670 (ePDF)
ISBN 978-111-9751-663 (ePub)

Cover Design: Wiley
Cover Image: © David Malan/Getty Images

SKY10026168_041621

"*The good life is inspired by love and guided by knowledge. . . . Neither love without knowledge nor knowledge without love can produce a good life.*"
—*Bertrand Russell*

"*We die. That may be the meaning of life.
But we do language. That may be the measure of our lives.*"
—*Toni Morrison*

Contents

Online Content

HOW TO ACCESS

This book is supplemented with videos and print-ready materials. Visit the link for additional content, found at http://www.wiley.com/go/lal. The password is the first word of the introduction, "students." (Only fitting as they are the reason for this book!)

PRINT-READY MATERIALS

These resources are included in the online *Reading and Writing Handbook:*

Resource	Description
Resources for Curriculum Complexity	Guiding questions to build a complexity curriculum and a sample book list. • Text Selection Criteria • Sample Books List, Grades 5–12
Resources for Reading and Analyzing Texts	Key handouts to support reading for meaning. • Claim: Reading and Annotating Non-Narrative Text • Theme: Reading and Annotating Narrative Text • Poetry: Reading and Annotating Language and Structure • Analyzing Author's Craft: MR. CUF

Resource	Description
Resources for Writing About Texts	Key handouts to support writing about fiction and nonfiction. • Writing Literary Analysis: NEZZ • Writing Non-Literary Analysis: NEZZ • Writing Conference Guidance
Resources for Monitoring Student Work	Strategies to maximize instruction during student work time. • Sample Seating Charts for Monitoring • Guidance for Classroom Monitoring • Sample Monitoring Key • Guidance for Feedback During Monitoring
Resources for Planning and Facilitating Discourse	Compilation of the habits of discourse and handouts to plan and assess student discourse. • Habits of Discourse 101: Create Conversation • Habits of Discourse 201: Deepen Discourse • Academic Discourse Rubric • Discourse Planning Template • Discourse Planning Example • Literary Discourse: One-Pager • Literacy Discourse: One-Pager with Remote Teaching Adaptations
Resources to Build Classroom Culture	Useful handouts to plan for moments of celebration and design a classroom space that instructs and inspires. • Ideas for Whole-School Peak Literacy Moments • Classroom Signage That Teaches • Classroom Signage Gallery
Resources for Self-Assessment	Self-assessment tool to determine the state of literacy in your classroom. • *Love and Literacy* Implementation Rubric • *Love and Literacy* Rubric Areas, Organized by Priority

Resource	Description
Resources for Planning and Rollout	Key handouts for rollout: tips, templates and sample lesson plans. • Classroom Habits Rollout Guidance • Classroom Habits Planning Template • Sample Rollout Plan: Independent Practice • Sample Rollout Plan: Independent Practice and Reading for Claim • Weekly Implementation Rollout Template • Yearly Implementation Rollout Template • Sample Rollout Script: Monitor Independent Practice Expectations • Sample Rollout Script: Reading for Claim • Sample Rollout Script: Revoice

VIDEOS

Introduction

Clip	Technique	Description	Where Referenced in the Book
1	Student-led Discourse	**". . .Do you think she's giving in to her sexual desire? Or is it that she is really oppressed?"** Beth Verrilli's students debate Offred's autonomy in *The Handmaid's Tale*.	p. 1

What's My Dream for Kids? (Part 1)

Clip	Technique	Description	Where Referenced in the Book
2	Zoom In—Middle School	**". . .Why would she choose the color red?"** Allison Metz's students seek meaning in color imagery by unpacking language.	p. 85

Clip	Technique	Description	Where Referenced in the Book
3	Zoom In/Out— High School	**". . .he takes his uncle's gun and puts it inside of his pants, which is a replacement of his phallus."** Mike Taubman's students analyze phallocentrism by investigating word choice and an author's purpose.	p. 88
4	Zoom In/Out— Middle School	**". . .Why is Rich using this diction?"** Vy Graham's students unpack poetic language using replicable, discrete steps.	p. 89
5	Zoom In—Student Writing	**". . .'should' indicates that you have a choice, but 'must' means that you don't."** Danny Murray's students apply what they know about analysis to give feedback to a peer's writing.	p. 90

What Will I See When Students "Get It"? (Part 2)

Clip	Technique	Description	Where Referenced in the Book
6	What-to-Do Directions	**". . .You have two passages to read and a prompt at the bottom."** Julia Dutcher sets students up for independent practice with clear, precise instructions.	p. 132
7	Monitoring— Go Lap by Lap	**". . .I'm coming around to look for. . ."** Nina Blalock monitors student work by announcing precise points of focus as she goes.	p. 137
8	Build Meaning Through Discourse	**". . .Turn to you partner. Whose response is stronger and why?"** Angela Thomas bridges a comprehension gap she uncovered while monitoring.	p. 141

What Will I Hear When Students "Get It"? (Part 3)

Clip	Technique	Description	Where Referenced in the Book
9	Frontload Background Knowledge	**". . .In seventh grade, you studied poetry. So how do poets utilize structure to communicate their meaning?"** Michelle Wallace activates prior knowledge by linking learning across years.	p. 160
10	Frontload Background Knowledge	**". . .What kinds of language and structure do we need to look for when we read poetry?"** Hadley Westman activates background knowledge to launch her lesson.	p. 160
11	Drop Knowledge	**". . .The first time you'd open [the books] and read them, you had to cut open the pages. How does this add to the evidence?"** Sarah Schrag introduces new knowledge to complicate analysis.	p. 162
12	Connect to Strategy	**". . .Think back. How did we know that the pearl was a symbol?"** Vy Graham activates strategy knowledge to clarify confusion.	p. 162
13	Connect to Background Knowledge	**". . .When we read bell hooks's reading. . ."** Rilwan, a student, enriches analytical discourse by linking it to outside scholarship.	p. 163
14	Start with a Broad, High-Rigor Question	**". . .What does Douglass want his audience to feel and how is he creating that feeling?"** Vy Graham invites students to lead analysis by launching with a broad, rigorous prompt.	p. 167

Clip	Technique	Description	Where Referenced in the Book
15	Leverage Universal Prompts	**". . .Build on that."** Matthew McCluskey minimizes teacher talk with short, specific prompts.	p. 173
16	Habits of Discourse 101—Create Conversation	**". . .Jahne, you go first."** Eric Diamon's students use the habits of discourse to foster conversation.	p. 178
17	Habits of Discourse 201—Revoice	**". . .Bangale is saying [x]. Am I interpreting what you're saying correctly, Bangale?"** Danny Murray's students revoice each other's ideas to advance discourse and check their own understanding.	p. 182
18	Habits of Discourse 201—Problematize	**". . .I'd like to play devil's advocate."** Danny Murray and his student John invigorate discourse by posing alternative interpretations.	p. 185
19	Habits of Discourse 201—Sophisticate (Zoom In and Out)	**". . .So what's [the author] trying to connect here?"** Hadley Westman guides students toward greater complexity by prompting students to analyze word choice.	p. 188
20	Habits of Discourse 201—Sophisticate (Narrow the Focus)	**". . .Go back to somewhere between 45 and 48 and see if you see anything that complicates that picture."** Sarah Schrag directs attention toward a pivotal section of the text without tipping her hand.	p. 189
21	Stamp the Learning	**". . .Can you tell us what our key learning is here?"** Matthew McCluskey asks students to underscore what's most important in the day's lesson.	p. 192

How Do I Build It? (Part 4)

Clip	Technique	Description	Where Referenced in the Book
22	Savor the Text	**". . .We just read a really intense part of the text. [Let's] stop for a second and enjoy that moment."** Reggie McCrimmon reads aloud to help his students experience the power and joy of language.	p. 226
23	Make It Personal	**". . .If you were living during this time. . .where would you have landed?"** Julie Miller's students pick sides in a historical debate.	p. 227
24	Roll Out a Habit	**". . .When we talk about poetry and speak about a narrator, we always refer to the narrator as the speaker."** Vy Graham rolls out a new habit to reinforce precision in language.	p. 249

Acknowledgments

It all began with a brief interaction at the end of a workshop—and a lasting impression of the desire to serve students better. That began a more than decade-long journey that included countless hours of teaching, observing, coaching, and learning.

Love & Literacy is the latest destination, and it hums with the voices of the teachers and leaders who have traveled with us on this path—those who encouraged us, those who challenged us, and everyone in between.

First and foremost, we want to thank Beth Verrilli, whose example and mentorship were a beacon for this work. Alongside Beth stands an army of literacy leaders we've had the privilege to work with and learn from. At a curriculum level, we'd like to thank the visionary leaders who helped develop and drive this work across so many classrooms: Christine Algozo, Liz Anderson, Kelly Dowling, Christy Lundy, Sarah Nager, Erin Michels, Amy Parsons, and Kathryn Perkins. Shoulder to shoulder stands a list of teachers whose names would stretch for pages. We'd like to highlight a few who have invited us into their classrooms to learn and coach, whose videos appear not only in this book but whose work lives on in all our trainings: Maja Almquist, Maya Bhattacharjee, Nina Blalock, Melika Butcher, Eric Diamon, Erin Dillane, Aisha Douglas, Julia Dutcher, Megan Fernando, Beth Garcia, Sean Gavin, Grace Ghazzawi, Rebecca Lord Gomez, Vy Graham, Mallory Grossman, Nikki Jones, Alonte Johnson, Hailey Karcher, Ashley LaGrassa, Amy Lehrian, Lee Marcus, Matthew McCluskey, Reggie McCrimmon, Allison Metz, Julie Miller, Danny Murray, Laura Palumbo, MK Pope, Gentaro Ramadhan, Rue Ratray, Sean Reap, Courtney Richardson, Zachary Roach, Sarah Schrag, Mike Taubman, Gabriela Tejedor, Angela Thomas, Alex Toole, Michelle Wallace, Hadley Westman, and Ulrica White. That list should include the wonderful

Taylor Martin and Lauren Isabel, who coordinate and coach teacher filming across our organization. Added to these names are the scores of lesson planners who turned these ideas into a rich middle and high school experience. Each one of you dramatically shaped our thinking about what was possible for a literacy program—not just because you believed in a dream, but because you had the skill and commitment to make it a reality.

We would also like to thank every teacher, professor, mentor, friend, and family member who pushed or nurtured us. It's an admittedly long list, and we are both the better for it.

We owe an unpayable debt of gratitude to Doug Lemov, Erica Woolway, Colleen Driggs, and the whole Teach Like a Champion team—a group of educators who have pushed the national conversation around literacy, pedagogy, and coaching in ways that have inspired an entire generation of teachers. It's an honor to call you colleagues and partners in this work.

Morayo Faleyimu and Aly Ross were the truest of writing partners. They organized ideas, trimmed sesquipedalian passages, and shaped our drafts until they gleamed like polished stones. Your partnership made writing this text a complete joy.

Paul would like to thank his family: Gaby (25 years of love and counting), Ana (our sunshine), Maria (our rock), and Nico (our joy). From reading together everything from *The Lion, The Witch and the Wardrobe* to *The Hunger Games* to *Stamped from the Beginning*, books have brought us closer together and allowed use to share the story of our lives. Keep reading—and teaching us how to live.

Steve would like to thank his parents, who taught him the magic of reading and raised him to seek the wonder in this world. He also sends limitless gratitude to his wife Charell, the love of his life. As a child, she saw herself in *Julie of the Wolves* and it helped her find her path: one that somehow led to a bespectacled literacy nerd who never knew his days could feel so full. May this book help others find their way, too.

Many thanks to our Wiley editors, Kezia Endsley, Amy Fandrei, Pete Gaughan, and Donna J. Weinson, who helped shepherd this book from draft to reality. Thanks to those who gave feedback to all or part of this draft: Liz Anderson, Charell Chiger, Meg Donhauser, Kim Marshall, Laura McKay, Amy Parsons, Kathryn Perkins, Jennifer Serravallo, Maria Smith, and Hadley Westman. This book is so much better for your support.

We appreciate the thoughtful leadership of Brett Peiser, Julie Jackson, and Michael Ambriz, who supported and encouraged this work; Juliana Worrell, whose expertise and passion for literacy drive so much of the work at our schools; and our team of incredible school leaders, people whose commitment to literacy has allowed their schools to become places where kids can fall in love with reading.

Finally, we'd like to close by thanking the ultimate heroes of this book: every English teacher we've worked with over the years. In the words of poet Antonio Machado, "We make the road by walking it." Thank you for carving this road for our students. It leads, as you've taught us, to someplace truly beautiful.

About the Authors

Paul Bambrick-Santoyo is the founder and dean of the Leverage Leadership Institute, creating proof points of excellence in urban schools worldwide, as well as Chief Schools Officer for Uncommon Schools. Author of multiple books, including *Great Habits, Great Readers; Driven by Data 2.0; Leverage Leadership 2.0; Get Better Faster;* and *A Principal Manager's Guide to Leverage Leadership 2.0,* Bambrick-Santoyo has trained over 30,000 school leaders worldwide in instructional leadership, including at multiple schools that have gone on to become the highest-gaining or highest-achieving schools in their districts, states, and/or countries. Prior to these roles, Bambrick-Santoyo cofounded the Relay National Principal Academy Fellowship and led North Star Academies in Newark, New Jersey, whose academic results rank among the highest in urban schools in the nation.

    Stephen Chiger is a director of literacy for Uncommon Schools. Combined with his work with the Relay Graduate School of Education and Uncommon's Impact program, he has trained thousands of educators in literacy instruction. Chiger taught high school English and journalism for more than a decade in New Jersey. He served as president of the Garden State Scholastic Press Association and was named 2015 Educator of the Year by the New Jersey Council of Teachers of English. As a literacy director, Chiger led Uncommon's Newark middle and high schools to out-perform their non–economically disadvantaged counterparts on state and national assessments. He holds a B.A. in English from Lafayette College, an M.S.J. in journalism from Northwestern University, and an Ed.M. in Educational Leadership from Columbia University. He can be found online at stevechiger.com.

About Uncommon Schools

At Uncommon Schools, our mission is to start and manage outstanding urban public schools that close the achievement gap and prepare students from low-income communities to graduate from college. For twenty years, through trial, error, and adjustment, we have learned countless lessons about what works in classrooms. Not surprisingly, we have found that success in the classroom is closely linked to our ability to hire, develop, and retain great teachers and leaders. That has prompted us to invest heavily in training educators and building systems that help leaders to lead, teachers to teach, and students to learn. We are passionate about finding new ways for our scholars to learn more today than they did yesterday, and to do so, we work hard to ensure that every minute matters.

We know that many educators, schools, and school systems are interested in the same things we are interested in—practical solutions for classrooms and schools that work, that can be performed at scale, and that are accessible to anyone. We are fortunate to have had the opportunity to observe and learn from outstanding educators—both within our schools and from across the United States—who help all students achieve at high levels. Watching these educators at work has allowed us to identify, codify, and film concrete and practical findings about great instruction. We have been excited to share these findings in such books as *Driven by Data, Leverage Leadership, Great Habits, Great Readers, Teach Like a Champion* (and the companion *Field Guide*), and *Practice Perfect*.

We thank Paul Bambrick-Santoyo and Stephen Chiger for their tireless and insightful efforts to support teachers everywhere with strong, practical insights like those found in *Love and Literacy*. We hope our efforts to share what we have learned will help you, your students, and our collective communities.

Brett Peiser
Chief Executive Officer
Uncommon Schools

Uncommon Schools is a nonprofit network of 57 urban public charter schools that prepare more than 22,000 K–12 students in New York, New Jersey, and Massachusetts to graduate from college. A CREDO study found that for low-income students who attend Uncommon Schools, Uncommon "completely cancel[s] out the negative effect associated with being a student in poverty." Uncommon Schools was also named the winner of the national Broad Prize for Public Charter Schools for demonstrating "the most outstanding overall student performance and improvement in the nation in recent years while reducing achievement gaps for low-income students and students of color." To learn more about how Uncommon Schools is changing history, please visit us at uncommonschools.org.

LOVE & LITERACY

A Practical Guide for Grades 5–12 to
Finding the Magic in Literature

Introduction: The Call to Love

Students in Beth Verrilli's 12th-grade English class are engaged in a passionate debate. They're discussing Margaret Atwood's *The Handmaid's Tale*, a dystopian novel in which a religious faction has overthrown the US government and stripped women of their rights. In this scene, Offred, the female protagonist, has been taken to a secret party by a character called "the Commander." Here is a video of the class discussion:

WATCH Clip 1: Beth Verrilli—Students Discuss *The Handmaid's Tale*

http://www.wiley.com/go/lal

The dialogue is transcribed below. What do you notice about the way students speak about *The Handmaid's Tale*? (The transcript has been edited for clarity and brevity.)

Sample Class Discussion

The Handmaid's Tale

Nathalia: A lesson that society needs to learn is that there is a power struggle between male and female, as we can see through Offred and the Commander, or the Commander and Serena Joy. Society, like the other group was saying, is reflected in this, and the women need to have a voice and need to stand up.

Steve: I want to disagree with that point, looking at Hammer's last paragraph. There's a circle of passivity and helplessness. I don't think there is a power struggle. Women accept this inferior role in society and give in to the sexual desires of men. . . If we look on page 171, it shows how despite the fact [Offred] had a bandaged mouth and blind eyes and had to rub off the makeup, she liked it, she liked getting dressed up. She *liked* having a man choose her outfit and take her to such a place where her body was on display. . . .

Layla: I don't agree. I don't think this part goes with what you're saying. Don't you think that the only reason that she liked it is that she didn't have it [getting dressed up, wearing makeup] in such a long time? She's restricted to wearing that white hat on her head.

Jamie: I would argue that—no. Before Gilead, before [Offred] was married to Luke, she was Luke's mistress. . . .

Nathalia: I disagree with that. What about the passage when she's having sex with the commander? Do you think she's giving in to her sexual desire? Or is it that she really is oppressed? She said she had to fake it. . .

Steve: I don't think there is sexual desire here. There is a task that society has given her, and she has to do it. She's following the rules of the authority, and the authority in this society is the dominant gender. What I was getting at was this black-market aspect. That men aren't supposed to have women on display, but they do it, and women like Offred still enjoy it.

Nathalia: I mean they're *oppressed*—they don't have another choice. If they show their true feelings, they're going to get killed.

Something powerful is at work here. Without prompting, students jump right to the heart of a moving, resonant text and go at its big ideas. Citing both the novel and scholars, they build arguments and defend their stances with passion and confidence. They treat each other as intellectual equals, and everyone speaks. This discourse is *theirs*, and the ideas it sparks are richly provocative.

To us, this is what love in a literacy classroom looks like: a love for the conversation, love for the text, and love for the ideas they both spark. When that includes all students, magic happens.

But love like this is not a simple act. In a typical classroom anywhere in the world, there will be some (or many) students who will struggle. They will come to class without a love of reading. They might also have significant learning deficits from previous years. Add to that the natural socioemotional state of middle and high school students, and you have a recipe for potential malaise and a lack of deep learning. Small divides in what students are able to do become large gaps, and these can mark the beginning of life-changing inequity. You may be familiar with the sobering statistics that attest to these gaps, both on the national level and between groups of students:

- On the National Assessment of Educational Progress (NAEP), 12th-grade reading scores have been flat for more than a decade and have declined since its 1992 inception. As of 2015, only 37% of 12th graders performed at or above the proficiency level. And in 2019, the 8th-grade average score decreased by 3 points, with most students earning a "basic" score in reading comprehension.[1]

- Inequitable outcomes still persist or have even grown for low-income and non-white students. In 2015, for example, the 12th-grade gap in literacy between white and Black students was greater than it was in 1992.[2]

- On the 2015 Programme for International Student Assessment (or PISA, NAEP's international cousin), US reading achievement ranked as average among its peer group.[3]

You've also likely experienced the challenge in responding. States tried to raise the bar by moving to a common set of rigorous standards. This set of national expectations was almost immediately mired in politics, pushback, and a leadership vacuum that left most attempts at implementation hobbled at best. A few years later, the combination of the COVID-19 pandemic and violence against Black Americans laid bare further inequities in our system, exposing to all the precarious ground on which all of our classrooms—not just English—stood.[4] It's in this aftermath that we write to you.

Faced with this world, what can we do? We choose to follow the lead of outstanding teachers who have blazed a trail for all of us.

Think back to *The Handmaid's Tale* discussion. There was one voice we never heard—Beth's. Although she set the stage, it was her students who stole the show.

How did she do it? Beth's story—and that of the many other teachers throughout this book—shows us that English teachers don't need to choose between relishing the joy of literature and academic achievement.

Beth taught in Newark, New Jersey, for years. Her students, who are predominantly low-income Black and Latino, have had to scale the north face of history on their way to achieving academic success.[5] Determined to knock down as many barriers for them as possible, in 2005 Beth began teaching AP English to a small cohort of 13 students. None of them passed.

Undeterred, Beth resolved to do better—and she did. By 2015, her pass rate had soared to more than 80%, even as her cohort size nearly quadrupled. Something had changed for Beth over the intervening years. You could see it in her students and in her results: real, replicable teaching moves were producing the magic of authentic engagement *and* measurable achievement.

Although Beth's story is remarkable, she is not alone.[6] We've had the privilege to observe outstanding English teachers leading classrooms across the country, and we're excited to honor their work in this book. They show us the luminous power of an English class at its best. The study of English orbits the great, human urge to shape meaning from the void: to say *something* beautiful and true and whole. When we do, the words we read, write, and speak become incantation, just like the magic we heard in Beth's classroom.[7] What we saw students say and do didn't happen by chance. Beth set the stage for it by making choices and moves that were purposeful, practical, and most importantly for teachers—replicable.

Core Idea

There's real magic in the teaching of literature—and that magic is replicable.

Paul, along with Aja Settles and Juliana Worrell, first addressed this idea in their book *Great Habits, Great Readers*, which focused on elementary school reading instruction. *Love & Literacy* takes the story into middle and high school, where our quest to get students to fall in love with reading meets the crucible of adolescence. During these years, our students' sense of self is perhaps at its most vulnerable. They need the nurturing power of stories—and a bit of classroom wizardry—more than ever.

While there is no shortage of guidance on English instruction, there is less support on its execution. *Love & Literacy* aims to fill that void. You may find some of these practices familiar, while others may be new. Try what strikes you as valuable. Ultimately, know that although we discuss the practices in broad categories by chapter, they are designed to work in tandem. Every piece is part of a larger jigsaw puzzle. When we link them together, the full possibility of English class becomes clear.

THE MOVES BEHIND THE MAGIC

Over the past decades, cognitive science research has become far more accessible to the interested public, and technology has allowed us to observe, film, and share good teaching like never before. In *Love & Literacy*, we share the concrete tools that teachers like Beth use to create replicable magic, including the day-by-day details that build the practices behind repeated success. Our students—and yours—deserve no less.

A "PRACTICAL GUIDE": WHAT YOU'LL FIND IN THE BOOK

The pages that follow are a concrete, step-by-step guide to building the lifelong reader in every student. Part 1 (What's My Dream for Kids?) defines the bar for lasting literacy success. Part 2 (What Will I See When Students Get It?) shows us what to look for during student reading and writing if we want to see them deeply engage with texts. Part 3 (What Will I Hear When Students Get It?) focuses on student talk and what it takes to make discourse a primary driver of learning. Part 4 (How Do I Build It?) begins with a chapter-long deep dive into the creation of a culture of literacy; it names the habits and moves necessary to build a classroom where students are encouraged to think boldly and share openly. It then helps you apply those tools to your classroom: it provides a pathway to assess your current practices, identify gaps, and build a plan to close them. To help in that journey, this book also includes additional sections: a list of frequently asked questions and a discussion guide that can be used for self- or professional development. Finally, we offer an online appendix, a full *Reading and Writing Handbook*, which compiles all the teaching resources mentioned in Chapters 1–8 in printable form.

TURNING ON THE LIGHT: SEE IT, NAME IT, AND DO IT

When Paul first started working with school leaders 20 years ago, the most common refrain after a training session was, "I'll believe it when I see it." This struck a chord: in so many other disciplines—physical fitness, medicine, music, etc.—we find mentors or models that we can follow as we get better. The web has accelerated that access—you can learn to cook, build a retaining wall, or fix a car, simply by watching a video online. Yet in the teaching profession we are often on our own, hopefully learning from a colleague down the hall, but given few opportunities to see a model in action.

See It, Name It, and Do It is the framework Paul utilized for *Leverage Leadership 2.0* to give guidance to the power of apprenticeship: *see* a model of excellence in clear detail; *name* the characteristics that make that model effective; and *do* those actions repeatedly—first behind the scenes in extensive practice sessions and then daily in the classroom.

Love & Literacy follows this same framework: we present powerful teaching in action (see it), describe the guiding principles (name it), then talk about how to bring it into your own practice (do it). Here is what it will look like.

SEE IT: VIDEOS AND WORK SAMPLES

Videos

Our videos come from real classrooms. Each one captures authentic classroom interactions between teachers and students. Video clips are indicated by this symbol.

 WATCH Clip 1: Beth Verrilli—Students Discuss *The Handmaid's Tale*

We use video because seeing teaching and learning in action is far more powerful than reading about it. Whenever possible, we recommend viewing each clip before reading the accompanying transcript and text. Although we strive to include the most meaningful aspects within the written description, watching those "aha" moments as they unfold is an experience unto itself.

Work Samples and Tools

Good teaching doesn't just happen—it's something teachers prepare for. To that end, we'll also show you the planning that teachers did to prepare for their classes: annotated lesson plans, tools to use in the classroom, etc.

NAME IT: CORE IDEAS AND ONE-PAGERS

Seeing best practices is one thing. Naming them is another. Although there are multiple ways to describe the same technique, if we all use different terms it will be difficult to work together to get better. We use consistent language throughout the text to make it easier to collaborate and share knowledge.

Core Ideas

These are the key ideas of each section. They simplify complex ideas or strategies into concise, sticky phrases.

Core Idea

There's real magic in the teaching of literature—and that magic is replicable.

Key Takeaways

At the end of each major part, a box will recap the core ideas we've discussed. Use it as a quick refresher or as a thumbnail to help preview some of the section's contents:

Key Takeaways

- To check that students get it, see if they can write it. Write first, talk second.
- You can't correct what you don't detect.
- You raise the bar when you spar with an exemplar.

Stop and Jot

This book is an interactive experience. Use the stop and jot boxes to record your thoughts.

One-Pagers

Through observations, working groups, and teacher-created exemplars, we've compiled a collection of "one-pagers" (brief guides) that describe or illustrate key aspects of instruction. These are printer friendly and easy to carry around with you when teaching or planning for instruction. Here is a snippet from the Habits 201 discourse guide:

Excerpt—Habits of Discourse 201

201 HABITS—MAKE IT MEANINGFUL

Core Habit	Ideal Student Actions	Teacher Talk Moves
Problematize	• Name or provoke debate: *"It sounds like we're divided between X and Y. I think. . ."* • Name contradictions: *"Rene and Gabriel have opposite readings of X. I think. . ."* • Play devil's advocate: *"I'm going to play devil's advocate here. I think. . ."*	• Name or provoke the debate: *"Some of you say X. Some of you say Y. What do you think?"* • Name contradictions: *"These two ideas are contradictory. How can we make sense of this?"* • Play devil's advocate: *"Allow me to play devil's advocate. I actually think. . ."* or *"Who can play devil's advocate?"*

Core Habit	Ideal Student Actions	Teacher Talk Moves
Sophisticate	• Zoom in & out: *"I want to focus on X", "X is important because. . . .", "Y creates or makes Z in the text."* • Dive deeper into the text: *"Let's turn to page XX. Does it support or challenge our theory?"* • Apply within different or new context/ perspective: *"What do you think ___ would think about X?* • Give a hypothetical: *"What if. . ."*	• Zoom in: *"What connotations does this diction have?"* • Zoom out: *"So What?" "What's the consequence of that choice?"* • Narrow the focus: *"Given what you've said, what do you make of pages. . .?"* • Feign ignorance: *"I don't understand. I was thinking. . ."* • Apply within different or new context/perspective: *"What would ___ think about this?"* • Give a hypothetical: *"What if. . ."*

Reading and Writing Handbook

We want this book to live on for you and your students long after you've finished reading it. To help you use the materials we've described, you'll find a *Reading and Writing Handbook* in the online appendix that consolidates all these guides into one place. The handbook includes teacher- and student-facing resources that you can use in class— everything from student reference sheets to classroom signage. We've organized it by chapter to make it easier to bring to life any new ideas you have after reading.

DO IT: MATERIALS TO MAKE IT HAPPEN

With all these resources in hand, all that's left is to plan how to make it happen. A comprehensive self-evaluation sets priorities, while our adaptable planning documents and teaching scripts provide a structure for rolling out new habits or skills and maintaining them.

Self-Assessment

At the end of each major section, a self-assessment guides you through a reflection of your own school/classroom: What are the strengths and what are the areas to improve?

All the habits and skills introduced in the chapter are listed within the box alongside a rubric score (the score is weighted according to the importance of that criterion in the context of the whole chapter). Score yourself at the end of each chapter to help prioritize your next steps. (In Chapter 8, we combine these self-assessments into a comprehensive evaluation to look at your class/school as a whole.)

Self-Assessment Sample—Part 1

Part 1: What's my dream for kids?	
• **Create a Complexity Curriculum:** My curriculum deliberately sequences texts so they increase in quantitative, qualitative, and task complexity over time. Across the year, students read a diverse set of perspectives, genres, and experiences, including those far different from their own experience.	____/12
• **Build Background Knowledge:** From my teaching, students receive the schema necessary to access texts.	____/8
• **Read for Claim:** My students find the claims and sub-claims in narrative and non-narrative texts.	____/6
• **Read for Analysis:** My students use consistent methodologies (e.g., MR. CUF, NEZZ) to analyze, discuss, and write about author's craft.	____/6
Score:	____/32

Planning for Action

Once you've evaluated where you stand, you are ready to take action. Found at the end of each major part, this section helps you choose the most helpful resources included in the chapter and provides space to plan for potential modifications or adaptations.

WHO SHOULD USE THIS BOOK AND HOW?

This book is for everyone who teaches literacy or coaches/influences its instruction. Our primary audience, then, is middle school and high school English teachers. Yet literacy instruction is one of the most important activities in any child's education, which means we are all—to one degree or another—literacy teachers. With that "big tent" in mind, this book is also designed to be useful to instructional coaches, department chairs, principals, curriculum directors, central office leadership, and any other staff who can affect the quality of learning for our students. Depending on your role, we recommend a few different pathways for reading this book:

- **New Teachers:** If you are near the beginning of your teaching journey, welcome! We are excited to have you join this fellowship. For you, we recommend beginning with Chapter 1, as a quality curriculum is the foundation for strong English instruction. From there, you could either continue in order or skip ahead to Chapter 7, which discusses classroom culture. If you skip ahead, also stop by Chapter 4 to read the section "Make Independent Practice a Habit." You'll need to have these components in place before you'll be able to introduce student annotation (Chapter 3) or discourse (Chapters 5 and 6). Chapter 8 will give you the tools you need to roll out the habits that you've prioritized for your students.

- **Experienced Teachers:** If you have been teaching literacy for a while, you probably have a number of systems and habits already built into your classroom. In that case, you can use this book as a tool to focus on areas where you want to improve. We still recommend starting with Chapter 1, because if the literature you are using is not complex enough, all the other practices will fall short. After that, turn to the chapters that will most help you improve your practice. While chapters build on one another, each one can be read as an independent unit of study. Review our rollout guide in Chapter 8 once you've determined which habits/skills you'd like to introduce. It's designed to save time and energy in planning a rollout, allowing you to devote the bulk of your attention to the day-to-day responsibilities of your classroom.

- **Department Chairs and Literacy Coaches:** We recommend starting with Chapter 1 to make sure that your grade-level curriculum exposes students to inclusive, challenging texts. After that, use Chapter 8 to assess the strengths and gaps of your department as a whole. Once you've identified a growth opportunity, look to the relevant chapter for strategies to address it. (Chapters 3 and 4 focus on student reading, Chapters 5 and 6 on discourse, and Chapter 7 on school and class culture.) If you're using this book as part of your professional development program or learning community, the discussion guide at the end is a useful tool to jump-start conversation and reflection.

- **School Leaders:** Principals or administrators who lead English departments should start with the evaluation checklist in Chapter 8. You may wish to complete some of the checklist with your department chair(s) or literacy coach(es) if they have more on-the-ground data about classrooms. The results will help determine the order in which you'll use the other chapters. Focus your attention on the chapters that discuss the priority goals for your school or targeted grade levels. From there, you can incorporate information from these chapters into your school's professional development sessions and the observation-feedback cycle.

- **Education Professors:** In order to make this guide as practical as possible, we have focused on describing the key actions that effective teachers take in the classroom. While many of these practices were honed through action research, we've cited and given commentary on the academic research that guided us. If you are using this text to teach pre-service teachers, we recommend assigning chapters and video viewing in chapter order. If you are teaching a specialized education course or working with more seasoned teachers, assign the chapters in an order that best meets the needs of the course and your students. The discussion guide at the end of this book can be used to generate class conversations or for student reflection at the end of each section.

- **Parents, Interventionists, Tutors, and Others Who Work with Readers:** While this book is written largely for teachers, anyone who works with middle or high school readers can take something of value away from it.

  ○ For those working with reluctant readers or readers in struggle, our chapter on literacy culture (Chapter 7) will help you identify ways to jump-start a love of reading. In addition, our chapter on building a complexity curriculum (Chapter 1) can help you determine whether your child is sufficiently exposed to books that will help them develop.

  ○ Literacy Interventionists and tutors who work one-on-one with students will find Chapters 1–3 directly applicable to their work. These chapters give students accessible entry points into non-narrative and narrative texts. You'll especially want to review Chapter 3, which focuses on annotation as a complement to reading comprehension.

  ○ If your work or relationships with students falls outside what we've mentioned, you can still turn to *Love & Literacy* for information and strategies to help you reach the young readers in your life, particularly in Chapter 7. Let your curiosity guide here. Do you want to pique a young person's interest in a new topic? Read our section on independent reading. Do you want to create rituals around literacy? Read our section on peak moments and use the cultural calendar as your guide. Remember that students learn both in and outside the classroom. Use this book to reach them wherever you meet them.

LITERACY AS A LOVE STORY

After years of working with Beth Verrilli as colleagues, we finally sat down for a formal interview with her. We asked her to share how she balanced rigorous coursework with joyfulness and excitement. She said, quite simply: "Kids fall in love with what they know how to do."

> ## Core Idea
>
> Kids fall in love with what they know how to do.

The power of Beth's words has stuck with us ever since. They remind us that love, when we get it right, comes from understanding. When students believe they are good or great at something, they'll persist—and even delight—in the face of challenge.[8] This belief doesn't just apply to students. As teachers, we love doing what *we* are good at too. And like our students, we don't have to be naturals. We wrote *Love & Literacy* to give all of us tools to nurture our confidence in a clear vision for instruction, content study, and action.

Teaching literacy is greater than the sum of its parts: it's more complex than the books students read, more nuanced than the essays they write, and more rigorous than the debates they hold. It's preparation for life.

But for what kind of life are we preparing our students? To answer, let's begin by defining our dream for the types of readers they can be.

What's My Dream for Kids?

INTRODUCTION

> *A writer's life and work are not a gift to mankind; they are its necessity.*
> —Toni Morrison, *The Source of Self-Regard*

Pulitzer and Nobel Prize–winning author Toni Morrison published her debut novel, *The Bluest Eye*, in 1970. The novel chronicles the life of Pecola Breedlove, a young Black girl whose obsession with white beauty leads to tragedy. Take a moment to dive into this excerpt from the novel's "Winter" section. What would the average student take away from this passage?

Excerpt—*The Bluest Eye* by Toni Morrison

By the time this winter had stiffened itself into a hateful knot that nothing could loosen, something did loosen it, or rather someone. A someone who splintered the knot into silver threads that tangled us, netted us, made us long for the dull chafe of the previous boredom.

This disrupter of seasons was a new girl in school named Maureen Peal. A high-yellow dream child with long brown hair braided into two lynch ropes that hung down her back. She was rich, at least by our standards, as rich as the richest of the white girls, swaddled in comfort and care. The quality of her clothes threatened to derange Frieda and me. Patent-leather shoes with buckles, a cheaper version of which we got only at Easter and which had disintegrated by the end of May. Fluffy sweaters the color of lemon drops tucked into skirts with pleats so orderly they astounded us. Brightly colored knee socks with white borders, a brown velvet coat trimmed in white rabbit fur, and a matching muff. There was a hint of spring in her sloe green eyes, something summery in her complexion, and a rich autumn ripeness in her walk.

Source: Toni Morrison, 1970 / Penguin Random House.

Most students would pick up on Morrison's vivid description of Maureen Pearl and the speaker's resentment over Maureen's relative wealth and perceived attractiveness. Students might also broadly catch Morrison's use of metaphor or at least appreciate that she's doing *something* with figurative language. In the end, they might settle on a reading like "Maureen is the rich, new girl, and everyone is jealous of her."

If they only did that, they'd be missing so much.

This scene, for example, takes place in 1941, well before the Civil Rights movement, and the passage simmers with racial tension even in the absence of white characters. Claudia, the Black narrator, describes Maureen's complexion as "high-yellow," an offensive and outdated term used to describe Black people with lighter skin complexions. Without background knowledge on colorism, students may miss the meaning of this term and its larger social implications in 1940s America. Lighter-skinned Black people were often of mixed racial ancestry and their closer proximity to whiteness gave them privileged standing in a society stratified by race. The narrator's rage at Maureen's luxurious clothing and green eyes becomes much more nuanced once we know that lighter-skinned Black people were often wealthier and deemed more attractive than darker-skinned Black people.

And then there's the matter of Maureen's hairstyle. Morrison describes the two braids as "lynch ropes," and this troubling description gives us much to mine. Here are a few potential readings:

- Maureen, although Black, is able to adopt some elements of white beauty standards by wearing a popular hairstyle of the time. However, by linking the hairstyle to racial violence, Morrison suggests these standards can be viewed as a type of threat to other characters.

- The lynch ropes that hang figuratively (and literally) about Maureen's neck remind readers that the threat doesn't simply come *from* her but also *toward* her. That is, both she and the narrator are under the sway of the cruel power she wields.

- The lynch ropes may allude to a poem by Jean Toomer, an early twentieth-century multiracial poet and writer. (Morrison was likely familiar with his work.) His poem describes a popular white hairstyle as "braided chestnut, coiled like a lyncher's rope" and its violent imagery suggests the real danger that Maureen poses.[1]

If we think of understanding literature as a journey, this depth of analysis is the destination many of us aim for when we teach. But how do we take students from "Maureen is the new, rich girl and the narrator is jealous" to "Morrison uses Maureen to embody exploitive, racialized classism and the attendant colorism"? And what would it take to help students read that way?

Recall Beth's students in the introduction to this book: their rich discussion of *The Handmaid's Tale* was the product of their deep understanding of the text and the context surrounding it. That depth allowed them to grapple with Atwood's text in an authentic, rigorous, and ultimately generative way.

A superficial reader, however, cannot yet access that level of analysis. Imagine what a "surface reader" thinks after reading this section of *The Bluest Eye*. Morrison's lyricism might make them scratch their heads or dismiss this section as overwrought. They might even abandon this book for one with a clearer, quick-chugging plot.

When we say we want students to love literacy, we mean more than the simple enjoyment of a text. Buddhist monk Thich Nhat Hanh describes love in a way that fits this need well. He says, "Understanding is love's other name. If you don't understand, you can't love."[2] Students can only love texts they understand.

> ## Core Idea
>
> Students can only fall in love with texts they understand.

Our dream for kids is something loftier than "getting the gist" or even just enjoying reading. We want them to experience literature for what it truly is: a compass, a salve, and most importantly—a spark that inspires. And we want them to be able to do it with any text to which their inclination leads them.

Seeing and connecting with literature in this deeper way is not innate. We cultivate it when we give students opportunities to richly engage with texts that are complex enough to merit it. That's why we teach English: to expose students to beautiful texts and give them the tools to experience them in their fullness. If we fall short of that, we might reach infatuation, but we won't have love.

Figure P1.1 The Cheshire Cat tells Alice that if she doesn't care where she's going, it won't matter which direction she takes. We do care, so it does.

Source: Image by Sir John Tenniel, in the public domain.

If students fall in love with texts they understand, then two of the most pressing questions for us to answer are:

- What will my students read? (Chapter 1: Build a Complexity Curriculum)
- What will it take for them to understand it? (Chapter 2: What Does It Mean to "Get It"?)

In *Alice in Wonderland*, Alice asks the Cheshire Cat for help finding a path forward. "That depends a good deal on where you want to get to," the cat replies. When Alice admits she doesn't really care, the cat replies, "Then it doesn't matter which way you go."[3] Clearly, we care where we're going; that's why we're doing this work. So, following the wisdom of the Cheshire Cat, let's spend some time envisioning the destination.

Chapter 1

Build a Complexity Curriculum

DEFINING THE DREAM

The universe is made of stories, not of atoms.
—Muriel Rukeyser, *"The Speed of Darkness,"* 2006

Steve's wife, Charell, did not have an easy childhood. She grew up in Harlem in the 1980s, where she bounced around its foster care system and public schools. Each turn brought new uncertainty about herself and her future. But Charell found a lifeline in books. She saw herself as the outsider in *Julie of the Wolves*, the Julie/Miyax who had every right to chart her own course, even and especially when adults made choices that were not in her best interests. In *Matilda* she learned from others, meeting a librarian named Mrs. Phelps who gave her (and Matilda) permission to read difficult things and work toward understanding them.

Charell took this wisdom and fused it with the lessons of her own experience to make something all her own. To this day, she cites both texts as helping her define the person she wanted to become. Isn't *that* the experience we dream of for each of our students?

Steve often thinks of his wife's journey when he plans curriculum—how her teachers' choices shaped the road she walked. Consider, for example, two hypothetical 11th-grade book lists. What is the difference between the pathway each creates for its students?

Two Possible Book Lists—11th Grade

Reading List 1	Reading List 2
Tess of the d'Urbervilles: A Pure Woman Faithfully Presented (Thomas Hardy)	*Their Eyes Were Watching God* (Zora Neale Hurston)
The Odyssey (Homer)	*The Odyssey* (Homer)
Of Mice and Men (John Steinbeck)	*Interpreter of Maladies* (Jhumpa Lahiri)
The Scarlet Letter (Nathaniel Hawthorne)	*Deaf Republic* (Ilya Kaminsky)
The Rime of the Ancient Mariner (William Wordsworth)	*The House of the Spirits* (Isabel Allende)
Great Expectations (Charles Dickens)	*Another Country* (James Baldwin)
Hamlet (William Shakespeare)	*Hamlet* (William Shakespeare)

Both book lists have rigorous, challenging texts that will stretch students. Each grapples with major life themes that connect to the human condition. But they represent highly different experiences.

Let's go back and consider Charell's experience—or that of any of our students. If Charell only got to read the list on the left, she'd be sent a pretty clear message of what she could find in books—and it wouldn't be herself. People of color aren't represented. To the degree that women are, their stories are told by men. The list on the right, meanwhile, doesn't ignore the voices on the left—it simply makes space for others. If literature has the power to shape who we become, the list on the right helps students encounter more paths on that journey.

At its best, literature offers a mirror in which we might more clearly see ourselves and a window through which we might better know others.[1] It affords us a sense of place, somewhere amid the universe, where we might find ourselves a bit less alone. In our dream curriculum, the deep, atomic pull of literature calls students to something larger than themselves.

Creating a curriculum like this is no easy task. For starters, there is the limit of time: in a given year, we might only get to study five or six texts as a whole class. How can we possibly choose? To begin, we propose a single question: Beyond what our students can say or do when they leave our care, what kinds of people do we want them to become?

Core Idea

Our curriculum shapes more than what students can do.
It shapes who they become.

This approach differs from the way that English curricula have been historically designed. The backbone of much of the US English curriculum is a "canon" of American and English literature that was first selected in the late 1800s—from both historic authors and those who were, at the time, contemporary. If you love some of those texts, or some of the others that have since been added to the list, you are not alone. They are some of our favorites, too. But these works are inevitably limited by the worldviews of their time and by the mechanisms that allowed white men to have voice while forcing others to the periphery—or out of the conversation entirely. The canon captures *a* past. Teaching literacy with love means sharing other pasts, connecting narratives to the present, and imaging a future together.

The growing diversity of our classrooms invites us to widen and deepen our curricula beyond those texts we've inherited.[2] This is a moment to think about whose voices get time in the books we choose: not only which characters students meet, but who gets to tell their stories. When students from underrepresented backgrounds engage with storytellers who share similar experiences[3]—and not solely when they're writing about trauma—they can more easily see themselves in the humanities. When all students, regardless of background, enjoy an inclusive curriculum, we share with them the strength of stories across cultures and experiences.

As #DisruptTexts cofounder Tricia Ebarvia writes, reconsidering our curriculum doesn't necessarily mean replacing all our books. Instead, it often means complementing them with additional texts that give previously marginalized voices a place at the table.[4] Teaching *Romeo and Juliet*? Consider interrogating Romeo's misogyny and teaching texts that portray healthy teen relationships. Teaching *To Kill a Mockingbird*?

Also teach texts about race written by people of color themselves, and perhaps investigate the text's difficulty portraying civil rights or characters of color (see one example in Chapter 2, and another in this endnote).[5]

The Canon in Schools: A Historical Perspective

Students of history know that the genesis of the US instructional "canon" was the product of a few converging forces: a list of texts used in Harvard's entrance requirements in the late 1870s, publishers seeking to profit from this list (with study aids and anthologies), and an 1894 report that effectively established "English" as a US discipline in secondary schools.[6] Then and today still, access to publication itself remains far from egalitarian. Some voices have been routinely excluded.[7] Outside the United States, the history of English instruction poses further problems. Its study was developed, for example, as a tool of the British colonial project in India.[8] Knowing this history can be discomforting, but it also invites us to look at our texts with clearer eyes.

As an adult, Charell is a fearless reader who devours everything from beach reads to biographies. When a coworker recently opined on utopias, Charell realized her educational experience didn't spend much time on the concept . . . so she picked up Thomas More's 1516 treatise on the topic and read it herself.

Charell's story highlights the power of a true complexity curriculum. It didn't just help her build a sense of empathy and identity; it gave her skill and confidence to tackle any text—even those that brim with sophistication.

A complexity curriculum sets students up to love reading in a meaningful and lasting way. Let's talk about how to build one.

Stop and Jot—Gut Check

The first step in thinking about our curriculum is evaluating what we use. We'll talk in a bit about how to consider new texts (if you feel you need to). For now, consider the current text list for the grade(s) you teach or your students' experience across your department. Ask yourself:

- Whose stories are told? Even if I can't represent all voices, am I over-representing certain voices at the expense of others?

- Who does the storytelling? Even when characters are diverse, are their stories only told by white authors?
- What are the stories about? For example, do non-white authors only speak about identity-based trauma?
- Where do my stories take place? Is my curriculum limited to just the United States or Western countries?
- When I use canonical texts, do I present counter-narratives?

List out your texts below, along with your takeaways:

(NOTE: Don't be afraid to write in this book. Poet Billy Collins counsels his students to get over their reverence for the texts enough to really interact with them. Not quite sure? Take a break and read his poem "Marginalia" to give you a nudge!)

_____

_____

_____

_____

_____

_____

_____

DEFINING COMPLEXITY

Some might use the word "complex" to describe the Toni Morrison excerpt in the introduction (or Thomas More's *Utopia* for that matter). But what does complexity mean and how much does it really matter when we think about preparing our students for the world? To answer, look at this excerpt of a newspaper article that was printed a few years ago.[9] As you read, jot some notes. What could make this text challenging for students?

Stop and Jot—Defining Complexity

"Black People Were Denied Vanilla Ice Cream in the Jim Crow South —Except on Independence Day"
by Michael W. Twitty

By custom rather than by law, black folks were best off if they weren't caught eating vanilla ice cream in public in the Jim Crow South, except—the narrative always stipulates—on the Fourth of July. I heard it from my father growing up myself, and the memory of that all-but-unspoken rule seems to be unique to the generation born between World War I and World War II.

But if Maya Angelou hadn't said it in her classic autobiography *I Know Why the Caged Bird Sings*, I doubt anybody would believe it today.

"People in Stamps used to say that the whites in our town were so prejudiced that a Negro couldn't buy vanilla ice cream. Except on July Fourth. Other days he had to be satisfied with chocolate."

Vanilla ice cream—flavored with a Nahuatl spice indigenous to Mexico, the cultivation of which was improved by an enslaved black man named Edmund Albius on the colonized Réunion island in the Indian Ocean, now predominately grown on the largest island of the African continent, Madagascar, and served wrapped in the conical invention of a Middle Eastern immigrant—was the symbol of the American dream. That its pure, white sweetness was then routinely denied to the grandchildren of the enslaved was a dream deferred indeed.

—Courtesy of Guardian News & Media Ltd

What makes this article complex? What would give your students difficulty if they encountered it on their own?

_____

_____

_____

_____

_____

This commentary appeared in *The Guardian*, a newspaper written at a reading level that most adults are supposed to access. Yet consider the demands of the third paragraph. Readers must decipher so many things to truly understand it. Among them:

- **Sophisticated vocabulary** (that often isn't discernable in context)—words like "indigenous" and "deferred."

- **Geographical knowledge**—knowing where Mexico, the Indian Ocean, or Madagascar is.

- **Historical knowledge**—understanding what colonization is and its implications.

- **Literary knowledge**—catching that the author is playing on the traditional (albeit toxic) association of whiteness with purity.

- **Long, complex sentence structure**—the final paragraph is composed of just two sentences—and the first is 65 words long!

- **Spotting the irony**—that everyone involved in the creation of vanilla ice cream is a person of color. This helps unlock Twitty's ironic tone.

- **Catching the allusion** to Langston Hughes's "A Dream Deferred"—and bringing their understanding of that text to bear on the one at hand.

That's no small order for a newspaper article written for the general public! As adult readers, we can see how Twitty supports his takeaway message as we read, a process made automatic by years of wide reading and analysis. While this process may feel effortless to us, we cannot assume the same is true for our students. Without the ability to recognize, connect, and synthesize these features, some students will never get Twitty's point. And if that's true, we can't expect it to matter much to them.

The task of understanding Twitty highlights the challenge our students face. In 2005, the ACT—maker of one of the two major college entrance exams in the country—released a study showing that the biggest obstacle for students on their assessment wasn't a single, isolated reading skill like drawing conclusions or identifying supporting details. It was that all students, even high-performing ones, struggled with reading comprehension when texts became difficult.[10] When the going got tough, our students got it wrong. (See Figure 1.1.)

Figure 1.1 The ACT's report helped reveal complexity as a major culprit behind student struggle. In the graphs above, it's the complexity of the text—not isolated reading skills—that distinguish the top scorers from those who are less successful on the assessment.

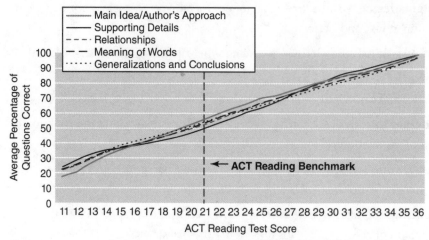

Performance on the ACT Reading Test by Textual Element
(Averaged across Seven Forms)

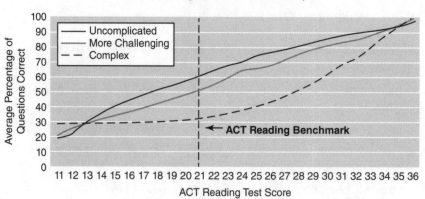

Performance on the ACT Reading Test by Degree of Text Complexity
(Averaged across Seven Forms)

Regardless of how you feel about college admissions or standardized tests, there's no measure of educational progress that says things are going well for our students. A 2010 study, for example, found that only half of Texas's 11th graders could read texts with the complexity they would encounter in college.[11]

What these studies reveal is that before we talk about how we teach literacy, we have to talk about the texts we give students. If they aren't complex enough, they won't push students' development. Education leaders Ross Weiner and Susan Pimentel write:

> System leaders who want to foster effective and relevant professional learning. . . should focus in the first instance on making sure the instructional materials reflect the full aspiration of college and career readiness. It's the professional learning equivalent of "you are what you eat."[12]

Core Idea

You are what you eat:
if you want students to grow, nourish them with challenging texts.

For many of us, this advice seems easier said than done. How does it apply to readers in struggle or those who are reading several years below grade level? Is a complexity curriculum even appropriate for them? The answer is yes, if we take care to provide supports. (We'll address this directly and show how in Chapter 2.)

Watering down the texts we give to students doesn't help them grow. Chowing down on comfort food is fine on occasion, but it's no way to raise a healthy eater. Students are nourished when we do the opposite—choose increasingly challenging, complex texts that allow reading skills to develop and flourish.[13]

If you want to push students to love reading—to enjoy it *and* be great at it—take the notion of a complexity curriculum to heart. Let's consider what that might feel like.

Steve has directed literacy curriculum for every grade from 5th to 12th and he likes to think about ways to organize units. Take a look at this sample sequence of novels for 8th grade. While novels aren't the only things students would read in class (students read scores of articles, poems, short stories, speeches, and other texts—and text complexity matters there, too), the list of texts gives a quick cross-section of a curriculum.

What do you notice?

Sample—8th-Grade Sequence of Texts

Texts
Persepolis (Marjane Satrapi)
In the Time of the Butterflies (Julia Alvarez)
Animal Farm (George Orwell)
The Narrative of the Life of Frederick Douglass (Frederick Douglass)
Othello (William Shakespeare)

Steve faced a number of choices when he selected these texts and he spent a good deal of time considering their complexity: curricular, quantitative, and qualitative. We can unpack them one by one.

CURRICULAR COMPLEXITY

A great literacy curriculum is always talking to itself. Books poke at big questions. Authors challenge each other. Students leave class not with answers, but with new questions and new perspectives. In essence, the curriculum as a whole is one large story, and the more cohesive the story, the more compelling it is to read.

Core Idea

Curriculum tells a larger story:
the more cohesive it is, the more compelling it becomes.

To tell the larger story, Steve will need to consider two ideas simultaneously:

- How do these potential texts talk to each other?
- Who gets to do the talking, and who are they talking about?

Let's see how these two questions work together.

Many educators are familiar with the concept of essential questions, popularized by the work of Grant Wiggins and Jay McTighe. An essential question is a broad, open-ended question that invites deep inquiry during the course of a year or unit.[14] In literacy class, these are the questions that will keep your students up at night (we hope!), the questions that link the books we read to meaningful topics: "What do we owe to each other?" or "What does it mean to really love someone?" or "Are people inherently good?" A good essential question shapes the story your curriculum tells and what you want students to take away from what they read.

Beyond intellectual magnetism, what else does an essential question need? Relevancy. Jump-start your thinking by reviewing your school's broader course materials. Ask yourself: What have students already discussed? What questions are coming up in other classes right now?

Let's use Steve's sample list. Imagine that last year in literacy class, students discussed the question "What is freedom?" and in history class, they studied the US revolution and other contemporaneous uprisings. This year, the social studies curriculum examines the mid-1800s and beyond, particularly domestic and international labor and civil rights movements. How could we complement this focus in English class? Steve proposes the following overarching questions:

- What is power? Does it corrupt people, do corrupt people seek it, or is it something else altogether?

- What should be the relationship between a government and the people it serves?

Steve chose these essential questions because they fit well within the broader school curriculum and because, as a former journalist, they still captivate him. Were he crafting a books list from scratch, these essential questions would guide him. If he were replacing one or more books on an existing list, these questions would help him choose.[15]

Steve picked these texts to bring multiple viewpoints to a topic our world still grapples with today.[16] But he also was careful to vary the genres selected. Scholar Peter Rabinowitz argues that exposing students to a wide range of genres helps them develop a stronger sense of how different types of writing work *and* inoculates them against any biases embedded within the traditional English literary canon. He notes that "intensive reading may well be a worthless skill for someone who has not already devoured a large and heterogeneous collection of texts. Deep reading, in other words, can complement wide reading, but it cannot replace it."[17]

Sample—8th-Grade Texts and Curriculum Complexity

Essential Questions:

- What is power? Does power corrupt people, do corrupt people seek power, or is it something else altogether?
- What's the right relationship between a government and the people it serves?

Text	Curriculum-level Complexity
Persepolis (Marjane Satrapi)	**Essential questions:** examines how a society can shift toward oppressive structure **Genre:** graphic novel, memoir
In the Time of the Butterflies (Julia Alvarez)	**Essential questions:** examines an oppressive regime and responses to it **Genre:** historical fiction
Animal Farm (George Orwell)	**Essential questions:** considers how good political intentions can be corrupted by power **Genre:** sociopolitical fiction, allegory
The Narrative of the Life of Frederick Douglass (Frederick Douglass)	**Essential questions:** demonstrates the consequences of a racist government that does not value its citizens' lives, as well as pathways to challenge it **Genre:** memoir
Othello (William Shakespeare)	**Essential questions:** demonstrates the consequences of a racist, misogynist, and xenophobic social structure **Genre:** drama

Steve hopes to offer experiences that will feel both familiar and new to students. But he's thinking about something else as well. Let's review Steve's list using two other considerations he had in mind, diversity and knowledge building:

Sample—8th-Grade Texts and Curriculum Complexity

DIVERSITY AND KNOWLEDGE BUILDING

Text	Curriculum-Level Complexity
Persepolis (Marjane Satrapi)	French-Iranian author describing childhood experience during the Islamic revolution; late twentieth century
In the Time of the Butterflies (Julia Alvarez)	Life during the Trujillo dictatorship in the Dominican Republic, as told by a Dominican-American; mid- to late twentieth century
Animal Farm (George Orwell)	Oft-referenced text and author; "Orwellian" is a common term in social discourse and this text is a staple example of allegory; early to mid-twentieth century
The Narrative of the Life of Frederick Douglass (Frederick Douglass)	African American icon describing a pathway out of slavery; early to mid-nineteenth century
Othello (William Shakespeare)	Play's themes (and Shakespearean tropes) have been replicated and expanded throughout the world of literature; Renaissance

Steve's selection expands the perspectives and voices student hear, but it also includes authors who would be considered canonical. Why? Because doing so introduces students to texts that will build on knowledge that other authors will presume they have. Canonical texts are deeply embedded in literary and broader culture. Reading them gives students a grounding to understand contemporary authors who will respond to, build on, and challenge the ideas they pose.[18] (This is in addition to any literary merit these texts have.) They are passports to an ongoing conversation, and to never discuss them deeply disadvantages students.[19]

As we mentioned earlier, discussing canonical texts, as with any book, doesn't mean doing so without challenge. Were Steve's students to read *Othello*, they'd most certainly be discussing the racism and misogyny of its characters, as well as investigating the perspectives of characters like Emilia, Desdemona, or Desdemona's nurse, all women who are sidelined by the text.

Curriculum shapes thought and belief, whispering to our students what the world is and what it might become. The books that we choose (or don't) establish the tone and tenor of that conversation, as well as who gets to participate in it. It might seem strange for us to call these decisions a type of complexity, but in our view, that's exactly what they are. A reductive or oversimplified curriculum presents the same ideas, voices, and genres again and again. It doesn't ask our students to challenge the status quo—a deep irony considering that's what many of the authors they read are famous for doing. Teaching a complexity curriculum means problematizing well-trod ideas in the exact same way great authors do. Our kids are all the better for it.

Following is a quick summary of the keys to curriculum complexity that we have discussed so far (you'll find a full list of factors you can use as a checklist in the online appendix's *Reading and Writing Handbook*).

Curriculum-Level Complexity

Factors for Text Selection and Sequence

- **Diversity and Inclusion**—Does this group of texts help us represent the broader diversity of the United States and the world? Does it resonate with our students' experience or offer a new one? Does it help center marginalized voices? Does it run the risk of tokenizing an experience or telling a single story about a particular group?

- **Presumed Knowledge**—Will these texts provide knowledge that is assumed by other texts?

- **Essential Questions**—Do these texts speak to each other in a way that will be fruitful for students?

- **Genre and Time Period**—Are we exposing students to a wide variety of genres and time periods throughout our curriculum?

Stop and Jot—Curricular Complexity

Apply this to your own classroom. Using your own curriculum, assess the strengths and weaknesses in the following areas:

1. Diversity and inclusion

2. Presumed knowledge

3. Essential questions

4. Genre and time period

Are there any key changes you would like to make to the text selection or the essential question?

Texts	Key Takeaways for Curricular Complexity

(If you review this list and have concerns, this is probably the first place you'll want to advocate for change at school. See the FAQ in Chapter 9 "What if I have a mandated curriculum and it is not diverse or complex?" to get started.)

We now have the beginnings of a curriculum that tells a compelling, inclusive story. Yet even if we craft a powerful essential question and link it with inclusive texts, it's still possible to fail—and fail spectacularly—in our goal of preparing students to read any text they choose. How?

If we don't give students practice reading complex text, they'll only be able to access (and love) a very limited subset of books. So the next place to look is the nitty-gritty details of what makes any specific book challenging. As we do, we'll need to do a gut check of our selections to see if they should stay on our list and to decide in what order we might teach them. There are two categories to consider—quantitative and qualitative complexity.[20] Let's discuss both.

QUANTITATIVE COMPLEXITY

Below are two versions of a news story. These paragraphs come from Newsela.com, a website that provides reading passages at various difficulty levels. Both passages have the same content—they describe a new Oreo cookie on the market—but there is a noticeable difference in complexity. Complexity in this case is measured by a Lexile score, one of the most well-known quantitative measures of text complexity. Take a moment to read both and jot down the differences between the two.

Stop and Jot—Lexile Level Comparison

Mondelez International just introduced its latest twist on the Oreo, the best-selling cookie in the world. Oreo Thins are slightly wider and just a little over half as thick as the original wafers. The sleek new cookies are also 7 calories lighter, though they are not meant to be a diet version of the classic. *Lexile 1180L*	Oreo is the best-selling cookie in the world. Mondelez International just came out with a new kind, called Oreo Thins. They are only about half as thick as regular Oreos and just a little wider. They have 7 fewer calories. They are not meant to be a diet cookie, though. *Lexile 640L*

What differences do you notice between the two passages?

_____

_____

_____

Two chief features are noticeable in the higher-Lexile text: more complex vocabulary (e.g. "sleek," "wafers") and longer sentences. That's what Lexile is: an algorithm that considers vocabulary and sentence length, assigning a numerical score based on how complex the text appears to be.[21] This is a reasonable way to get a quick readout, though critics will point out that it is imperfect. If we relied on Lexile alone, we'd call *The Hunger Games* (810L) much more complex than *The Sun Also Rises* (610L). And while we consider ourselves proud members of Katniss's resistance, we're not quite ready to swap Hemingway to 5th grade.[22] Similarly, the memoir *Night* (570L) challenges students in some ways that the higher-Lexile *The Giver* (760L) does not.

Lexile gives us objective—albeit incomplete—information about complexity. It's our initial gut check to the question: Are we exposing our students to increasingly complex texts on their pathway to understanding?

Let's reconsider Steve's original list with the Lexile levels included:

Sample—8th-Grade Texts and Curriculum Complexity

Text	Lexile
Persepolis (Marjane Satrapi)	N/A*
In the Time of the Butterflies (Julia Alvarez)	910
The Narrative of the Life of Frederick Douglass (Frederick Douglass)	1080
Animal Farm (George Orwell)	1170
Othello (William Shakespeare)	N/A*

* Lexile measures cannot be used with graphic novels or plays, but at least in terms of quantitative measures, *Persepolis*—a graphic novel—would be one of the least complex texts of this sequence and *Othello*—written in highly dense and archaic language—would be the most complex.

Let's break down the decisions we see here: overall, students are being stretched with texts of different quantitative measures over the course of one year, beginning with texts whose language will be accessible to most students (*Persepolis* and *In the Time of the Butterflies*) and ending with a few that will stretch all of them (*Othello*).

Stop and Jot—Quantitative Complexity

Using your current curriculum, look up the quantitative complexity of the texts you teach (you can find these listed online by many publishers or at lexile .com). Based on your state's guidance, how close are you to the range for your grade?* Do your texts increase in challenge over the course of the year?

Text	Lexile (or other quantitative measure)

If useful, here are the Lexile guidelines provided by the Common Core:

- *Grades 4–5 (770–980)*
- *Grades 6–8 (955–1155)*
- *Grades 9–10 (1080–1305)*
- *Grades 11+ (1215–1355).*[23]

While we use Lexile as our initial complexity gut check, sequencing is not as simple as ordering texts numerically. With any text, there are other dimensions of complexity that we need to factor in. And as in the case of Steve's list, these qualitative components can encourage us to rearrange the order of texts being offered.

QUALITATIVE COMPLEXITY

A book's quantitative score can help us place it within the right grade span, but after that, we should take qualitative measures into account. Plenty of AP-level books have low Lexile levels (e.g. *The Grapes of Wrath*—680L) but are rich in qualitative or thematic complexity, meriting their instruction.

Take this case study of two poems. Which is more complex, Ezra Pound's "In a Station of the Metro" or Joyce Kilmer's "Trees"?

Case Study—Two Poems

"In a Station of the Metro"
by Ezra Pound

The apparition of these faces in the
   crowd;
Petals on a wet, black bough.

"Trees"
by Joyce Kilmer

I think that I shall never see
A poem as lovely as a tree.

A tree whose hungry mouth is prest
Against the earth's sweet flowing
   breast;

A tree that looks at God all day,
And lifts her leafy arms to pray;

A tree that may in Summer wear
A nest of robins in her hair;

Upon whose bosom snow has lain;
Who intimately lives with rain.

Poems are made by fools like me,
But only God can make a tree.

Kilmer's poem is longer, yet it relies on relatively simple structure and imagery and its message feels more straightforward. (Of course, its antiquated language and sentence structure might confuse younger readers.) Pound's text, in contrast, is far shorter, but it also presents the potentially challenging word "apparition," and, more significantly, offers more complex ideas to analyze.

In *Three Genres*, Stephen Minot uses these two poems to make a case that while neither is better than the other, Pound's is the more sophisticated. "In a Station of the Metro" uses language in an unexpected way—juxtaposing commuters with wind-tossed petals— and its message is elusive.[24] Minot's assessment sounds accurate; we'd expect far more high school or college students to struggle with Pound's text than with Kilmer's.

Qualitative complexity is easier to categorize than to measure: what *types* of qualitative complexity appear in a given text? We're indebted to the work of Doug Lemov, Erica Woolway, and Colleen Driggs in *Reading Considered*, where the authors describe the array of forms qualitative complexity can take as the "five plagues of the developing reader."[25] These create a manageable framework for analyzing texts:

A Few Words on . . . Qualitative Text Complexity

The Five Plagues of the Developing Reader
based on *Reading Reconsidered*

- **Archaic Text**—Language pre-1900 worked differently. Sentences were longer, passive voice was more common, and subjects and predicates had more complicated relationships.

  Example from *Barnaby Rudge,* by Charles Dickens:

  In the year 1775, there stood upon the borders of Epping Forest, at a distance of about twelve miles from London—measuring from the Standard in Cornhill or rather from the spot on or near to which the Standard used to be in days of yore—a house of public entertainment called the Maypole; which fact was demonstrated to all such travellers as could neither read nor write (and at that time a vast number both of travellers and stay-at-homes were in this condition) by the emblem reared on the roadside over against the house, which, if not of those goodly proportions that May-poles were wont to present in olden times, was a fair young ash, thirty feet in height, and straight as any arrow that ever English yeoman drew.

- **Non-Linear Time Sequence**—Texts can skip from past to present to future without warning and some texts make use of this frequently.

  Example: David Mitchell's *Cloud Atlas* is a series of nested stories, moving forward, then backward in time. *Time's Arrow*, by Martin Amis, uses a reverse chronology.

- **Complexity of Narrator**—Texts can have unreliable narrators, multiple narrators, non-human narrators, and these perspectives add complexity.

  Example: Patricia Smith's excellent poetry collection, *Blood Dazzler*, describes Hurricane Katrina from multiple perspectives, including that of the storm. Toni Morrison's *The Bluest Eye* jumps between characters multiple times in the novel, as does George R.R. Martin's *Game of Thrones*.

- **Complexity of Story**—Some stories make extensive use of symbolism, extended metaphor, or allegory. In other cases, they have particularly labyrinthine plot structures.

  Example: *Animal Farm*, by George Orwell, takes on substantially more complexity when considered as an allegory. Stephen Graham Jones's *Mapping the Interior* is both horror story and social commentary on the Native American experience.

- **Intentionally Resistant Text**—Some texts (especially poems) have structures that intentionally resist easy meaning-making. That is, part of the meaning is created from deliberate gaps in clarity.

  Example: Claudia Rankine's "Citizen" is a book-length poem that experiments with form and defies easy categorization. Tim O'Brien's *The Things They Carried* makes ample use of paradox:

  Right here, now, as I invent myself, I'm thinking of all I want to tell you about why this book is written as it is. For instance, I want to tell you this: twenty years ago I watched a man die on a trail near the village of My Khe. I did not kill him. But I was present, you see, and my presence was guilt enough. I remember his face, which was not a pretty face, because his jaw was in his throat, and I remember feeling the burden of responsibility and grief. *But listen. Even that story is made up.*

Texts vary in the type and amount of qualitative complexity they offer. Edgar Allan Poe's "The Telltale Heart" includes multiple challenges: archaic language, complexity of story, and complexity of narrator, while Tommy Orange's *There There* relies on non-linear time sequence and a complex set of narrators.

Keeping the qualitative complexity of text in mind, let's revisit Steve's sample text choices:

Sample—8th-Grade Texts & Qualitative Complexity

Text	Selected Factors of Qualitative Complexity
Persepolis	Complexity of story (a graphic novel, pairing images and text)
In the Time of the Butterflies (910)	Complexity of narrator (multiple narrators) Non-linear time sequence Complexity of story (symbolism)
Animal Farm (1170)	Complexity of story (symbolism, allegory)
The Narrative of the Life of Frederick Douglass (1080)	Archaic language Complexity of story (irony)
Othello	Archaic language (Shakespearean!) Complexity of story (figurative language)

When we look at these texts from this perspective, we see that Steve gives students multiple at-bats with increasingly complex symbolism at the beginning of the sequence. We also see that he reordered the texts despite Lexile—shifting *Animal Farm* before Frederick Douglass's narrative—so that students could stick with symbolism and then spend the latter half of the year working with archaic language. With this additional insight, the care behind Steve's sequencing choices becomes clearer.

Stop and Jot—Qualitative Complexity

Analyze the qualitative complexity of your texts in the same way Steve did. What are your takeaways?

Text	Factors of Qualitative Complexity

When put together, curricular, quantitative, and qualitative complexity create a rich journey for students to deepen their understanding of literature and the world. The final aspect of a quality curriculum is what we ask students to do with the texts they read.

TASK COMPLEXITY

If the complexity of the text matters, so does the task that accompanies it. Take a moment to review these four possible essay assignments for Elie Wiesel's *Night*. As you read, consider: How does each assignment determine the complexity of students' experience with the text during the unit?

Stop and Jot—Defining Task Complexity

Task 1: Connect the lessons of *Night* to another event in history: How are they similar or different?

Task 2: What is a theme of *Night*? Cite examples from the text.

Task 3: How does Wiesel use the idea of night, both literally and figuratively, to recount his experience in the Holocaust? Consider this concept throughout the book and in relation to his trilogy (*Night, Dawn, Day*).

Task 4: Elie Wiesel's original draft of *Night* was 865 pages long. Choose three sections and their revisions and explain: How do Wiesel's changes in structure and language affect the meaning of the passage? Which version do you believe is stronger, and why?

* * *

How does each assignment determine the complexity of students' experience with the text during the unit?

_____

_____

_____

_____

As you read through each task, one takeaway is certain: the work a student must do for each one is strikingly different. Each successive task asks students to get closer and closer to the text. In the first, a student could write about *Night* without having read it. Listening to class discussions or using a cheat sheet summary of the text would be enough to get by. The second task requires reading, but the amount of analysis required depends on how specific and precise the cited examples are. The third task asks students to read closely for a single idea woven throughout the text and two additional texts. The final task demands the most: a comparative close rereading of specific passages alongside their original counterparts.

Depending on which task you chose as the culminating assessment, you'd get very different measures for what students are able to do by the end. What's more, your unit would probably look a lot different depending on this final task. As Paul notes in

Driven by Data and *Leverage Leadership*, standards are meaningless until you define how to assess them. So, too, in curriculum planning. The journey to understanding a text is not clear until you determine the destination task(s) and how you will evaluate them. The destination defines the path.

Core Idea

The destination defines the path.
Assessment tasks are the starting point for instruction, not the end.

The tasks we assign can greatly enhance or decrease what students will need to do with the text, and thus the depth of their reading. So it's crucial that we create the task before—not after—we teach the text. For example, if you were to choose the fourth task, the one Steve and his planners decided on, you'd pay particular attention to opportunities for close reading of language and structure, and you'd develop lessons and rubrics aligned to your expectations.

Generating a quality task takes time, but it's well worth the effort. The questions below will help you begin.

- What do I want students to be able to say about this text?
- What task will require them to closely read the text to be able to answer it?

Let's imagine we were planning a destination assessment for John Steinbeck's *The Pearl*. A straightforward prompt might simply ask students to explain the symbolism of one object in the text (e.g. the pearl). It's important for the text, and it requires pulling evidence from multiple sections. But we might decide that this will lead to too superficial of a unit.

Instead, we might decide we want students to be able to explain the critique of capitalism embedded in Steinbeck's text. We could say: "*The Pearl* takes place in Mexico, but many argue it is really about the United States. Agree or Disagree, citing the text and two additional articles/essays." This prompt would ask students to explain Steinbeck's critique and whether they agree or disagree with it. It would pair well with a unit on argumentative writing and give students an authentic opportunity to workshop their new writing skills.

Or perhaps we've already worked on argumentative writing and want to focus on text structures. One of the challenging aspects of this text is hidden in its resolution. A character dies (no spoilers, we promise), and a close reading of the text reveals that the murderer is never actually named—the reader needs to decide who it is. This is a pretty provocative omission, and analyzing it requires really thinking about Steinbeck's messages. Were we working on text structure, we might ask: "In your opinion, who killed X? Why wouldn't Steinbeck make this clear, and why does the answer to this question matter for his themes?" We could imagine kicking this task off with an energetic class debate.

Not every destination needs to be an essay, and students often benefit from the ability to choose between multiple options.[26] If your expectations are clear, students can do the same level of analysis and thinking in creative writing (e.g., adding and performing a scene for *Othello*), performance tasks (e.g., holding "character court" and writing "legal briefs" defending or attacking a character's motives), or interdisciplinary study (e.g., explaining how characters would respond to moments being studied in history, or how historical figures would have interacted with characters). In addition to more traditional essays, students can write reviews, blogs, letters, articles, or direct short films.

While we are not limited in the types of tasks we create, the key to making them a true reading task (versus something they can do by simply listening to class discussion) is to answer these two questions effectively:

- **What do I want students to be able to say about this text?**
  - o Does my task require students to understand this text in its fullness?
  - o What aspects of this text do I want students to analyze? What task will push them beyond their comfort zone and into a place of intellectual risk?
  - o What concepts have we already studied this year, and what haven't we discussed yet?

- **What task will require students to closely read the text to be able to answer it?**

  - o Do they need to marshal evidence, or could they get by on just a summary?
  - o What types of tasks have my students already completed this year?
  - o Is there an opportunity to be creative or allow my students some choice?

At first, it can be difficult to generate a "perfect" task, so lean on your fellow teachers to build one together. This will take time. But combined with quantitative, qualitative, and curricular complexity, your work with task complexity will take you a long way toward developing a curriculum of real elegance and depth.

Stop and Jot—Task Complexity

Use these questions to evaluate the tasks for one of the texts you teach.
What do you want students to say about the text?

_____

_____

_____

_____

What task will require them to closely read the text to be able to answer it?
Would you keep your original task or modify it?

_____

_____

_____

CONCLUSION

By now, you may already have some thoughts on where you might push your curriculum in the coming year. At the end of Part 1, we'll share some resources to help you start doing this. (And in Part 4, we'll help you put together everything you learn reading this book.) For now, take a moment to jot down the ideas you want to explore further.

Stop and Jot—My Takeaways

What are your top takeaways for your classroom so far?

_____

_____

_____

_____

A complexity curriculum defines the dream. But by its nature, an ambitious dream will bring in its wake more students in struggle. As we've mentioned before, students can't fall for a book if they don't know what it's saying. So what does understanding look like, especially with a challenging text?

Chapter 2

What Does It Mean to "Get It"?

UNDERSTANDING COMPLEX TEXTS

Alison Bechdel's 2006 graphic novel *Fun Home* is a memoir of her youth. It focuses on her complex relationship with her father and the different paths their lives take when they confront (or choose not to confront) their sexual orientation. Since its publication, *Fun Home* has garnered much acclaim, including being named one of *The Guardian's* top 100 books of the twenty-first century.[1] In this scene, Alison walks in on her father, Bruce, as he reads in their home library. What can you infer about him based on the information in these two panels? (See Figure 2.1.)

Figure 2.1

Source: © Fun Home by Alison Bechdel.

Here's what we might say about Bruce, at a few different levels of depth:

- **First Reading:** Bechdel draws a comparison between her father and Jay Gatsby, the protagonist of F. Scott Fitzgerald's *The Great Gatsby*. Bruce, like Gatsby, has a well-stocked library. In the second panel, Bechdel notes that their libraries signal a preference for fiction over reality—hinting, perhaps, that these men share a love of stories. (We know from earlier in the novel that Bruce teaches literature.)

- **Second Reading:** Bechdel refers to the library scene in *The Great Gatsby* in the first panel. First, she notes a partygoer's surprise that Gatsby's books are real, and then she quotes his exclamation, "What thoroughness! What realism! Knew when to stop, too! Didn't cut the pages." Although we know both scenes take place in a library, why does Bechdel make mention that Gatsby's books are real? And what does the partygoer mean by "Didn't cut the pages?"

Let's bring some additional background knowledge to our analysis by reading (or recalling) the corresponding scene from *The Great Gatsby*. The narrator and partygoer have entered the library for the first time:

> "What do you think?" he [the partygoer] demanded impetuously.
>
> "About what?" [asks Nick, the narrator]
>
> He waved his hand toward the book-shelves.
>
> "About that. As a matter of fact you needn't bother to ascertain. I ascertained. They're real."
>
> "The books?" He nodded.
>
> "Absolutely real—have pages and everything. I thought they'd be a nice durable cardboard. Matter of fact they're absolutely real. Pages and—Here! Lemme show you."
>
> Taking our skepticism for granted he rushed to the book-cases and returned with Volume One of the "Stoddard Lectures."
>
> "See!" He cried triumphantly. "It's a bona-fide piece of printed matter. It fooled me. This fella's a regular Belasco. It's a triumph. What thoroughness! What realism! Knew when to stop, too—didn't cut the pages. But what do you want? What do you expect?"
>
> He snatched the book from me and replaced it hastily on its shelf muttering that if one brick was removed the whole library was liable to collapse.

The partygoer calls Gatsby "a regular Belasco." David Belasco was an American theater producer known to use lighting to stage things that *looked* real. So the partygoer isn't impressed that the library *is* real, but rather that it *appears* real; this is what he praises when he cries, "What thoroughness! What realism!" This tension between reality and the appearance of reality occurs again when the partygoer notes the books' uncut pages. With some background knowledge on this era, you'll know that in the 1920s books were printed on large sheets of paper that were folded several times to make pages. Today, the printer cuts these. But to read a book back then, one needed to cut the pages apart by slicing the fold that ran along the top or the side of joined pages. Books in this pre-cut state were known as "unopened." All of Gatsby's books are unopened; he hasn't read a single one.

So, Gatsby is not the man we thought he was—he's projecting an image of himself as he *wants* to be seen. With this new insight, Bechdel's comparison of the two men takes on a new shade of meaning: although Bruce has read his books, the fiction that both he and Gatsby prefer is not found in books but in how they live their lives.

- **Third Reading:** Let's take a second look at the specific book Bruce is reading in these panels. It's *Zelda,* a biography of Zelda Sayre Fitzgerald, F. Scott Fitzgerald's wife. After looking up some information about the book, we find out that Zelda was in some ways the real-life inspiration for Daisy, the tragic character that Gatsby hopes to win over with his facade. Bechdel took years to write *Fun Home,* and her research included rereading the books she alludes to.[2] Why import both *The Great Gatsby* and *Zelda* to talk about Bruce? Perhaps she wants to link Bruce to Gatsby and the Fitzgeralds because of the way their stories, and the lives they led, end.

Gatsby's world crashes down around him when he can no longer sustain it. The novel's library scene foreshadows this end when the partygoer mutters, "If one brick was removed the whole library was liable to collapse." The metaphor is telling: the books, like bricks, seem solid, but the structure they support is fundamentally unsound. This same fate, as Bruce will read in *Zelda,* awaits the author of *Gatsby* and his wife. Bechdel's comparison is now more robust: Bruce, like Gatsby, is unable to maintain his double-life. And like the Fitzgeralds, his world comes crashing down.

In just two panels, Bechdel imports an entire novel's worth of self-abnegating tragedy to link her father with Gatsby's—and the Fitzgeralds'—ultimately dark fate. For us, each new reading was an invitation to see more in the text, peeling back its layers to find multitudes. That's what it means to "get it."

Core Idea

Texts are like diamonds: they sparkle when we see multiple angles.

Some students might get the full depth of Bechdel's passage at first glance. But for many, an analysis like this may feel more like sleight of hand or, worse yet, the exclusive province of professional academics. But it isn't. "Getting it"—understanding and appreciating a text in all its complexity—isn't a magic trick. It's a multilayered process that requires three building blocks: background knowledge, the ability to dissect claims, and knowing when (and how) to read for analysis.

- **We used background knowledge.** We brought specific knowledge to bear on the text, and not just at the surface level. To enrich our analysis, we used knowledge about *The Great Gatsby*, David Belasco, "unopened" books, and F. Scott and Zelda Sayre Fitzgerald.

- **We read for the text's claims.** We read the panels for the overall meaning that Bechdel was signaling, noting her central claim in the second panel that focused on the shared preference of Bechdel's father, Gatsby, and Fitzgerald for fiction over reality.

- **We knew when and how to analyze more deeply.** We looked for moments of deeper meaning to enhance our understanding of the text thus far. For example, we paused to note that Bechdel's decision to compare her father to Gatsby was an important and likely key message to analyze. We scoured the panels for additional clues: we looked closely to note the presence of *Zelda* in Bruce's hands and asked about its significance. Then we stepped back to consider what all of this might mean for the work as a whole.

If we build and share each of these components with our students, we'll go a long way toward helping them "get" literature in a deeper way.[3]

BUILD BACKGROUND KNOWLEDGE

In our earlier section on complexity curriculum, we broke down a Michael Twitty article to see what it took to fully understand a text. A large part of the answer was background knowledge.

Schema, commonly referred to as background knowledge,[4] can make or break our understanding of a text, just as scholars like E. D. Hirsch have argued for years. Consider, for example, these sentences Hirsch shares from philosopher Immanuel Kant.[5] What is Kant trying to communicate?

> A manifold, contained in an intuition which I call mine, is represented, by means of the synthesis of the understanding, as belonging to the necessary unity of self-consciousness; and this is effected by means of the category.

Need a little more context? No problem—here's the next sentence.

> This requirement of a category therefore shows that the empirical consciousness of a given manifold in a single intuition is subject to a pure self-consciousness a priori, just as is empirical intuition to a pure sensible intuition, which likewise takes place a priori.[6]

Still stuck? Narrow your options with this multiple-choice answer set.

The main idea of this passage is:

a. Without a manifold, one cannot call an intuition "mine."
b. Intuition must precede understanding.
c. Intuition must occur through a category.
d. Self-consciousness is necessary to understanding.

Stop and Jot—The Meaning of Kant

What was the text about?

_____

_____

_____

Critical thinking or rereading is insufficient to crack a passage like this. Instead, what we need is context: an understanding of Kant's vocabulary and what these terms meant to him, the problem he was trying to solve, his goals and viewpoints, and the other topics about which he wrote. In other words, we need background knowledge. Without it, we can't unlock Kant. (If you're curious, the actual answer is C—but the real challenge is in justifying why that answer is correct. We'll leave that to the philosophers!)

When we talk about background knowledge, we mean more than a scattered collection of facts or dates. Background knowledge is most useful to readers when it is thorough. In fact, the amount of difficulty that a text presents is often based on what and how much prior knowledge we bring to bear on it. And there's the rub—there is no way to provide all the background knowledge we'd want students to have. That makes background knowledge the most difficult hurdle to comprehension for students to overcome.[7]

How does this insight support our teaching, especially our work with readers in struggle? It tells us that students need to draw from a rich pool of knowledge as they learn and practice comprehension strategies, especially as they grapple with the kinds of complex texts we want them to read. In this way, literacy instruction is like learning to drive. Yes, you need to know the methods for turning, braking, and accelerating. But without a car, you aren't going anywhere. Teaching strategies without background knowledge is like teaching driving without a car.

> ## Core Idea
>
> Teaching strategies without schema is like teaching driving without a car.

For English teachers, the importance of background knowledge presents an additional challenge. As cognitive scientist Daniel Willingham points out, "Adults with broad background knowledge (which helps them to be good readers) got that background knowledge by reading." In other words, readers get better at reading by reading more.

For avid readers with large pools of knowledge, this is a virtuous cycle. But for those who don't yet have vast knowledge, complex texts—and all the richness in language and ideas they offer—remain out of reach. This catch-22 is sometimes referred to as the Matthew Effect: the rich get richer, and the poor get poorer.[9] (See Figure 2.2.)

Figure 2.2 An illustration of Matthew writing. Researchers often talk about the Matthew Effect for knowledge: the rich get richer and the poor get poorer.

Source: Image from the Lindisfarne Gospels, in the public domain, Courtesy of Wikimedia Commons.

As our colleague Doug Lemov notes, this quickly becomes a question of equity: "The ability to build knowledge by reading and to learn from texts is a crucial driver to student success. . . . It is crucial to equity because many students' lack of background knowledge causes them to fall further and further behind."[10]

Willingham makes the following point:

Data from the last thirty years lead to a conclusion that is not scientifically challenge-able: thinking well requires knowing facts, and that's not true simply because you need something to think *about*. The very processes that teachers care about most—critical thinking processes such as reasoning and problem solving—are intimately entwined with factual knowledge that is stored in long-term memory (not just found in the environment).[11]

He explains that when we group knowledge into chunks, our working memory is freed up to think about more complex materials. The power of background knowledge becomes twofold: it makes reading easier and it frees up mental processes for deep thinking. For this reason, educators from Lemov to Daisy Christodoulou have challenged the common misunderstanding of Bloom's Taxonomy that subordinates factual understanding to analytical skill.[12] Why, they reason, do we treat knowledge as if it's simple and ignore the fundamental role it plays in comprehension?[13]

While it takes a lifetime of reading to build background knowledge, the way that we select and order texts can spark this process on a smaller scale. Models of vocabulary acquisition suggest that reading progressively challenging texts on a topic builds neural models that help readers understand words that aren't even in the texts themselves. (For example, students might understand "extraterrestrial" if they previously learned "subterranean.")

This appears to work not just for vocabulary, but for the complex ideas that the words represent. "As a simplistic example," writes cognitive scientist Marilyn Jager Adams, "when we read about tigers, then, by dint of both similarities and contrasts, we learn more about all sorts of cats and, further, about every subtopic mentioned along the way. The more deeply we read about tigers, the more nuanced and complex these concepts and their interrelations become."[14] According to Jager Adams, the solution isn't just breadth of reading, it's also depth of complexity. Progressively assigning complex texts on a topic—sometimes referred to as the "ladder of complexity"—allows students to access more challenging concepts that simpler texts or high-low reading materials trim out. Building schema in this way empowers all readers, but it is particularly effective in building the knowledge base and confidence of readers in struggle.

Figure 2.3 In Greek mythology, the blind giant Orion carried Cedalion on his shoulders to act as his eyes. When we build background knowledge, we allow students to climb on the shoulders of other texts they've read. They see farther.

Source: Courtesy of Wikimedia Commons, in the public domain.

In 1675, Isaac Newton famously said that "If I have seen further, it is by standing on the shoulders of giants."[15] (See Figure 2.3.) All readers stand on the shoulders of their schema; it helps students see farther to more complex ideas, and these texts in turn give them a more complete pool of background knowledge.

> ### Core Idea
>
> All readers stand on the shoulders of their schema.

So if we want to make complex texts understandable, how do we determine the most important background knowledge to teach and when to teach it? We can take the following steps.

Step 1: Start with the End in Mind—What You Want Students to "Get"

Many texts are so rich and layered with complexity that you could teach them from four different angles and still not unpack everything. As such, your first step is to decide the approach(es) you want students to take with the text—and what task can measure this. Think back to the questions we used in Chapter 1:

- What key task/prompt do I want to give students once they finish reading?
- What, ideally, do I want students to be able to say or do when completing that task?

Once you have a clear vision of your goal, you can begin to think about what it takes to get there.

Step 2: Identify What They Need to Do to "Get It"

This next step is the most difficult. You need to unpack all the knowledge you brought intuitively to your reading of the text so you can identify where a student might not have the knowledge to do the same. Ask yourself:

- What knowledge is *most* essential for grappling with the text and my lesson/unit goals?

First, think about both historical and literary knowledge. For example, if students don't know anything about Communist Russia, or how an allegory works, they can't really access George Orwell's *Animal Farm*. If students don't know what the Jacobean period was or what a soliloquy is, they'll miss much of *Macbeth*.[16]

After that, though, broaden your scope to consider your unit themes.[17] Ask yourself:

- What understanding will help my students see the relevance and power in this text? What knowledge is *most* essential for the way this text explores its themes?

For example, if students are reading *Animal Farm*, you might go beyond the back-grounder on Communism and share the history of a few global uprisings—those that succeeded, and others (as in Orwell's text) that did not. Likewise, students reading Rita Williams-Garcia's *One Crazy Summer* of course benefit from knowing about the Black Panther Party, which features prominently in the book. At the same time, they benefit from thinking about the meaning and power of names (including their own), since that's thematically important to the text.

Just like highlighting essential questions, this approach helps ensure our novels—especially any written more than a decade ago—feel relevant to our students. Connection is key. Regardless of what book we are teaching, our students need to know why the texts in the curriculum matter to them. Thematic schema is powerful to introduce at any time, but we have found it particularly useful on the first days of a unit, as we preview the text and why it is worthy of our students' time and attention.

Step 3: Tier It—Build Knowledge with Increasingly Complex Texts

Most likely, some of the background knowledge you'll identify is quite basic (e.g. students need to know a few key vocabulary terms that can be memorized). Other background knowledge is more complex and well beyond the easy reach of your students. For that sort of knowledge, we can tier the information by providing a text set. As Jager Adams pointed out earlier, providing students with a series of increasingly complex texts on a single topic supercharges their conceptual networks. Sequencing tiered materials to build background knowledge for units takes time, however, and Jager Adams admits it cannot be easily completed by individual teachers or even schools.[18] The good news is that in the past few years it has become much simpler to locate high-quality texts at various levels of challenge. Here are some concrete steps to do this:

How to Locate Tiered Schema

1. **Hit the stacks:** The library is a great resource. Databases such as EBSCO's *Middle Search Plus* and *Explora Secondary Schools* allow users to filter results by Lexile.

2. **Work your textbooks:** Textbooks written for various grades can be additional resources both above and below the complexity of your own grade level. If the topic you're seeking connects with your school's history or science curricula, these may be on hand to borrow.

---

3. **Google it:** The Internet's cup runneth over with informational articles, and these can be assessed via Lexile.com's analyzer or another complexity assessment tool. Make sure to carefully review the source of the information you're reading and weigh what you find for accuracy and bias.

4. **Find a partner:** In the past few years, many organizations, from Newsela to CommonLit to the Smithsonian's TweenTribune have curated materials searchable by complexity, even providing multiple versions of the same text at various Lexile levels. Student Achievement Partners provides an assortment of text sets for commonly taught topics, as well as guidance on how to leverage text sets to enhance an independent reading library. In many cases, materials are free to use and are suggested for commonly taught novels, allowing teachers to search curated materials to build text sets. Links to get you started are in the next endnote.[19]

Step 4: Plan Where to Build or "Drop" Knowledge

Once you know the knowledge your students will need, determine when and how you will provide it:

- Do you need to add pre-reading to the unit to build background knowledge?
- Are there key points during the reading process where you could "drop knowledge"—give students a small bit of information like the definition of a key term—to unlock meaning?

For any given lesson or unit, we can ask ourselves these questions to test where we need to embed additional information. The right knowledge at the right time is a powerful tool.

Core Idea

The right knowledge at the right time is a powerful tool.

Case Study: Putting It All Together

Let's see what this could look like. For this sample unit on Harper Lee's *To Kill a Mockingbird*, we've decided we want students to grapple with the novel's themes as they read and, at the end, consider these themes through a contemporary lens on social justice. Specifically, for the final prompt we want students to make a case that readers today should or should not consider Atticus a hero. Based on our end goal, the essential background knowledge for students follows:

- **Thematic Knowledge:**
  - **Polarization:** the increasing, contemporary concern that people have lost the ability to understand each other because we do not have shared notions of reality
  - **Gradualism:** the belief, implicit in Atticus's approach, that social change comes by small degrees. Again, this is a live debate in our society.

- **Historical Knowledge:**
  - **The Great Depression:** how it shaped the 1930s South, the degree of poverty in the town of Maycomb, and its similarities to, and differences from, the poverty of today
  - **Jim Crow laws:** the impact of these laws on the freedom and opportunity of African Americans and their fear of state-sponsored violence
  - **The Scottsboro trials:** what was unjust about The Scottsboro trials and why Harper Lee might have wanted to allude to these by the way she created her own

- **Literary Knowledge:**
  - **The bildungsroman:** the characteristics of these coming-of-age stories, their focus on the moral and intellectual development of a character, and the life lessons the characters often encounter
  - **The legal and scholarly debate about Atticus:** the debate about whether Atticus would have supported racial justice on his own, his membership in the state legislature, and his self-comparison in the novel to white supremacist James "Cotton Tom" Heflin[20]

We might launch the unit thinking about political polarization, a hot topic in the past few years and one for which it would be easy to find current articles and essays. We could also consider showing a clip from 2020's *The Social*

Dilemma, a documentary that questions whether social media is creating a world in which people operate from separate sets of facts. Prior to starting the novel, we'd also teach lessons on the Great Depression, the Jim Crow South, and the bildungsroman genre. Why these topics? The historical knowledge will help students understand the setting and dispositions they encounter, while familiarity with the bildungsroman genre will give students a stronger template to make predictions as they read.

Other information could be introduced later. The information about the Scottsboro trials will be most powerful if we introduce it during chapter 17, right as Tom Robinson's trial begins, as this will keep the comparison fresh in students' minds. Finally, we'd save the literary and legal criticism about Atticus until after students finish the book, so they can draw their own conclusions about him before scholars weigh in. Likewise, this would be a great time to review the idea of gradualism, perhaps listening to and analyzing the lyrics of Nina Simone's "Mississippi Goddam," with its refrain of "do it slow," or studying the part of Martin Luther King Jr.'s "I Have a Dream" speech that warns against the "tranquilizing drug of gradualism."

The final element of this process involves tiering schema-building texts. We've identified at least four areas of background knowledge for *To Kill A Mockingbird*, and it could be a big lift to tier readings for all of these. In some cases, a single article or two might be enough to share the knowledge needed. But for more complex ideas, it's worth it to tier. If you are pressed for time or lack high-quality resources, begin with a single essential topic—say the Jim Crow South—and tier just those texts. It could look something like this:

- **Textbook/Article:** "What was the Jim Crow South?" (750L); paired with short **video or image gallery** (n/a)
- **Interview:** Interview with someone who lived in the Jim Crow South (880L)
- **Article:** "Alabama votes to remove a vestige of the Jim Crow South" (1100L)
- **Textbook:** AP history review on the Jim Crow South (1250L)

Walk through this process with a text of your choice and fill out the following box.

Your Turn! Design Your Own Background Knowledge for a Text

Choose one of the books that you currently teach or would like to teach in the future. After you've completed reading the text, answer the following questions.

Start with the end in mind: What do you want students to "get"?

Design the final assessment for the text—the task you want students to complete and what you want them to be able to write:

_____

_____

_____

_____

What do they need to "get it?"

What knowledge is essential to unlock the deeper meaning of the text?

_____

_____

_____

_____

Tier it:

Do the students need to start simple to access the knowledge and slowly build up the Lexile level on the same topic? If so, propose those texts here:

_____

_____

_____

_____

When do they need it?

Go back to your list above and add a notation for the timing of each piece of knowledge:

- Pre-reading (they should do before starting the novel)
- During reading (right before or after they read a particular part of the novel)
- Post-reading (after completing the novel to prepare for the task)

Background knowledge is necessary to access texts fully, but—as we mentioned earlier—it's insufficient on its own for deep reading.[21] If we're reading complex texts, we'll need some enhanced moves to discern their central messages. Let's start with how to coach students to read for claim.

READ EVERYTHING FOR CLAIM

The work of Indiana University history Professor David Pace offers insight into where we can sharpen students' reading instincts. A recurring challenge plagued him: his first-year students struggled to separate the essential from the non-essential when they read.[22] Pace decided to model for students how he made sense of complex texts, using the following passage. What information do you think struck him as essential?

Stop and Jot—What Matters Most?

The Jewish apocalyptic genre emerged from earlier prophetic tradition but is distinct from it. The Jewish prophets from the eighth to the sixth centuries BC—Amos, Joel, Isaiah, Jeremiah, Ezekiel, and the others—functioned primarily as preachers, focusing on the people's transgressions and foretelling the Lord's renewed favor if they repented and further woes if they did not. The prophets were present minded and specific as they addressed a people beset by enemies and continually straying from the path of righteousness.

* * *

What information mattered most to Pace?

_____

_____

_____

Pace noted that his students weighted the details heavily when they read. Facts like these stood out to them:

- Apocalyptic genre
- Eighth to sixth century BC
- Jewish prophets—Amos, Joel, Isaiah, Jeremiah, Ezekiel
- Prophets addressed people beset by enemies

Pace, however, read for the full picture, not just the details. Look at his version of the text. He enlarged what mattered most and shrunk the less important. (See Figure 2.4.)

Let's compare the two approaches. The student version is heavy on the details (the *who*, *what*, and *when*) but light on purpose. We don't know *why* this information matters or how it connects to the text's overall meaning. If this is how Pace's students initially read about history, we can see why they struggled to remember the big ideas or link trends across time—their information lacked a connecting thread. Pace, however, read differently. He hunted first for the overall claim (the "story" as

Figure 2.4

"The Jewish apocalyptic genre emerged from the earlier prophetic tradition, but is distinct from it. The Jewish prophets of the eighth to the sixth centuries B.C.—Amos, Joel, Isaiah, Jeremiah, Ezekiel, and the others—functioned primarily as preachers, focusing on the people's transgressions and foretelling the Lord's renewed favor if they repented and further woes if they did not. The prophets were present minded and specific as they addressed a people beset by enemies and continually straying from the path of righteousness."

he called it) and then he looked for the sub-claims that supported it. Pace's process articulates something powerful. Text is claim: the heart of any writing is the statement it makes.

Core Idea

The heart of any text is the claim it makes.

Asking students to read for claim presupposes a philosophy that we want to name: *all* texts—from Instagram posts to Victorian novels—make arguments. For those who struggle to believe this, here's a thought exercise. Imagine a box of cereal that reads "Fortified with 12 essential vitamins; a great way to start your day!" Many of us would skim right past this line and miss two big claims: (1) that the cereal *is* fortified with vitamins and (2) that this cereal (along with its vitamins) is a great thing to eat in the morning. Although these claims seem innocuous, take a closer look. Even if the cereal has the vitamins it advertises, the support for supplementing our vitamin intake isn't nearly as ironclad as we imagine it to be.[23]

If all texts make claims, we have a choice as readers to accept or reject their messages. This is what it means to read well. In other words: everything's an argument. Our job as readers is to find the claims—and decide if we accept them.

Core Idea

Everything's an argument.
Our job as readers is to find the claims—and decide if we accept them.

Experienced readers read for claim all the time; it's an unconscious habit shaped by years of experience. In *Before Reading*, scholar Peter Rabinowitz argues that authors expect readers to read in certain ways—to know what is important in a text—and that this is often signaled by the conventions of genre as well as what readers know about how literature works.[24] What's more, authors use signals or "calls to attention" to direct readers' attention to key moments. With enough experience, we internalize the ways in which these appear.

Literacy experts Kylene Beers and Robert Probst translate Rabinowitz's theories into classroom-friendly "signposts" in their book *Notice and Note*. They argue that students will be far more equipped to figure out themes and big ideas if they are attuned to moments when texts are trying to tell us something. Macbeth's clothes *never* fit right? That matters. Zora Neale Hurston crafts a two-page description of a pear tree with charged, sexual diction? That matters. How about Jay Gatsby's library—full of real books that no one will ever read? That's important too.

These unspoken rules call our attention to key moments and messages. Some patterns are so pervasive we can map them across texts, like Joseph Campbell's "hero's journey" outline or the predictable structures of TV comedies from *Seinfeld* to *Rick and Morty*.[25] When we teach students to look for the signals that an author provides, we invite them to see the hidden operating system that runs in the background of literature. This approach, academics have since argued, applies to nonfiction as much as fiction.[26] And once we become sensitive to how texts work, it becomes far easier to develop a radar for the important moments.

So how do we bring all of this to life for students? Let's test it out by reading a short news article.

How to Read for Claim in Informational Texts

"The Hive Mind" is an article that New York State included on its 2018 8th-grade literacy assessment. The full article is about 1,000 words long with a Lexile between 1000 and 1100, so it's a good midpoint for secondary school study. Let's read part of it for claim. What's the big message in the text? And how do you know?

Stop and Jot—Reading for Claim in "The Hive Mind"

Read the very beginning of the article (feel free to mark it up!). As you read, keep track of how you make sense of it.

Figure 2.5

The Hive Mind

by Avery Elizabeth Hurt

1   Honeybees are the picture of hard work and cooperation. They pollinate plants, helping to ensure that humans will have enough food to eat. They also make honey, protect themselves from predators, and keep the interiors of their hives at just the right temperature. But even though they are pretty impressive as a group, individual bees don't have much going on in the mental department—or so science has always thought. What would you expect from a single bee, anyway? It has a brain roughly the size of one of the sesame seeds on your hamburger bun.

2   It has only about one million neurons, compared to the 90 billion neurons of the human brain. It's only by working together as a colony that bees manage to pull off the impressive feats they are so well known for. A colony of bees is like one big brain, and the bees are like brain cells, explains animal behaviorist and bee expert Thomas Seeley. "Even though each unit (bee or neuron) has limited information and limited intelligence, the group as a whole makes first-rate collective decisions," Seeley writes in a description of his research.

Source: Avery Elizabeth Hurt, 2015 / Carus Publishing Company.

Without realizing it, you probably made several moves to help you identify the claim, beginning right with the opening words. Here's our thought process:

Read the Beginning to Identify the Topic and Opening Claim

The first thing we notice is the headline: "The Hive Mind." We know this phrase often refers to groupthink, and "hive" makes us think of bees. After finishing the first two paragraphs, we have enough information to jot a note about the topic:

- Topic: Honeybee intelligence

We also noticed that this article is written in a type of journalistic prose. If we recall what we know about that genre, we can be on the lookout for how it communicates information through its structure. For example:

- News articles usually have headlines that signal their content.

- News articles are generally written in a neutral register, which means we need to look for claims that are made directly by sources. (In this case, we can see Thomas Seeley makes the claim that bees, collectively, are smart.)

- News articles often state their key claims a few paragraphs in. Journalists call this a delayed lede. This means we may need to read a bit further to determine what this text is really about.

After we've considered the genre and identified the topic, we can look for the claims the text makes about that topic.[27] Here's what we have after reading the first two paragraphs:

- Claim 1: As a group, the intelligence of bees is impressive. (A margin note could have been: *bee group intelligence=impressive*)

Read the Middle for Sub-Claims and Shifts

We're now in the meat of the article. As we continue to track the claims in this text, a few calls to attention catch our eye. Try it for yourself:

We finished reading paragraph 3 and *aha!* A new sub-claim becomes clear:

- Claim 2: Individual bees are smarter than researchers thought, even more than many mammals. (Margin jot could be: *New evidence: 1 bee brain ≥ many mammals*)

How did we figure that out? Look more closely at paragraph 3. The article gave us a clue with the word "however." Authors use transitions like "however," "nevertheless," or even "but" to signal a shift in ideas, and this is a great place to find a new claim. That's precisely what happens in the first sentence of paragraph 3; the author contradicts the earlier claim that bees are unintelligent.

As the passage continues, the author continues to use features of the genre to build a case for bee intelligence. A subhead between paragraph 3 and 4 directs our attention to the new topic. Paragraph 4 signals us next, posing a rhetorical question to introduce the author's next claim: how to study bee cognition. Rhetorical questions are great set-ups for direct claim statements. Their answer *is* the claim.[28]

Level Up When Struggling

The average 8th grader might find this next section a bit tougher than the rest (Figure 2.7):

Stop and Jot—Reading for Claim in "The Hive Mind," Part 3

Review this next section in its entirety. Where might a reader in struggle stumble?

Figure 2.7

How to Study a Bee Brain

4   It's hard enough to study the minds of humans, who can actually tell you what they're thinking. So how does one look into a bee's brain?

5   Clint Perry, a scientist working at Queen Mary University of London, has spent a lot of time studying how bees think. He says studying bees is not very different from studying other animals. "A major difficulty is designing an experiment that will actually test what we want," he says. "With humans, we can ask them a question and get an answer. But bees don't know that we want to know what they are thinking. They are just trying to get sugar. Bees like sugar."

6   This fact can be very helpful when designing experiments to study bees. For example, in one experiment, Perry gave bees a choice between landing on a spot above a black bar or a spot below it. If they landed above the bar, they would find a delicious sugary drink. If they chose the spot below the black bar, they found a nasty-tasting bitter liquid. (Perry made the test easier or harder by moving the landing spots farther from or closer to the black bar.) Most experiments with bees involve training them to go to a particular spot to find a reward. Many studies use artificial flowers with sugar water at their centers. In some experiments bees even learn to go through mazes.

7   So experiments with bees are not that different from experiments with our favorite lab mammal, the rat. Rats press bars to get food pellets; bees land on targets to get sugary drinks. And humans try to figure out what it all means.

Source: Avery Elizabeth Hurt, 2015 / Carus Publishing Company.

A reader in struggle would likely need additional support to make sense of this section, especially without background knowledge on animal intelligence testing. (Admittedly, it's not a common topic of conversation.)

What if we taught students that this struggle was natural and gave them—in advance—some moves to use when faced with a challenging section of text?

- **Slow down and reread:** Starting at the point of confusion, have students reread the text line by line, jotting annotations more frequently as they go. In the case of "The Hive Mind," students should start at paragraph 6 and set a purpose for their reading—rereading and annotating the text to better visualize the bee and rat experiments.

- **Paraphrase the most difficult lines:** Another technique is to spend time paraphrasing the most difficult sentences. Identify the subjects and verbs, chunk the sentence into smaller parts, and try to paraphrase each part. This could involve using context clues for challenging vocabulary or phrases.

- **Skip ahead and come back later:** Sometimes the best way to break through is to skip ahead, learn that content, and use it to come back and understand. This happens intuitively to most of us when faced with a daunting task, but we can teach this explicitly to students.

- **Scan the end (leverage your knowledge of text structure):** The end of a subsection often ties together the claims it makes, which is exactly what happens here. Paragraph 7 makes a direct claim that researchers draw conclusions about animal thinking through their reward-seeking behaviors in lab experiments. For particularly challenging texts, it can even be helpful to read the final paragraphs or closing sentences of the larger passage. These often reveal key arguments, allowing students to then go back to earlier sections.

- **Gut check your knowledge:** There are times that a text might assume knowledge of readers that they simply don't have. For example, if we had no conception of what lab testing for rats entails, the comparison to bee testing holds little meaning. Kylene Beers and Robert Probst advocate for students to be thoughtful about what an author thinks they already know. It's a beautiful metacognitive moment that invites students to forgive themselves when they realize they're missing key background knowledge—and then do something about it.[29]

Struggle isn't something to be avoided. In fact, struggle is the hallmark of learning; it tells us students are being challenged. When students have trouble with a text, we want them to notice this frustration, pause, and select more targeted strategies: rereading, paraphrasing, and leveraging other parts of the text. We call this process "leveling up." A number of students we've worked with affectionately call it "beast mode."[30]

Generate an End Note that Captures the Claim

Once we've read all the way to the end, we need to make sense of the overall text. Here is the list of claims that we jotted as we continued reading the full text. (Were we writing in the margins, we'd use our own shorthand, but we've expanded our jots here for clarity.) Review these notes and consider: What would an overall statement of claim be for the full text?

Stop and Jot—"The Hive Mind" Claims

- **Topic:** Bee intelligence
- **Claim #1 (opening claim):** As a group, the intelligence of bees is impressive.
- **Claim #2:** Individual bees are smarter than researchers thought, even more than many mammals.
- **Claim #3:** Scientists study bees by looking at reward-seeking behavior.
- **Claim #4:** Research suggests that bees appear to act based on the likelihood of success.
- **Claim #5:** It's unclear to what level bees actually think. Studying bees helps us better understand how brains (theirs and ours) work.

* * *

What's the main idea of this article?

_____

_____

_____

Here's our note on the overall claim (main idea):

- Researchers are discovering that bees have a greater capacity for reasoning than previously thought, though it's still unclear to what extent they can "think."

Reading for claim has multiple benefits. As teachers, students' claim notes help us peek inside their heads. We can see which aspects of a text students have understood and which aspects have gone misunderstood or unnoticed. For students, annotations and claim notes help them track their understanding as they read. This process signals that texts rarely have simple main ideas; they are often the result of multiple sub-claims working in concert.

Reading for claim creates a path through the thicket. We've compiled the moves we used to clear the way in the guide that follows.

Reading and Annotating for

Claim

Make sense of the most challenging informational texts.

Every text is arguing something. Read to find the topic and claim about the topic, and you can unlock the most challenging texts.

Beginning	**Read the Beginning to Identify the Topic & Opening Claim**

	• Start with the title, blurb, and the first paragraph(s)—carefully read and annotate:
	  ○ Identify the speaker and genre; note any obvious bias
	  ○ Jot the topic in the margin after 1–2 paragraphs
	  ○ Jot the opening claim

Middle	**Read the Middle for Sub-Claims & Shifts**
	Annotate words/lines that develop the initial claim and/or establish additional claims:
	
	• Annotate arguments:
	  ○ Underline sentences that make a "how" or a "why" claim (esp. at beginning of paragraphs)
	  ○ Circle key words that signal arguments and author's perspective (e.g. "similarly," "in other words," "surprisingly," rhetorical questions, charged diction, "I" statements)
	  ○ Jot a claim note next to key claims, sub-sections and charts/graphs
	• Annotate shifts in thinking/transition words:
	  ○ Circle words that show a shift in thinking (e.g. "however," "although," "despite this," "in fact")
	  ○ Circle phrases that signal the author is addressing counter-arguments (e.g. "critics say," "some might argue," "while many people believe")

End	**Generate an End Note That Captures the Claim**
	• Review your annotations: How do all of my notes connect to reveal the author's claim about the topic?
	• Write a final end note: What is the claim about the topic that this text makes (the central idea)?
	• Check your end note for precision:
	○ Does it articulate the author's perspective on the topic?
	○ Does it synthesize all of the key sub-claims you annotated?

When You Struggle, Level Up

If the paragraph or sentence is challenging	**Anytime you Struggle with a Paragraph or Sentence, Level Up**
	• Slow down and reread—increase your annotations to every 2–3 lines
	• Paraphrase the most difficult lines
	○ Identify subjects and verbs (particularly when there are unclear pronouns and/or multiple subjects)
	○ Chunk a sentence into smaller parts and try to paraphrase each
	○ Unpack challenging vocabulary—use context clues to define terms or for connotation
	○ Review the surrounding text for phrases that provide additional context
	• Skip ahead and come back later
	○ Learn the future content and use it to come back and understand
If a larger section looks challenging	**Scan to the End [difficult texts only]**
	• Shorter text: read the final paragraph & opening/closing sentences of each paragraph to ID key claims
	• Longer text: read the final section, subheadings, and text features to identify key claims
	Gut Check Your Knowledge
	• Ask yourself: Does this text assume I know something I don't? If so, look it up.

Right now, you might be thinking that reading for claim in an informational text—especially something like a news article—is dramatically different from working with a piece of fiction. Some might even argue that novels don't make claims the way non-narrative texts do.

Yet narrative fiction is no stranger to claims. In fact, it makes some of the boldest claims of all. Consider what a work of fiction asks of its readers: an author presents us with an imagined set of people, places, and details so that, through a sequenced set of imaginings, we arrive at a new understanding.

Narrative texts build arguments just like non-narrative ones. They just use a different set of techniques to signal their message, and so we describe their claims differently—as themes. Essentially, a theme is a claim made by a narrative text.

Core Idea

A theme is a claim made by a narrative text.

Themes in fiction work differently than non-narrative claims. They can be more subtle, self-contradictory, and so multifaceted that they inspire critical debates that never get resolved. As students develop as readers, they'll be able to read with new and powerful lenses that suggest multiple interpretations, none of which is singularly "correct." That's the beauty of fiction.

Think back to Alison Bechdel's novel *Fun Home*. Take a moment to contemplate what you did intellectually when we first looked at those two panels in Bechdel's text. Likely, even subconsciously, you did the following: you began with the genre (in graphic novels, images are essential parts of the reading). Next, you read the lines to get the text's perspective—that of an intellectual daughter reflecting on her father. After that, you tried to figure out what this text was claiming—in this case, about Bruce. But while your opening moves with narrative text were similar to what we did to understand "The Hive Mind," they started to shift as you sussed out the excerpt's claims.

Narrative claims are often more implicit than non-narrative ones, so we can't simply ask students to underline claims when they see them. Instead, we can guide students toward the breadcrumbs that will allow them to draw their own inferences from the text. We teach these clues to students as the 4 C's—characterization, conflict/resolution, changes in the narrative, and the author's craft—and we give them a system to annotate for them as they read.

Teaching students a base system for reading narrative texts carries the same benefits as the framework we provided for reading non-narrative ones. It helps students to develop a radar for authors' calls to attention and to see how texts—even fictional ones—construct the claims they make. With the above information in mind, students can begin to propose a potential theme.

We have captured our approach to reading narrative texts in the following guide. As you review, note the similarities and differences between it and reading for claim in a non-narrative text:

Theme

*Make sense of challenging
narrative texts.*

*Every text is arguing something. Themes are claims that narrative texts make
about the world, humanity, or society.*

Beginning	**Read the Text About the Text and the Beginning** • Start with the blurb, title (and book jacket, if applicable) to ID the genre and topic • Carefully read the first paragraphs and annotate the text's narrative perspective

Middle	**Read the Middle to Spot Themes: Look for the 4 C's:**
	Underline sentences that hint at themes and jot a 1–4 word margin note by key ideas:
	
	• **Conflict/Resolution**—what the conflict is, and how the conflict is resolved, are huge clues about the author's message
	• **Characterization**—how the author develops the personality of characters. What are your initial theories? (Consider how the setting is "characterized," too.)
	• **Changes**—big shifts in characterization, chronology (flashback), setting, or narrative perspective
	• **Craft**—calls to attention in an author's language (MR. CUF)
	   ○ <u>**M**ultiple Meanings</u>: images/words/ideas that appear to have multiple meanings (allusions, symbols, wordplay)
	   ○ <u>**R**epeated images</u>/words/ideas
	   ○ <u>**C**harged connotations</u> with images/words/ideas
	   ○ <u>**U**nexpected or surprising</u> images/words/ideas
	   ○ <u>**F**igurative language</u> (simile, metaphor, imagery, personification, etc.)

Theme Note	**At the End of the Text or Chapter, Generate an End Note on the Theme:**

	• Review your annotations and ask: How do all of my notes connect to build to a theme for this section? (Theme = a universal topic and a claim about that topic)
	• Write a final end note: theme(s) (or how this chapter helps support a theme(s))
	   ◦ If you struggle, review the list of universal topics/conflicts that follows. Choose one that applies. Think: What does the text say about this subject?
	
	• Check your end note for precision:
	   ◦ Does it match your annotations?
	   ◦ Is it text-based?
	   ◦ Does it avoid clichés?

When You Struggle, Level Up

When you struggle, level up	**Any Time You Struggle with a Paragraph or Sentence, Move to Level Up Strategies:**
	 • Slow down and reread—increase your annotations to every 2–3 lines. • Reread challenging areas twice, then skip and come back if still stuck. **Paraphrase the Most Difficult Lines** • Identify subjects and verbs (particularly when there are unclear pronouns and/or multiple subjects). • Chunk a sentence into smaller parts, try to paraphrase each. • Unpack challenging vocabulary—use context clues to define terms or for connotation. • Review the surrounding text for phrases that provide additional context.

Universal topics and conflicts	A theme is a statement about the world, humanity, or society, so it should always be a full sentence. However, there are many topics that occur throughout literature. If you're stuck thinking about how to articulate a theme, review the following universal topics and conflicts. Answer the questions:
	1. What topics or conflicts does this text discuss? Is there one that isn't on the list?
	2. What message does the text have about this topic or conflict?

Universal Topics		Universal Conflicts	
Loss of innocence	Circle of life	Youth v. Experience	Slavery v. Freedom
Personal growth	Coming of age	Love v. Hate	Darkness v. Light
Justice	Family	Appearance v. Reality	Good v. Evil
Overcoming oppression	Self-knowledge	Safety v. Freedom	Ignorance v. Knowledge
Beauty	Freedom/ Independence	Individual v. Society	
Love			

Teaching our students to read for claim and theme gives them habits of mind they can bring to any text. Once we've done that, we can teach them how to think about what they've read.

READ FOR ANALYSIS

> Literature, real literature, must not be gulped down like some potion which may be good for the heart or good for the brain—the brain, that stomach of the soul. Literature must be taken and broken to bits, pulled apart, squashed—then its lovely reek will be smelt in the hollow of the palm, it will be munched and rolled upon the tongue with relish; then, and only then, its rare flavor will be appreciated at its true worth and the broken and crushed parts will again come together in your mind and disclose the beauty of a unity to which you have contributed something of your own blood.
>
> —Vladimir Nabokov, *Lectures on Russian Literature*

Analysis is a tantalizing topic—and we mean that in the "mythological Greek torture" sense of the word.[31] While we know great analysis when we see it, pinning it down in the affirmative can be a challenge. As students, many of us were taught to simply talk about "what matters" or to "go deep" on the text. That sort of guidance is simply too vague to sharpen our craft or that of our students.

So let's use Ezra Pound's "In a Station of the Metro" to get more specific. (You'll recall it from our discussion of qualitative complexity in Chapter 1.) Read Pound's poem again. What do you think it's about?

Stop and Jot—Read for Analysis

"In a Station of the Metro"
by Ezra Pound

The apparition of these faces in the crowd;
Petals on a wet, black bough.

* * *

What is this poem about?

_____

_____

_____

Although Steve loves to teach Pound's poem now, he hated having to read it in high school. Back then, it was easy to dismiss. How could you call it a poem if it was only two lines? What could anyone say in just two lines? But Steve has learned a thing or two since high school. Now he can see the meaning bursting from the poem's seams. Let's peek inside his head: What thinking does Steve do as he analyzes this poem?

So how did Steve go about analyzing this poem? We can look to the world of photography and filmmaking to find some helpful terminology for his process.

Photography is an incredible art form that relies heavily on composition. One of the first skills a photographer learns is how to frame an image. Knowing where to zoom in and zoom out is key. For lush detail, they zoom in. For a sense of scale, they zoom out. Let's apply this approach to Steve's moves.

The first thing Steve did to analyze the poem was to get close to it—he zoomed in to unpack its language. He paused at words like "apparition" and thought about what that diction signaled. He did the same for the poem's "wet, black bough" image. Then, he zoomed out to consider the implications of Pound's language and the greater message it conveyed.

Core Idea

Analysis is like camerawork:
zoom in to unpack language, zoom out to identify the "so what."

The terms "zoom in" and "zoom out" apply just as well to literary analysis as they do to the world of visual art. Just like the lenses of a camera, we can train our analysis on the trees or widen it to encompass the forest. To get a clear picture of a text, we need to do both. Let's unpack what this looks like for students.

Zoom In

Step into the 6th-grade classroom of Allison Metz. Her students are reading Gwendolyn Brooks's "The Last Quatrain of the Ballad of Emmett Till." Brooks's poem relies on color imagery, so as you watch consider what students note as they zoom in on the colors in the lines "she sits in a red room" and "chaos in windy grays through a red prairie."

WATCH Clip 2: Allison Metz—Students Discuss Color Imagery

http://www.wiley.com/go/lal

Sample Class Discussion

"The Last Quatrain"

Allison: So I want you to think for a moment: What do you typically associate with the color red?

Onye: I would associate red with blood.

Allison: Let's write that down. What else?

Onye: Angry faces.

Allison: Let's write that down. Anger. Any other associations that I'm missing?

Odie: Heat.

Allison: Let's look at the harder question. Why would she use the color red? She could have chosen any color. Someone told me earlier we were describing a red room. Why use the color red?

[Off-screen student]: I think it means that she's describing blood. . .I think that means the blood of Emmett Till.

Ismat: I agree with you, and I'd like to add on. I think the author used red to show Mamie Till's anger.

Understanding that Emmett Till was lynched as a teenager and that his mother mourns his loss affects the way in which students read the color imagery. They use their knowledge to help them consider a range of connotations for red. This sensitivity sets them up to consider what these connotations bring to bear on the text.

"Zooming in" like this is a time-honored tradition. Samuel Taylor Coleridge remarks on his own education in his *Biographia Literaria*:

> I learnt from him that Poetry, even that of the loftiest and, seemingly, that of the wildest odes, had a logic of its own as severe as that of science; and more difficult, because more subtle, more complex, and dependent on more, and more fugitive causes. . . I well remember that, availing himself of the synonimes to the Homer of Didymus, he made us attempt to show, with regard to each, why it would not have answered the same purpose; and *wherein* consisted the peculiar fitness of the word in the original text." (145)[32]

Although Coleridge speaks of poetry, reading for analysis considers the effect of specific language in any given text.[33] Every word has a purpose, and when we analyze we consider the particular implications of an author's choices. Why this word? Why not another? How would a different word change the text? Zooming in distinguishes literary analysis from other forms of reading—it shifts the focus from the surface to the music beneath.[34]

Zooming in on word connotations can offer major benefits to developing readers,[35] but in analysis, it is only valuable when applied to language that warrants it. If a character is hungry and orders "lunch," it may not be worth the time to unpack the craft moves there. They may just want a sandwich. When should we zoom in? When the evidence is a piece of author's craft—something regularly used to call our attention. Craft can come in many forms: words with multiple meanings, repeated language, charged connotations, unexpected phrases, or figurative language. To help students stay on the lookout for these techniques we use the acronym MR. CUF (Figure 2.8). (Feel free to use whatever acronym works for you!)

MR CUF—An Acronym for Authors' Craft

Source: Courtesy of The Graphics Fairy LLC.

Multiple Meanings
Repeated Language/Images/Ideas
Charged Connotations
Unexpected Language/Images/Ideas
Figurative Language

☞ **Multiple meanings**—These are words or images that might mean more than one thing. In Theodore Roethke's "My Papa's Waltz," the phrase "beat time on my head" could mean keeping a rhythm or it could mean abuse. In August Wilson's *The Piano Lesson*, the piano symbolizes different things to different characters.

☞ **Repeated words/images**—Authors often use repetition to make a point, whether it's in words—"of the people, by the people, for the people"—or images, like blood in Shakespeare's *Macbeth*.

☞ **Charged connotations**—Words carry with them oceans of meaning, rife with associations we make based on our culture and life experience. When Julio Noboa Polanco writes a poem in which the speaker says he'd rather be a weed than a flower "harnessed to a pot of dirt," we know that "harnessed to" contains a series of associations—control, confinement, even subjugation—that an alternative like "planted in" does not.[36]

☞ **Unexpected language/images/ideas**—Things we don't see coming are a great way for authors to grab our attention. This can be a cruel act from a character we expected to be kind, or a helpful act from a character we expected to be treacherous. This occurs at the word level, too—for example, the Greek tragedian Aeschylus writes of the "awful grace of God"—an unexpected combination that creates friction and new meaning, at least to the modern ear.

☞ **Figurative language**—Figurative language is the classic and most commonly taught way to call attention to craft. If Paul calls Steve a *prince*, it means something very different than if he calls him a *troll*.

Source: Image Courtesy of The Graphics Fairy LLC.

The MR. CUF acronym reminds students what to look for while reading and makes them more likely to zoom in on these techniques. But zooming in is just the first part of the analytical process.

Zoom Out—"So What?"

Once students have zoomed in on language, they are ready to zoom out to consider its implications. This is when they provide the "so what" for the evidence they're considering: what implications this language has in the text, and why this evidence matters in the context of the discussion they are having or argument they are making.[37] A good zoom-out pushes beyond paraphrasing and can often be as simple as answering "so what" or "what effect does that line have on readers or the text?"

Let's see this in action with Mike Taubman's 12th-grade students. His class is reading Junot Díaz's *The Brief Wondrous Life of Oscar Wao*.[38] At this point in their education, students are sensitive enough to the text to zoom in independently on the imagery in a pivotal scene. Oscar has stuck a gun down the front of his pants as he confronts the aptly named "Manny," a stand-in for toxic masculinity.

As you watch, think about the following: building on instruction like Allison's, what are Mike's students able to do on their own? Then, how do they zoom out?

WATCH Clip 3: Mike Taubman—Students Zoom Out in Oscar Wao

http://www.wiley.com/go/lal

Sample Class Discussion

The Brief Wondrous Life of Oscar Wao

Sylvon: We know he [Oscar] can't use his phallus in order to gain power, so he takes his uncle's gun and puts it inside of his pants which is like a replacement of his phallus. And so he's going to use violence in order to gain power, to gain power that he can't get through his phallus.

Mike: Can you paraphrase what Sylvon just said?

Izhane: Basically, Oscar is trying to make up for what he lacks, so he's using the gun. He could have put the gun anywhere, but he specifically chose to stick it in the front of his pants, so that shows how he may not be able to use phallocentrism because I believe he still is a virgin. So now he has a gun in the front of his pants and he's in front of Manny's building and it shows that. . .he's going to use the gun to kill Manny and that's going to be his way to gain masculinity and make up for his status of being the underdog of masculinity.

As students get older, we can pull back our support until they instinctively pick apart language in a text. Mike's students are able to identify and zoom in on the phallic symbolism of the gun and then zoom out to consider how it supports Díaz's portrayal of masculinity and power.

Zoom In, Zoom Out—Making It Explicit

Mike's students have had a lot of practice zooming in and out, but younger students need us to make the framework a bit more explicit. For a middle school example of zooming in and out during discourse, watch Vy Graham's 7th graders discuss symbolism in Adrienne Rich's "Aunt Jennifer's Tigers":

WATCH Clip 4: Graham—Students Zoom Out on Aunt Jennifer's Tigers

http://www.wiley.com/go/lal

The framework of zooming in and zooming out is not just useful while reading—it also influences and guides student writing. Danny Murray's 8th-grade students are reading George Orwell's *Animal Farm* and have read and written about a speech by

Joseph Stalin as part of their schema-building. What do you notice about how they talk about the craft of writing?

WATCH Clip 5: Danny Murray—Students Analyze Their Own Writing Craft

http://www.wiley.com/go/lal

Sample Class Discussion

Analyzing Diction in Student Writing

Danny: [reads a student's summary statement] "Russia should industrialize, or else the country will become weaker, and the other countries will become superior." With your partner, evaluate Sarah's summary.

. . .

Naim: I recommend next time, Sarah, that you add that Russia should have industrialized faster because they were already industrializing, and Joseph Stalin made the point that it is not possible for the tempo to be slowed down.

Kaylin: Sarah, I recommend two things. One, when you say "should," I think you should change that to "must" or some sort of stronger language because what Stalin is communicating isn't, "You can do it"; he's saying that if you don't do this, then I'm going to kill you. So I think it's "must."

Danny: What did Kaylin do?

Sydney: She analyzed Sarah's diction.

Danny: Just like we close read every intentional word of an author, when we're looking at our peer's work, every word matters. In this case, the difference between should and must—What's the difference?

Omari: The difference is that "should" indicates that you have a choice, but "must" means that you don't have a choice. You have to do it.

As we see in Danny's classroom, zooming in and out can apply to informational text just as easily as it can to fiction. More importantly, the act of zooming in and out gives students a language to use when discussing their own written work. It provides terminology you and your students can use to demystify the process of analysis.

Go ahead, give it a try. Choose one or both of the following writing samples and see if you can identify where the student is zooming in and zooming out on the author's word choice.

Stop and Jot—Student Writing Samples

The House on Mango Street—middle school	The Kite Runner—high school
In the novel, The House on Mango Street, author Sandra Cisneros uses symbolism to show how Sally, who is abused by her husband and father, is haunted by abuse. Describing Sally's house, Cisneros uses the imagery of "linoleum roses" to describe the kitchen floor. Cisneros could have used tiles or wood, but instead she uses "linoleum roses." Linoleum is cheap material used on floors. From far away it looks perfect, but if you look closely it is cheap. Cisneros uses this symbol to convey that Sally's life isn't what it seems to be. Sally hides her abuse in hopes of portraying a perfect life. Instead, she is masquerading as someone she is not. Cisneros' symbol points out the falseness of trying to ignore abuse, a theme we can see later in her novel. . . .	Amir's inner thoughts as a young child demonstrate his mentality and how he is able to justify betraying Hassan when they are older. One day, after winning the kite running tournament, and as Hassan ran to retrieve the prize of the fallen kite, Amir chooses to betray his brother. After finding the kite, Hassan is cornered and confronted by Assef and his friends in order to punish Hassan for previously protecting Amir. From behind a concrete wall, Amir watches as Hassan is raped by Assef for not giving him the kite that Amir won. In order to reassure his friends, Assef states that "It's just a Hazara" (75). By referring to Hassan as an "it," Assef reveals that he truly does not believe that Hassan is a human being worthy of respect or unalienable human rights. Instead of protecting Hassan as he did so many times before, Amir chooses to "watch them close in on the boy [he']d grown up with..." (71). As he runs away in cowardice, he rationalizes his lack of action by thinking, "He was just a Hazara, wasn't he?" (77). Amir's ability to betray his own kin demonstrates the power of social hierarchies and their irreparable effects on human bonds. . . .

Where are students zooming in and out to build their argument?

_____

_____

_____

_____

Once students become familiar with the language of zooming in and out, you can integrate it directly into the way you teach writing. The following guides, which incorporate all of the elements of a full analytical paragraph, are designed to be student-facing. These can be found in your *Reading and Writing Handbook* in the online Appendix.

Analyzing writing with

NEZZ

Know the moves for analyzing author's craft.

A paragraph is a fully developed idea. Use (and, when you wish, reorder) the following components to write paragraphs that analyze author's craft. You can reorder and change this as you become more confident and experienced.

Argument	Begin each paragraph with an argument that states how or why: • *"Smith's imagery in chapter 7 helps establish that Christina is independent and bold."* • *"The structure and imagery in Whitman's text both under-score its rejection of lecture-style learning in favor of experience."*
Name It	Name the literary device or technique being used (<u>at any moment</u> in your writing): • *"Here, Morrison uses a <u>metaphor</u> to describe Pecola."* • *"Lincoln's <u>diction</u> helps him associate the battle with spirituality."*
Explain It	Provide context for the quote that shares the *what* and *when* for the evidence. • *"Shakespeare uses the words "wreckful siege," "battering days." and "gates impregnable" to establish that time is at odds with beauty."* • *"When John puts the saxophone to his mouth for the first time, Lewis writes that it 'bleeds song' (34)."*

| Zoom In [only if analyzing author's craft] | [Use as needed when analyzing **author's craft**—not always!]

Pull out a powerful word and zoom in on its connotation (do this when unpacking the connotations of a word or image helps prove your argument):

• **Zoom in on "MR. CUF" words:**
   ◦ **Multiple meanings**: images/words/ideas that appear to have multiple meanings (allusions, symbols, wordplay)
   ◦ **Repeated images**/words/ideas
   ◦ **Charged connotations** with images/words/ideas
   ◦ **Unexpected or surprising** images/words/ideas
   ◦ **Figurative language**
• **Consider: Why is *this* choice meaningful? How would this text be different if a different word were chosen?**
   ◦ *"Lowry intentionally uses the word "labor" instead of "work" to describe the birthmothers' duties. "Work" can refer to tasks we accomplish with our minds or bodies, but "labor" refers solely to physical tasks."*
   ◦ *"Taken together, the pattern of diction in the second quatrain evokes the notion of war (5-8)."*
   ◦ *"Alvarez writes the rain is "slapping" down for a reason: it reminds readers of Minerva physically smacking Trujillo just a few pages earlier."* |

Zoom Out	Always zoom out to answer "So what?"
	
	• The zoom out usually takes at least two sentences: (1) Explain the effect/importance of the evidence you selected;
	• (2) Explain how this evidence supports your argument:
	
	    ○ **Zo1:** *"Tan's comparison helps her convey how embarrassed her narrator is by her own culture."*
	
	    ○ **Zo2:** *"Her narrator rejects her own identity in favor of someone else's, underscoring how dangerous this can be."*
	
	    ○ **Zo1:** *"Poe signals that his protagonist clearly isn't someone who can be trusted."*
	
	    ○ **Zo2:** *"As a result, the entire narrative becomes suspect, in a way that adds tension for the reader."*

Clincher	End your paragraph with a statement that transitions or reaffirms its overall argument: ○ *"By establishing a clear connection between beauty and virtue, Smith implies that to be fair is also to be good, a sentiment clearly at odds with this next quatrain."*

Discussing and evaluating nonfiction with

NEZZ

Discuss or evaluate informational texts with this structure.

A paragraph is a fully developed idea. Use the following components to help you marshal multiple informational texts.

Argument	Begin each paragraph with an argument that states how or why: • *"A combination of an oily coating on their legs and tiny hairs called setae help spiders avoid getting tangled in their webs."* • *"While some argue that the Civil War was caused by economics, it is undeniable that the issue of slavery lay at its core."*
Name It	Name the specific key terms (e.g. a historical event, scientific term) at any moment in your writing: • *"The industrial revolution was known as a time of. . ."* • *"Energy gets generated during the process of photosynthesis, as the plant. . ."*
Explain It	Provide context for a quote or paraphrased key evidence so the reader can understand it. Good context explains the *what* or *when* behind the source material: • *"Listing their many grievances against the British monarchy, Jefferson argues that he. . ."* • *"Spiders' sticky nets are used as an "excellent hunting tool," but the existence of these nets has led experts to question how spiders avoid getting caught in their own threads. . ."* NOTE: Reserve quotes for first-person accounts or language that is particularly striking. Otherwise, paraphrases are fine.

Zoom In **[rarely]**	[When analyzing historical or informational text with rich and complex rhetoric] Pull out a powerful word and zoom in on its diction. NOTE: This technique should be used rarely with informational texts—only if you are analyzing author's craft. Consult the NEZZ for Analysis one-pager if you think a zoom-in is appropriate.

Zoom Out	Always zoom out to answer "So what?"
	
	• (1) Explain the author's purpose. (You may also discuss the intended audience, point of view, or provide additional context.)
	• (2) Link the evidence back to your argument by explaining why it is important.
	   ◦ *"Smith's statistics demonstrate the danger of assuming the world will get better on its own. That is, while the townspeople feel the world is improving, local crime statistics seem to suggest otherwise. The reality is far different from what people assume, which has major consequences for how new policies are created."*
	
	   ◦ *"When examined together, both studies highlight the unique and adaptive qualities of spiders' legs. Because of these adaptations, spiders are best equipped to capture prey in their webs."*

Clincher	End your paragraph with a statement that transitions or reaffirms its overall argument: ◦ *"Hammurabi's code of laws didn't just provide order for Babylonian society; it provided a template for many others to come."*

Conclusion

"All [people] dream: but not equally. Those who dream by night in the dusty recesses of their minds wake in the day to find that it was vanity: but the dreamers of the day are dangerous [people], for they may act their dreams with open eyes, to make it possible."

—T.E. Lawrence, *Seven Pillars of Wisdom*

Many of us have been fortunate enough to see ourselves in a character who lives within the pages of a book—be it John Grimes in *Go Tell It on the Mountain*, Miyax in *Julie of the Wolves,* or Alison Bechdel's self-rendering in *Fun Home*. We've experienced the insight, healing, or sheer delight that comes from seeing oneself reflected in literature. And for every character who gives us that spark of recognition, many more have shown us new, less familiar perspectives. Those discoveries expand our humanity—allowing us to see ourselves and those with whom we share the world with a little more grace and wisdom.[1]

But this level of understanding won't come with surface-level reading and analysis. "A guy turns into a bug, and his family acts like jerks" is not only an inadequate interpretation of Kafka's *Metamorphosis*, it's a kind of theft. The reader who settles there has been robbed of the opportunity to find something provocative and deep tucked into the creases of the text. We *get* literature when it makes us shake our head in wonder, ball our fists, or call a friend. We *get* it when it reveals things about our world that we've never known—or refused to see. And when our students *get* it, our dream for them begins to take shape.

But the question remains: What does it look like in action? What will I *see* when students get it? Let's find out.

THERE AND BACK AGAIN—PART 1 SUMMARY

Key Takeaways

- There's real magic in the teaching of literature—and that magic is replicable. (Introduction)

- Kids fall in love with what they know how to do (Introduction).

- Students can only fall in love with texts they understand.

- Our curriculum does more than shape what our students can do. It shapes who they become.

- You are what you eat: if you want students to grow, nourish them with challenging texts.

- Curriculum tells a larger story: the more cohesive it is, the more compelling it becomes.

- The destination defines the path. Assessment tasks are the starting point for instruction, not the end.

- Texts are like diamonds: they sparkle when we see multiple angles.

- Teaching strategies without schema is like teaching driving without a car.

- All readers stand on the shoulders of their schema.

- The right knowledge at the right time is a powerful tool.

- The heart of any text is the claim it makes.

- Everything's an argument. Our job as readers is to find the claims—and decide if we accept them.

- A theme is a claim made by a narrative text.

- Analysis is like camerawork: zoom in to unpack language, zoom out to identify the "so what."

Self-Assessment

A summary of key techniques from Part 1 is listed here. Take a moment and step back to self-assess your own class or school: Where are you already strong, and where are your opportunities to grow? You'll notice that some categories are weighted more than others. That's because some categories are more important. In Chapter 8, you'll be able to integrate your results with the other ideas in this book, and we'll discuss how to plan and prioritize your next steps.

Part 1: What's My Dream for Kids?	
• **Create a Complexity Curriculum:** My curriculum deliberately sequences texts so they increase in quantitative, qualitative, and task complexity over time. Across the year, students read a diverse set of perspectives, genres, and experiences, including those far different from their own experience.	___/12
• **Build Background Knowledge:** From my teaching, students receive the schema necessary to access texts.	___/8
• **Read for Claim:** My students find the claims and sub-claims in narrative and non-narrative texts.	___/6
• **Read for Analysis:** My students use consistent methodologies (e.g., MR. CUF, NEZZ) to analyze, discuss, and write about author's craft.	___/6
Score:	___/32

Planning for Action

- What resources from Part 1 will you use to adjust your instruction? (All of these are available in the online *Love & Literacy Reading and Writing Handbook*.)

    o Text Selection Criteria: Questions to Consider When Selecting Books (*Handbook* p. 3)

    o Sample Books List, Grades 5–12 (*Handbook* p. 4)

    o Claim: Reading and Annotating Non-Narrative Text (*Handbook* p. 5)

    o Theme: Reading and Annotating Narrative Text (*Handbook* pp. 7–8)

    o Poetry: Reading and Annotating (*Handbook* p. 9)

    o Identifying Author's Craft: MR. CUF (*Handbook* p. 11)

    o Writing Literary Analysis: NEZZ (*Handbook* p. 12)

    o Writing Non-Literary Analysis: NEZZ (*Handbook* p. 14)

- How will you modify these resources to meet the needs of your class(es)?

_____

_____

_____

Action	Date

What Will I See When Students "Get It"?

INTRODUCTION

"There's something about the pen that focuses the brain in a way that nothing else does."

—David McCullough, *Humanities Magazine (National Endowment for the Humanities, 2003)*

To the untrained eye, Angela Thomas might look like a mind reader. In lesson after lesson, she always seems to know if her students get it or don't, and this knowledge makes her instruction precise—Angela spends the bulk of her time on trouble spots, not on moments of consensus. In a single school year, Angela's students gain months more of additional instruction than they would otherwise.[1] But if you didn't know what to look for, you might assume it's just her charisma or some other inimitable pedagogy.

Figure P2.1   Angela knows that when students "get" it, she can see it in their writing.

Source: © Uncommon Schools. Used with permission.

On this particular day, Angela's 6th-grade students are reading the lyrics to "Birmingham Sunday." Written by Richard Fariña and popularized by Joan Baez, the song mourns the loss of four young girls in the 1963 Ku Klux Klan bombing of an African American Baptist church. Fariña's lyrics still ring true today: violence against Black people and communities continues as a twenty-first-century problem.

Before we watch Angela in action, take a moment to read this brief excerpt, which describes the second of the four victims of the bombing:

Stop and Jot—Unpack the Lyrics

"Birmingham Sunday" by Richard Fariña (Fourth Stanza)

The clouds, they were dark and the autumn wind blew
And Denise McNair brought the number to two
The falcon of death was a creature they knew
And the choir kept singing of freedom

* * *

What is Fariña's message?
How does figurative language bring that alive?

_____

_____

_____

_____

_____

Once students finish reading, Angela lets the lyrics sink in for a moment. She asks, "What's going on here—what is Fariña's message? Pay close attention to the figurative language to help you figure this out."

No hands go up—instead, each student picks up a pen and begins to write their response. Angela walks from desk to desk as they work, looking over students' shoulders to read their writing. She jots down what she sees: what students underline and annotate, where they struggle, where there are different perspectives that could spar with each other, and what she should focus on when class resumes.

So far, Angela has noticed that students have a pretty solid understanding of the message, but they're struggling with the figurative language. Here's what two of her students, Kymani and Amma, wrote about the figurative language in the poem.

Stop and Jot—Analyzing Student Responses

Kymani: [The author] chose to use a falcon because falcons have strong eyesight and they can see vast amounts of things. Falcons are scavengers so people can know if something dies by looking for falcons. In the text it states, "falcon of death." A falcon is a beacon or symbol that something is in a dire situation where there is death. Falcons are attracted to death, so they are affiliated with it.

Amma: [The author] chose a falcon because a falcon is a bird of prey and has good ways to get its prey—just like the bomber had good ways to get its prey, the Blacks.

* * *

How do their responses compare?

_____

_____

_____

_____

_____

From reading responses, Angela has noted that most students have a superficial understanding of the fourth stanza's key metaphor, the "falcon of death." ("The falcon of death was a creature they knew.") Kymani's writing, while ample, reflects the same error. He attempts to find meaning in the metaphor and concludes that falcons are somehow connected with death. After that, he's stuck. To use the language we introduced in Chapter 2, Kymani is struggling to "zoom in"—or unpack the connotations of the metaphor. It's possible the skill is weak, or that he simply lacks background knowledge. Amma's writing, on the other hand, indicates deeper understanding: she links the predatory nature of both the bomber and the falcon.

The timer buzzes, and Angela strides to the front of the room.

At first glance, it might appear that little has happened so far—discussion hasn't begun, and student voices haven't been heard. But Angela already knows where her students are. She sees what they get and what they don't, even before they share, and she's ready to steer them through the challenge. Although she hasn't changed the trajectory of their learning experience yet, she will. How? By focusing on what they write. We'll study this in two stages:

- Chapter 3—Make It Visible (Student Annotations and Writing)
- Chapter 4—Look for It (Monitor Student Work)

Chapter 3

Make It Visible

E. M. Forster, Flannery O'Connor, and Joan Didion were all visionary writers: prolific and piercingly insightful. It is easy to imagine them as limitless reservoirs of wisdom. But each of them argued that, on the contrary, they saw the world the same way everyone else did. So what made the difference? How they came to know their thoughts:

> "How do I know what I think until I see what I say?" (Forster)
> "I write because I don't know what I think until I read what I say." (O'Connor)
> "I don't know what I think until I write it down." (Didion)

All three insisted that their understanding of the world wasn't complete until they wrote it down.

Angela Thomas uses the same principle to guide her instruction. Until students articulate their understanding in writing, she doesn't fully know what they comprehend, and on some level, neither do they. Moreover, if Angela falls for the trap of having the class talk about the text before they write, the writing becomes a regurgitation of what was said rather than a record of original student thought. Writing before talking reveals initial understanding, both to students and to teachers like Angela.[1] So write first, talk second.

> ## Core Idea
>
> To check if students get it, see if they can write it.
> Write first, talk second.

In *The Skillful Teacher*, Jon Saphier and his colleagues remind us that a huge component of teaching is making students' thinking visible.[2] As Angela walks from desk to desk and reads student work, she is building a picture of what understanding looks like in her classroom. Simply by noticing, Angela does something powerful during independent practice: she detects the challenges and opportunities before anyone speaks. She knows you can't correct what you don't detect.

> ## Core Idea
>
> You can't correct what you don't detect.

By focusing the beginning of class on observation instead of discussion, Angela can see what every student thinks, allowing her to shift instruction to focus on the places where her kids need it. It's a move that pays dividends for her students, because it allows her both to close gaps in understanding and coax her students toward the places that will challenge them most.

If we want to understand how Angela makes this possible, we need to begin at a surprising place—the end.

SET THE BAR WITH AN EXEMPLAR

Imagine that you are preparing to teach "Sonnet 65" by William Shakespeare. Read the sonnet to yourself and respond in one paragraph to the prompt below.

Stop and Jot—Create an Exemplar

"Sonnet 65" by William Shakespeare

Since brass, nor stone, nor earth, nor boundless sea,
But sad mortality o'er-sways their power,
How with this rage shall beauty hold a plea,
Whose action is no stronger than a flower?
O, how shall summer's honey breath hold out   5
Against the wreckful siege of battering days,
When rocks impregnable are not so stout,
Nor gates of steel so strong, but Time decays?
O fearful meditation! Where, alack,
Shall Time's best jewel from Time's chest lie hid?   10
Or what strong hand can hold his swift foot back?
Or who his spoil of beauty can forbid?
    O, none, unless this miracle have might,
    That in black ink my love may still shine bright.

* * *

What strikes you about this poem?
What is Shakespeare's theme and how does he convey it?

_____

_____

_____

_____

_____

_____

_____

_____

_____

Now take a moment and compare your response to Steve's:

> ### Lesson Exemplar—Sonnet 65
>
> In many ways, Shakespeare's "Sonnet 65" is a poem about the transcendent power of writing: that writing, despite the entropic processes of the natural world, is ultimately what sustains beauty. Here, time plays the role of the aggressor, devastating all that lies in its path. For instance, the extended, mixed metaphor in lines 5–8 frets that "summer's honey breath" cannot hold out against time's "wreckful siege" (5–6). These lines cast time as a conquering army with the power to destroy "rocks impregnable" and "gates of steel." Clearly, this is an uneven matchup. Shakespeare engineers a similar contrast during his first quatrain, where he offers up the concrete, natural diction of "brass," "stone," and "boundless sea," only to remind the reader that they will be shuttered by time (1). With all of this in mind, the imagery at the poem's final couplet takes on increased weight. The speaker hopes the "miracle" of his writing "may still shine bright," implicitly comparing it to a star. Set against the earthly imagery used in the first two quatrains of his poem, the speaker claims that writing (or at least *his* writing) is celestial: more powerful than an army, more powerful than stone, more powerful than the earth itself. By coding this hierarchy into the very level of his language, Shakespeare emphasizes the speaker's faith in the power of his writing to conquer even earthly fragility.

Perhaps the bulk of your analysis is similar to Steve's, or perhaps you found different or additional perspectives and depth to add. Perhaps you disagree and want to challenge Steve's take. Or perhaps, like Paul, you didn't pick up on some of the subtlety of Shakespeare's craft until you compared your response. Whatever your experience, something important happened in the act of writing your own response and sparring with Steve's: you got smarter.

All boxers prepare to compete by sparring. Some sparring partners are better than they are, others are equal, and some are worse, but the act of sparring strengthens their ability to compete, and in the end makes them better boxers. The same holds true for English teachers: we raise the bar when we spar with an exemplar.

> ## Core Idea
>
> You raise the bar when you spar with an exemplar.

Starting with another analysis doesn't just bolster our own understanding; it helps set the end goal for class. Going through this process means that you've personally struggled with the texts you're teaching—you know the possible challenges and you've thought about some of the many possibilities for analysis. This preparation is essential before we step foot in the classroom, because you ultimately cannot know where to focus until you know where you are headed. As Paul described in *Driven by Data 2.0*, assessment is the starting point for instruction, not the end.[3]

<u>An</u> Exemplar, Not <u>The</u> Exemplar

Were our job solely to teach reading comprehension, that would be hard enough. But the power of literary study is the multitude of approaches that can be taken with any text. If you search the academic literature on any great text, you will likely find many contrasting interpretations—some of which directly contradict each other. Meaning is slippery: writing, like people, contains multitudes.

In this context, crafting exemplars is not the same as writing an answer key for class: your response will be *one* exemplar, not the *only* exemplar (in fact, your instruction would be severely limited if you thought so!). We recommend this process not to narrow our focus to one right answer but to sharpen our vision for the depth of understanding that will be needed to unpack the text, which requires us to spend time on our own grappling with its meaning. When we do so, we're far more prepared in class to hear new ideas—even ones we didn't anticipate—and consider them against the depth of analysis we ultimately want students to do. It's *that* sense that helps us know when our class needs a push—and when they are doing just fine without us. There are few greater moments in English instruction than when students posit ideas we'd never considered ourselves—provided they can support and defend them with skill.

Creating an exemplar and sparring with others gives us a hard-won intimacy with our curriculum. It prevents both an "anything goes" atmosphere in class (if every analysis is correct—regardless of evidence—nothing is really meaningful) and also a "one correct interpretation" of each text where we are the arbiters. By starting at the end, we open multiple pathways for our students.

So how did Steve spar to prepare for a lesson on "Sonnet 65"? He used a few simple steps.

Read the Text and Identify Significant Aspects

Take the text you are going to teach and read it—savor it—and answer the following question: Why is this text valuable for my students to read? What do I want them to gain from it?

There are many approaches a teacher might take to a text, especially as they become increasingly complex. "Sonnet 65," for example, has much to offer. Students could look at the poem's structure and organization—how it builds to a theme and where its volta, or turn, appears. Or they could examine where the poem breaks from iambic pentameter and which ideas get stressed as a result. There could be a lesson devoted to deciphering the poem's dense language or on how this sonnet compares with others that Shakespeare or others have written.[4]

Ultimately, there are many meaningful ways to look at a text, and the first step is to identify many of them. After that, you'll need to winnow these down—because where you want students to end up will define the path it takes to get there.

Set the Prompt and Craft Your Response

Once you've identified as many significant aspects of the text as you can, you'll need to decide what you want the final class prompt, or "exit ticket" question, to be. While the term "exit ticket" can vary in meaning, we use it to mean a written prompt that assesses just how far students can get after the day's instruction. As others have written, exit tickets are a fantastic, formative assessment you can use to see how well students understood what you taught.[5] We have found asking students to write in response to an analytical prompt is the best way to assess their learning. After all, articulating understanding at the end of class is the truest measure of it (and fantastic writing practice, to boot).

What we choose for the final prompt says a lot about how we'll focus instruction. Texts do not demand a singular reading—a 12th-grade Literature class might analyze "Sonnet 65" quite differently from an 8th-grade one. Regardless of grade level, what matters most when setting a prompt is choosing what you want students to do with the text. Ask yourself: Based on the needs of my students and the complexity of this text, where is the most valuable place to direct our attention? What will my students most benefit from grappling with? What have they learned so far this year, where have they struggled, and what do I want them to be able to do by the end of the year?

In the case of "Sonnet 65," Steve and his grade-level team decided to focus on Shakespeare's extended metaphor and use of imagery. These were skills of literary analysis that the class had been working on, and they would help unlock the parts of the poem that resonated most to Steve and his colleagues. On this day, they crafted a straightforward final prompt: "How does Shakespeare's use of figurative language develop his theme?" Steve encourages planners to get playful with these once they feel comfortable. To get at these same ideas, a teacher could also ask: "Who does the speaker care more for—his subject or himself? Make a case citing figurative language." Prompts that encourage debate, as we'll discuss in Chapter 6, add complexity to class discourse.

With the final prompt set, Steve and his colleagues each draft an exemplar response. Their goal is to generate a written response that reflects the depth of understanding that they want the class to achieve. Steve and his team write this exemplar at an adult level of comprehension, instead of in the voice of a student, to keep the quality of thought and level of analysis high.

Spar with an Exemplar

Once the responses are fully fleshed out, the team is ready to compare answers with each other, just as you did moments ago. Depending on your school's context, sparring can take a few different forms. You can spar with fellow teachers or with an instructional leader. Or you can follow the lead of so many English teachers and professors and spar with giants in the field. Look up what academics have written about what you're studying and compare your notes to theirs. You likely haven't spent a lifetime analyzing "Sonnet 65," so why not lean on the analysis of those who have? We first applied Newton's words to schema, but they fit equally well here: stand on the shoulders of giants to enhance your own understanding.

Sparring helps us set a high bar for excellence. Students rise to the level of our expectations, so we owe it to them to keep these sky-high.[6]

Plan Anchor Prompts

With an exemplar prompt and response in hand, we can draft a few anchor prompts to guide the lesson toward the final prompt. These are the prompts you'll use to launch discourse or assign as stop-and-jot moments in class like Angela's prompt, "What is Fariña's message? How does figurative language bring that alive?"

Creating prompts is careful business. The biggest pitfall to avoid is feeding our analysis to students rather than letting them build one for themselves. Consider these two examples for "Sonnet 65." What makes the second prompt more effective?

Stop and Jot—Analyze the Prompt

Prompt 1	Prompt 2
How does the mixed, extended metaphor in the second quatrain help show that time is more powerful than beauty?	How does the second quatrain contribute to the text?

What makes the second prompt more effective?

_____

_____

_____

Prompt 1 is loaded; it gives away the deep analysis and mainly leaves it to students to justify the meaning. Even a well-intentioned prompt like "explain the extended war metaphor in the second quatrain" has already done much of the hard work by identifying the metaphor for students. When possible, an open-ended prompt like the second one is far more fruitful. Here are two of the best types of anchor prompts to use in class:

- **Go Broad:** What's going on? What strikes you? (These are particularly strong as opening prompts.)

- **Go Broad with a Specific Section of Text:** How do pages 17–19 contribute to the text?

These won't cover every scenario, but they will get students started. Then, you can go even deeper during the discourse (which we'll discuss in Chapter 6).

The prompts you create establish the depth of thinking that follows. In a 2015 study, researchers compared two groups of students—one that made remarkable gains on standardized tests and another whose scores improved much less significantly—and considered the kinds of writing tasks the students in each group received. The results were dramatic.

Students in the higher-achieving group were far more likely to have been assigned rigorous writing prompts in class and to have received feedback on their responses.[7] When we give students a chance to write about challenging questions before discussion, we set a threshold for what we expect of them and what they should expect of themselves.

With an exemplar and anchor prompts in hand, we can shift our focus to our students—and the moments in which they struggle.

TEACH STUDENTS TO TALK TO THEIR TEXTS

It's a brisk September morning, and Mallory Grossman has assigned her 6th graders a text about the fight for gun control—an excerpt of Emma Gonzalez's "We Call B.S." speech. Her class works independently as Mallory winds between the desks to review their work. Midway through her circuit, Mallory notices that students have glossed over a key idea: that Gonzalez is speaking about *student* activism, not just actions by adults. She pauses the class and asks them to reread two paragraphs where this idea appears and discuss what they've read. Students chatter softly with their partners. They share out what they overlooked, and class moves on. (See Figure 3.1.)

Figure 3.1 Mallory Grossman has a technique that allows her to remediate student misconceptions while they read.

Source: © Uncommon Schools. Used with permission.

In a few brief moments, Mallory has prevented a major misconception about Gonzalez's speech, one that would have led to a shallow or confusing reading experience. How did Mallory know students had missed an idea? And how did she know where it happened?

Mallory's secret is that she read students' annotations. The error, it turns out, was written all over their pages.

Annotate Purposefully

The process of annotation likely dates back as far as written text, ranging from doodling to sublime commentary. In the Middle Ages, the margins of a text took on special meaning, contrasting the often austere doctrine at the page's center with playful or even irreverent images.[8] But if something was important, scholars made sure it was noticed, drawing a small hand, or manicule, to quite literally point it out. (See Figure 3.2.) Centuries later, we're still talking to our texts; indeed, many literacy advocates argue for annotation as a means to improve student literacy.[9]

Annotation will always be a somewhat personal process: some of what we write connects to things we've read in the past, and some of it reflects our own personal responses to a text. Many of us stop annotating altogether when we read for pleasure. But in the context of literacy instruction, annotation is an invaluable tool.

Figure 3.2 Medieval manicule: annotation was a bit more artful in the Middle Ages.

Source: Photograph courtesy of Darry Green, Wikimedia Commons.

Consider Mallory's classroom. The magic of her instruction is that she knows where the big ideas in the text occur, and she can pause students there—in real time—when their annotations show they have missed those moments. Students use annotations to better understand texts, but teachers can use them to better understand students.[10]

> ## Core Idea
>
> Students can use annotations to better understand texts.
> Teachers can use them to better understand students.

Of course, highlighting *everything*—as some overzealous students tend to do—is as useful as highlighting nothing. (See Figure 3.3.) Annotating without intention is just decoration.

> ## Core Idea
>
> Annotation without intention is just decoration.

Helping students develop judgment about what is worth their ink is a huge benefit to them as a comprehension aid, and it helps us quickly spot when they miss the

Figure 3.3 Highlighting everything rarely reveals anything.

Source: Photograph courtesy of Piqsels.

mark—just like Mallory does. How do students know what matters most? Let's return to one of our core learnings from Chapter 2 and guide students, first and foremost, to read for claim.

Annotating Non-Narrative Texts

Following is an excerpt of the text that students read in Mallory's class.[11] Take a moment to underline information related to the key sub-claim in the paragraph and jot any notes in the margin (Figure 3.4).

Stop and Jot—Annotate for Claim

Figure 3.4

"We Are Going To Change The Law"

6   We are going to be the kids you read about in textbooks. Not because we're going to be another statistic about mass shootings in America, but because we are going to be the last mass shooting. We are going to change the law. That's what you'll read about Marjory Stoneman Douglas in textbooks, and it's going to be due to the tireless effort of the school board, the teachers, the family members and, most of all, the students.

How did you figure out the key sub-claim in paragraph 6?

_____

_____

_____

You likely used the strategies described in reading for claim (such as looking for key words and claim-revealing statements) to help you find the key argument of this paragraph—that students were going to be the changemakers in the gun control debate. Gonzalez makes this claim explicit when she writes, "We are going to change the law."

Now let's compare Mallory's annotations with a sample student's (Figures 3.5 and 3.6). What do you notice?

Exemplar Teacher Annotation

Figure 3.5

_____

"We Are Going To Change The Law"

6   (We) are going to be the kids you read about in textbooks. Not because we're going to be another statistic about mass shootings in America, but because (we) are going to be the last mass shooting. (We) are going to change the law. That's what you'll read about Marjory Stoneman Douglas in textbooks, and it's going to be due to the tireless effort of the school board. the teachers, the family members and, most of all, the students.   Students will change law

---

Sample Student Annotation

Figure 3.6

_____

"We Are Going To Change The Law"

6   We are going to be the kids you read about in textbooks. Not because we're going to be another statistic about mass shootings in America, but because we are going to be the last mass shooting. We are going to change the law. That's what you'll read about Marjory Stoneman Douglas in textbooks, and it's going to be due to the tireless effort of the school board, the teachers, the family members and, most of all, the students.   Laws must change

---

This student is partially there. Key language in the paragraph is highlighted, showing their sensitivity to the author's message. What catches Mallory's eye is the paragraph 6 jot, "Laws must change," which makes no mention of who should change the law. This trend appears in the work of many students and ultimately spurs Mallory's whole-class intervention—she knows students are overlooking a key part of the claim.

Following is the annotation guidance that Mallory has given her students. It's what she looks for as she reviews student work. You'll notice that it aligns with the Reading for Claim guidance we shared in Chapter 2:

Annotating Narrative Texts

Narrative text annotation has a similar end game (understanding the ideas and messages of the text) but getting there requires a different process. We'll apply it to the excerpt of Toni Morrison's *The Bluest Eye* from the introduction. Here's the text, to refresh your memory.

Excerpt—*The Bluest Eye* by Toni Morrison

By the time this winter had stiffened itself into a hateful knot that nothing could loosen, something did loosen it, or rather someone. A someone who splintered the knot into silver threads that tangled us, netted us, made us long for the dull chafe of the previous boredom.

This disrupter of seasons was a new girl in school named Maureen Peal. A high-yellow dream child with long brown hair braided into two lynch ropes that hung down her back. She was rich, at least by our standards, as rich as the richest of the white girls, swaddled in comfort and care. The quality of her clothes threatened to derange Frieda and me. Patent-leather shoes with buckles, a cheaper version of which we got only at Easter and which had disintegrated by the end of May. Fluffy sweaters the color of lemon drops tucked into skirts with pleats so orderly they astounded us. Brightly colored knee socks with white borders, a brown velvet coat trimmed in white rabbit fur, and a matching muff. There was a hint of spring in her sloe green eyes, something summery in her complexion, and a rich autumn ripeness in her walk.

Source: Toni Morrison, 1970 / Penguin Random House.

As experienced readers, our instincts might tell us to spend time thinking about the description of Maureen's hair as "lynch ropes" or the internal conflict she sparks in the narrator, but students might not pick up on these. How can we teach them?

When students read narrative text, we can ask them to annotate for the 4 C's: characterization, conflict/resolution, changes, and craft.

Annotating Narrative Text

Annotations are geared toward identifying the author's THEMES

Annotate for the 4 C's:
- Characterization
- Conflict/resolution
- Changes (especially in characters)
- Craft (MR. CUF)*

   ° Multiple meanings
   ° Repeated words/images
   ° Charged connotations
   ° Unexpected images/words/moments
   ° Figurative language

After reading: jot the theme (a claim the author makes about the world, society, or humanity)

*You saw MR. CUF unpacked in detail in the Chapter 2 section on reading for analysis.

On the next page, you'll see what that could ideally look like with *The Bluest Eye* (See Figure 3.7.). Notes focus on the characterization of Maureen and craft techniques used in her description. In this case, we'll assume that students have already learned about colorism and would likely catch the reference to it in the passage. If we reviewed student annotations and didn't see notes on it, we'd know this would be a fruitful place for class conversation (Figure 3.7).

Exemplar Teacher Annotation

Figure 3.7

The Bluest Eye (excerpt) – Winter Section – Toni Morrison

> By the time this winter had stiffened itself into a hateful knot that nothing could loosen, <u>something did loosen it, or rather someone.</u> A someone who splintered the knot into <u>silver threads that tangled us, netted us, made us long for the dull chafe</u> of the previous boredom.
>   This disrupter of seasons was a new girl in school named <u>Maureen Peal. A high-yellow dream child with long brown hair braided into two lynch ropes</u> that hung down her back. She was rich, at least by our standards, as rich as the richest of the white girls, swaddled in comfort and care. The quality of her clothes <u>threatened to derange</u> Frieda and me. Patent-leather shoes with buckles, a cheaper version of which we got only at Easter and which had disintegrated by the end of May. Fluffy sweaters the color of lemon drops tucked into skirts with pleats so orderly they astounded us. Brightly colored knee socks with white borders, a brown velvet coat trimmed in white rabbit fur, and a matching muff. There was a hint of spring in her sloe green eyes, something summery in her complexion, and a rich autumn ripeness in her walk.

[handwritten annotations: "MP disrupts winter but causes :-" on left; "colorism + threat" on right]

When you introduce this type of annotation to students, you will likely find that characterization, conflict, and changes are familiar to most. Craft, however, takes a bit of unpacking.

Recall the acronym MR. CUF from Chapter 2. When students notice components of craft in a text, we ask them to pause and consider if the author might be flagging important ideas that might otherwise go unnoticed. Think about *The Bluest Eye*. The words "lynch rope" feel unexpected. (That's the "U" in MR. CUF.) It's not the typical phrase one would use to describe someone's hair, so we know it's worth a second glance. Likewise, the imagery of the seasons, used to describe Maureen certainly merits probing. This sort of sensitivity—call it "reading radar"—takes practice. Giving these craft moves a nomenclature helps students develop a sense for key moments in a text. Over time, this develops

Figure 3.8 MR. CUF is our mnemonic for author's craft techniques. (See Chapter 2.)

Source: Courtesy of The Graphics Fairy LLC.

into an instinct for which sentences might be most valuable to unlocking the big ideas in a work.

A Word on. . . Annotating Poetry

With a few tweaks, the annotation systems we've outlined earlier can be applied to poetry. Poetry is a genre that, by nature, defies many of the expectations and systems of prose. Poets have spilled much ink to define the genre, but for pedagogical purposes we can say that poetry is writing where structure matters as much as language.[12] And because poetry is so compressed—it plays with the conventions of language and often organizes it in new ways—our students need an approach that allows them to engage with the text multiple times, in multiple ways.

- **First read: Breathing Room**—Read the poem out loud at least once, without expectations. Just experience it. Listen for the speaker, the topic, and the rhyme/rhythm.

- **Second read: Literal Meaning**—Reread the lines of the poem and paraphrase the basic meaning. What does the poem say? What's being described? Jot a hypothesis about the poem's theme, even if it's just a note on the topic to which our attention is drawn.

- **Third read: Language and Figurative Meaning**—Underline figurative language in the poem. Consider the effect and how it contributes to (or works against) your initial theory. Refine your theme hypothesis.

- **Fourth read: Structure and Sound**—Consider the form and organization of the text. Does it contribute to the meaning of the poem? Reconsider how the poem has been designed to sound: Do rhythm, rhyme, or cadence help emphasize words, lines, or ideas? Again, refine your theme hypothesis.

When students tell Steve they don't like poetry, he often responds that it's likely because they were never taught how to *really* read it. Poems aren't meant to be read in the same way as prose. We build students' sensitivity to language and structure (as well as their frustration tolerance) by asking them to read poetry in laps. What's more, this process reveals to us where and when breakdowns occur. Why spend the class period discussing imagery when a deep dive into cadence is where the class is struggling?

Following is a sample set of poetry annotations.[13] (See Figure 3.9.) We engaged in the same process we'd ask students to, reading Dunbar's text in four rounds to attend to its different aspects.

Figure 3.9

The Debt
by Paul Laurence Dunbar

[Annotated poem with handwritten notes:]

Boxes labeled: 1st read, 2, 3, 4

This is the debt I pay
Just for one riotous day,
Years of regret and grief,
Sorrow without relief.

massive debt for 1 day
debt is unnamed — figurative?

Pay it I will to the end—
Until the grave, my friend,
Gives me a true release—
Gives me the clasp of peace.

must pay until death
repetition → hyperbolic misery

Slight was the thing I bought,
Small was the debt I thought,
Poor was the loan at best—
God! But the interest!

regrets choice
Breaks meter — emphasizes long-term toll on speaker

Possible theme: the consequences of owing someone ($ or otherwise) lie in its long-term repercussions.

- **First read: Breathing Room**—After reading the poem out loud, we prepared for annotation. The boxes in the top right corner, developed by our colleague Amy Parsons, are a way to remind students to read in rounds. Students check off the boxes as they complete each lap.

- **Second read: Literal Meaning**—On the left, we jotted notes around the literal meaning of the poem before diving into figurative language. It's where we'd intervene first if we saw breakdowns in student notes.

- **Third read: Language and Figurative Meaning**—During this read, we noted how language contributed to the poem's meaning. For example, the first line begins with an ambiguous pronoun, "this." Why would Dunbar have not been specific about the debt? Is it possible that this debt isn't financial? In the second stanza, the repetition drew emphasis to the final two lines, which emphasized the speaker's misery and felt a bit hyperbolic. Is the speaker truly wishing for the release of death because of a debt? Again, we wondered— what kind of debt?

- **Fourth read: Structure and Sound**—In our fourth reading, we thought specifically about the meter of the poem. The poem holds a steady meter throughout, save for the fifth and last lines. Breaking a meter that is this predictable feels like a deliberate choice, like dissonance in music. In these lines—and especially in the poem's final word—the meter emphasizes the compounding toll of the debt, whatever it may be.

(You can find student-facing guidance on how to read poetry in the *Reading and Writing Handbook* in the online materials.)

Students sometimes speak of finding the "hidden meaning" in a text, but this is a bit of a misnomer. Most of the time, meaning isn't hidden at all—it just requires sensitivity to the ways authors present it.

Mallory and Angela build powerful habits of mind in their students by coaching them to talk to their texts. These habits sharpen the precision of their reading radars, allowing them to unlock understanding they wouldn't have had otherwise. In return, Mallory and Angela have a much more accurate sense of what their class understands and what they don't: a true win-win.

But annotations are just one window into student thinking. Written responses throw the doors wide open.

GENERATE A WRITTEN RESPONSE

As we observed in Angela's room, formative writing—ungraded, in-class jots about the text—can give us valuable insight into student thinking. The act of writing compels every student to communicate what they believe and commit that interpretation to paper, making it a powerful tool to improve reading achievement.

Earlier we showed responses from Kymani and Amma, two of Angela's students, where they wrote about the figurative language in the lines "And Denise McNair brought the number to two. / The falcon of death was a creature they knew." Here is their work again:

Both students know the lyrics hinge around the symbol of the falcon and they've both spotted reasons why the author has chosen it. Kymani's response is the lengthier one, and to the untrained eye, it would be easy to accept its length as a proxy for true understanding. But his response fails to unpack the connotations of the falcon image and contains incorrect information (that falcons are primarily scavengers). Amma's response is shorter, but it's conceptually stronger. She recognizes that the phrase "falcon of death" calls attention to the predatory intent behind the bombers' murder of the young girls.[14]

Angela can see that Kymani needs support to deepen his interpretation, and Amma's writing could be the bridge to help him and the class close the gap. What should she do about it? That's what's coming next.

CONCLUSION

In this chapter, we've explored the power of an exemplar to elevate the quality of instruction. From there, we explored how annotations and written responses gave us vital clues about where our students are succeeding and where they might be in struggle.

These practices may already be routine in your classrooms, or you may be thinking about when and how to launch some or all of them. At the end of Part 2, we'll again include a self-assessment rubric and list of resources to support you. For now, use the following box to record your takeaways.

Stop and Jot—My Takeaways

So far, what are your top takeaways for your classroom?

_____

_____

_____

_____

_____

Writing makes student thinking visible, but it only makes a difference when a teacher knows how to respond. To make your teaching impactful, you have to look for the point of struggle—and then act on it.

Let's see what it takes to do this.

Chapter 4

Look for It

Angela and Mallory, whom we met in Chapter 3, are expert teachers because they are expert listeners. As they read student work, they listen for the messages that bubble up from the annotations and written responses. What they observe shapes what and how they teach. While these actions may look effortless, they mask the concrete, deliberate steps that Angela and Mallory take every day to make them happen—steps we all can do.

It all begins with how both teachers treat independent work. Angela and Mallory know that before they can respond to their students' ideas, they need to provide space for their class to have them.

MAKE INDEPENDENT PRACTICE A HABIT

Consider this scene and how it differs from Angela's and Mallory's classrooms. Mr. Bradshaw asks his students to write in advance of the day's discourse. He cues students to write, and a third of them promptly begin. It's a different story for the rest: a large group slowly copies down the prompt as they wait out the clock, and the final group is cheerfully unengaged. By the time discourse begins, it won't matter how prepared Mr. Bradshaw is—only a third of his students are ready for the journey.

Independent practice is the prime time for students to push and try out their thinking, but it requires engagement, structure, and accountability. Without all three, students won't grow, and none of the techniques described in this chapter will be effective. As our colleague Julia Dutcher frequently reminds her students, "It's okay not to know, but it's not okay not to try."

Core Idea

The best time to try is when a task is trying.

How can Mr. Bradshaw bring Julia's words to life? Rather than just parroting her philosophy, he can look at how Julia infuses that message into every aspect of her independent practice.

Step 1: Launch Practice with What-to-Do Directions

In *Teach Like a Champion*, our colleague Doug Lemov writes about the power of clear, bite-sized directions.[1] The start of independent practice is the best time for them. When you launch practice, keep instructions brief, specific and clear. For example, Julia might say: "All eyes. *[wait for all students to focus]* Team, when I say go, you'll have 6 minutes to respond independently to the first question. Take notes in your notebook. Pens ready. . . go!" These directions give students a clear, observable task. Watch Julia and her middle school students in action:

WATCH Clip 6: Julia Dutcher—Set up students for independent practice

http://www.wiley.com/go/lal

Step 2: Make Sure Everyone Is at Work—at the Launch and Throughout

During the first 30 seconds of student work, Julia takes a quick look around the room to make sure everyone has begun, narrating the students who have immediately gotten to work and gently redirecting those who have not. Then, while giving individual feedback during independent practice, Julia periodically checks the room to ensure students remain focused and productive. No fancy moves need apply here. Instead,

Figure 4.1 During work time, occasionally swivel to check that students are engaged, something Jesse Rector calls "prairie dog stance."

Source: Photo by Sheila Brown, Courtesy of Public Domain Pictures.

she swivels her head to sweep the room, an action that Jesse Rector, national dean of leadership programs at the Relay Graduate School of Education, calls the "prairie dog stance." (See Figure 4.1.)

Step 3: Offer Time Checks

Give students time checks as they work so they can learn to pace themselves: "We have about 2 minutes remaining. By now, you should be writing your second piece of evidence." (Make sure that your students with accommodations know how or if these time checks apply to them.) Posting a countdown timer in a visible area also builds the same skill. Over time, Julia spaces out these reminders to help students work longer independently.

DON'T JUST CIRCULATE, MONITOR

Once you've created a climate where students use independent practice time consistently, you can spend most of this time reviewing the content of student work, just as Mallory did in the "We Call B.S." lesson. As you'll recall, Mallory pauses her students mid-reading when they miss a key claim near paragraph 6. How can she spot the error? It's because of what she does during independent practice: she collects data.

Monitoring while students work helps Mallory keep tabs on what students get and what they don't. Even better, she can point them in the right direction as they read and write. For this reason, Mallory describes independent work time not as a break from instruction, but as the heart of it.

> ## Core Idea
>
> Independent work time is not a break from instruction: it's the heart of it.

Imagine if Mallory did something other than look at student work: she could have simply circulated the room or held 1–2 conferences with individual students. Although these activities are useful in some contexts, both come with major instructional limitations. Skip monitoring student work, and most students' struggles might go unnoticed—either temporarily (as discussion breaks down and you scramble to figure out why) or permanently (if those students remain quiet during class discussion).

Monitoring as precisely as Mallory and Angela requires a conscious shift in what we do during independent practice time. We'll need to adjust a few of our practices, beginning with how we move around the room.

Create a Pathway

Take a look at Mallory's seating chart (Figure 4.2). What do you notice about the arrangement? (For context, the number 1 reflects the student with the greatest proficiency on the latest assessment; 30 is the student who struggled the most.)

Students are grouped by proficiency, but not in a fixed way. When students turn and talk with the person behind them, they talk with someone of a similar proficiency level, and if they turn to the person to their side, they work with a peer of a different, but proximal, proficiency level.[2] This setup means Mallory can easily partner students for varied, enriching experiences.

What's more, the seating chart guides Mallory's movements during independent practice: her pre-planned pathway allows her to quickly get a sense of class errors. She starts with her speedier students, since they'll have something substantive written down first. If she sees that they are struggling, she knows that most of the class is likely confused. This strategy allows Mallory to quickly clarify her directions or focus

Figure 4.2 A monitoring pathway sample showing Mallory's seating chart

front of class

5	20	10	25	15	30
4	19	9	24	14	29
3	18	8	23	13	28
2	17	7	22	12	27
1	16	6	21	11	26

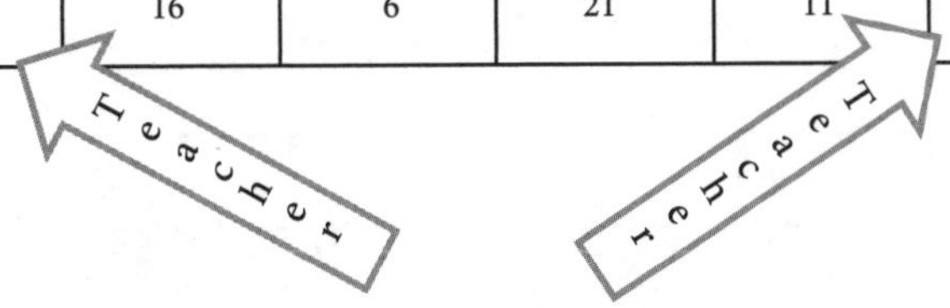

students on rereading before they get too far lost. Then, when she reaches her students with lower recent proficiency, she can see the trends that they share with their peers and the gaps that are unique to them. All of this is accomplished simply by leveraging the class's seating.

There is a useful pathway for every classroom setup. On the next page are the same principles applied to a U-shaped seating arrangement (Figure 4.3), a layout which allows students to more easily face each other during discourse. Notice that students can turn to the person next to them to be paired with someone of proximal proficiency or teamed up with students in front of or behind them for heterogeneous grouping. This setup has further value in that it allows for quick differentiation: the inner U sits closer to the teacher, allowing for small-group coaching during independent work time.

Seating arrangements are not set in stone; they should shift in response to student growth. But for the cost of some brief strategic planning, they create an opportunity for you to pulse check your students' progress—just as Mallory and Angela do.

Strategic seating can help you quickly collect a cross-section of class performance, but even with a pathway, trying to monitor everything students write is like drinking a glass of water through a firehose! We need a method to narrow our focus, especially on longer tasks when we want to review multiple components of student work.

Figure 4.3 A monitoring pathway sample for a U-shaped classroom

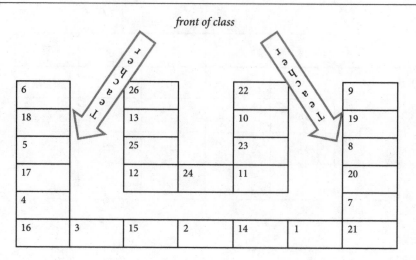

front of class

Go Lap by Lap

In her famous writing text *Bird by Bird*, Anne Lamott tells the memorable story behind the title of her book:

> Thirty years ago my older brother, who was ten years old at the time, was trying to get a report on birds written that he'd had three months to write. It was due the next day. We were out at our family cabin in Bolinas, and he was at the kitchen table close to tears, surrounded by binder paper and pencils and unopened books on birds, immobilized by the hugeness of the task ahead. Then my father sat down beside him, put his arm around my brother's shoulder, and said, "Bird by bird, buddy. Just take it bird by bird." (17–18)[3]

When students write, or annotate, or do just about anything in a literacy class, the volume of material they produce can feel overwhelming. By taking a page from Lamott, we can make this process much clearer for students and manageable for ourselves.

Nina Blalock is reading *Othello* with her 8th graders. Her students have a lengthy annotating and writing task, but she has taken care to build clear habits around independent practice and seat her students strategically. Still, there's a lot for her to take in during the day's independent practice session. As you watch, consider: How does Nina's monitoring allow her to manage multiple aspects of her students' work?

WATCH Clip 7: Nina Blalock—Monitors Student Work on Othello

http://www.wiley.com/go/lal

Figure 4.4 Nina Blalock plans to monitor in laps so she can effectively partner with student writers in class.

Source: © Uncommon Schools. Used with permission.

Notice what Nina does. At the start, she tells students that she is looking for their first paraphrases of difficult lines. Next, she tells them that she is looking for their description of the play's turning point. As students work, Nina breaks down what she plans to observe, moving lap by lap. (See Figure 4.4.) She solves the puzzle of her class's comprehension one piece at a time.

> ### Core Idea
>
> Start small: solve the puzzle one piece at a time.

When we name laps, we signal how students should pace their work and frame any feedback we provide. They know what we're looking for and when. But there's an even greater benefit for teachers. By breaking down what she's reviewing into smaller pieces, Nina can keep her monitoring manageable and her directions clear. As she walks around the classroom, Nina doesn't try to read everything a student has written: instead, she hones in on the element that she names at the start of each circuit. And although Nina only reviews one aspect a time, she sees a great deal! Here is a list of what she reviews and responds to during a 15-minute stretch of independent practice:

- Lap 1: First annotations—Are students noting the right evidence?
- Lap 2: Margin notes—First paraphrases of difficult lines or sub-claims
- Lap 3: End notes—Students' first attempt drafting a claim or argument
- Lap 4: Analysis—Students' first attempt to support their argument
- Lap 5: Clincher (closing lines)

Each lap is quick—just 15–30 seconds per student. And by the end of a single session of independent practice, Nina has a trove of information about her students as writers.

Chunking the review helps us collect valuable information about what students understand. With each round, we can drill down to specific skills and content, collect data on strengths and gaps in real time, and make our teaching more targeted.

Of course, finding the errors is one challenge. Knowing how to respond to them is another. Let's see what that looks like.

PEN IN HAND—GIVE QUICK FEEDBACK

In Chapter 3, we talked about the power of writing an exemplar response before teaching. Doing this sharpens our vision for how a lesson could go right and increases our sensitivity to how it might go wrong. But this process truly shines while giving students feedback. Here are some of the ways we've seen Angela, Mallory, and Nina transform the work they did before class into great feedback during it.

Turn to the Exemplar

Review your exemplar to determine which aspects of the analysis are most likely to give students pause. For example, Angela predicted that students would struggle with the connotations of the falcon in "Birmingham Sunday," so she planned prompts in case she needed to pause there and work with students to unpack that line.

Use Universal Prompts to Name What to Do

Prompts like "Go back and reread that paragraph" and "How do you know?" and "What's your evidence" are the Swiss Army knife of responding to student error: keep them on hand, and you'll be ready for nearly anything. Nina uses one when she prompts a student to include "the *how* piece" in her argument while she monitors. (When student claims are incomplete, we often ask them to "explain how or why.")

Mallory does the same. Here is sample feedback from her "We call B.S." lesson:

- "Clear, concise sub-claim by paragraph 10. Keep it up!"

- "Great work on your opening notes. You're missing a key claim in this section [brackets it]. Go back and see if you might spot it."

- "Very clear claim note by paragraph 6. Reread this section [brackets it]: Why did the author include it?"

What is most striking about this feedback is not only its precision but its brevity. The more targeted and precise the feedback, the more students you can reach. The more students receive feedback, the more quickly their learning accelerates. The point isn't to be frantic or to run; it's that simple precision has a dramatic effect on student learning.

Core Idea

Bite-sized feedback is far more digestible.

Although longer conferences with students have their place in the classroom,[4] you will accelerate student growth with multiple bite-sized pieces of feedback given day after day.

Quick, universal prompts like Nina's and Mallory's unpack a student's errors and point them in the right direction. However, sometimes larger trends will emerge that are impacting most of your class. What do you do then? Let's return to Angela's class to find out.

COLLECT DATA ON THE TREND AND ACT ON IT

Below is a class handout like the one Angela carried around with her when teaching "Birmingham Sunday." It's a copy of what Angela shared with students, but it is annotated in some specific ways. What stands out to you?

Stop and Jot

What is Fariña's message? How does figurative language bring that alive?

Exemplar Response:

Fariña mourns the loss of innocent lives at the hands of the KKK. He chooses a "falcon" to symbolize the KKK murders because it is a predator that kills smaller animals. The KKK members prey on the innocent souls of the 16th Street Church. This symbol illustrates the violent and murderous nature of the crime that the KKK committed against the little girls.

Lap 1: overall message
Lap 2: falcon zoom in
Lap 3: falcon zoom out

On-Track	Partially There
Amma	Kymani
Briceyda	Joshua
Tyla	Alonna
Andrew	Paola

How does Angela's annotated class handout prepare her for class discussion?

_____

_____

_____

Angela's handout shows lots of evidence of what we've discussed so far: key words are underlined and laps are mentioned. There is also a simple T-chart that lists students who are on track to meeting the depth of the exemplar and those who aren't quite there. What's the value of this? Angela knows precisely what her students need prior to starting the discourse. If you want to spend more class time on learning, focus less on what students already know and more on what they need.

Why lose class time reviewing questions students got right or establishing concepts that students already know? Skip these well-worn paths, as Angela does, and lead students right to the area of growth.

Watch how Angela challenges students to bridge the gap by directing their focus right to it, and the role that Kymani and Amma's work plays in that analysis.

WATCH Clip 8: Angela Thomas—Students Analyze "Birmingham Sunday"

http://www.wiley.com/go/lal

In this beautiful moment, all the work that Angela puts in pays off. Angela knows exactly whom to call on to showcase the trend she sees. She's ready to activate the missing background knowledge on the falcon and guide her students to zoom in on it as effectively as Amma did. Her preparation lets her students have the last word.

A Word on. . .The Power of Monitoring Student Work Schoolwide

In recent years, shows like *CSI* have popularized the career of forensic science, adding a high-tech gloss to the detective work made famous by Sir Arthur Conan Doyle's Sherlock Holmes. Fans are captivated by the detectives' meticulous study of the crime scene, be they enthusiasts of modern gadgetry or adherents to the school of good ol' "elementary" deduction. After all, crime scene analysis is a powerful way to answer the question: *What happened?*

This same question drove Kelly Dowling when she led Newark's Downtown Middle School. Her post-mortems, however, looked quite different. Dowling met weekly with her teachers to analyze student writing from exit tickets or class essays, using the data meeting protocols that Paul details in *Leverage Leadership 2.0*. Teachers analyzed the exemplar response for each lesson and then scored a cross-section of class responses to see where breakdowns occurred.

Kelly's key insight was that when students' topic sentences were off, it signaled a reading breakdown—and to know where that breakdown occurred, teachers had to examine student annotations. Analyzing data in this way sharpened teachers' insights about where, specifically, students were struggling. They moved from "they didn't get the theme" to "they didn't spot the conflict in paragraph 3." In doing so, teachers moved one step closer to helping their students read more effectively.[5]

Stop and Jot—My Takeaways

So far, what are your top takeaways for your classroom?

_____

_____

_____

_____

Part 2

Conclusion

By focusing on what students write, you improve their reading. And by monitoring that writing, you gain a clear sense of where students are and where they've yet to go. That's the perfect platform for fruitful, productive discussion—the subject of Part 3. It's in this moment that your instruction moves from individual interaction to a team sport.

THERE AND BACK AGAIN—PART 2 SUMMARY

Key Takeaways

- To check if students get it, see if they can write it. Write first, talk second.
- You can't correct what you don't detect.
- You raise the bar when you spar with an exemplar.
- Students can use annotations to better understand texts. Teachers can use them to better understand students.

- Annotation without intention is just decoration.
- The best time to try is when a task is trying.
- Independent work time is not a break from instruction: it's the heart of it.
- Start small: solve the puzzle one piece at a time.
- Bite-sized feedback is far more digestible.
- Want more time with your students? Spend less time on what they already know, and more on what they need.

Self-Assessment

A summary of key techniques from the chapter are listed here. Take a moment to score yourself now; we'll return to these ideas in Chapter 8.

Part 2: What Will I See When Students "Get It"?	
• **Spar with an Exemplar:** I analyze the texts I teach to generate an exemplar class product before teaching. My exemplar includes potential evidence that students might use, exemplary analysis for that evidence, and any additional ideas uncovered during sparring with others.	___/6
• **Teach Students to Talk to Their Texts:** When students read, they underline key claims and create brief margin notes around them. With shorter texts, students jot an overall claim or theme note after reading.	___/6
• **Honor and Monitor Independent Practice:**	___/8
○ 90% of my students use work time for purposeful, independent practice. I provide clear, what-to-do guidance and feedback to ensure they use this time effectively.	
○ I reach every student at least once a day during independent practice. I mark up their papers, give them written or oral feedback, and I collect data to guide my instruction.	
Score:	___/20

Planning for Action

- What resources from Part 2 will you use to adjust your instruction? (All of these are available in the online *Reading & Writing Handbook* in print-ready format—download and print at will!)

- ○ Sample Seating Charts for Monitoring (*Handbook* p.16)
- ○ Guidance for Classroom Monitoring (*Handbook* p. 17)
- ○ Sample Monitoring Key (*Handbook* p. 17)
- ○ Guidance for Feedback During Monitoring (*Handbook* pp. 18–19)
- How will you modify these resources to meet the needs of your class(es)?

_____

_____

_____

_____

Action	Date

What Will I Hear When Students "Get It"?

INTRODUCTION

"I don't know what he means by that, but I nod and smile at him. You'd be surprised at how far that response can get you in a conversation where you are completely confused."

—Jodi Picoult, *House Rules*[1]

Matthew McCluskey's 9th graders are getting ready to discuss Walt Whitman's poem, "When I Heard the Learn'd Astronomer." It's one of his favorites, a compact master class in Whitman's craft:

> When I heard the learn'd astronomer,
> When the proofs, the figures, were ranged in columns before me,
> When I was shown the charts, the diagrams, to add, divide, and measure them,
> When I sitting heard the learned astronomer where he lectured with much applause in the lecture room,
> How soon unaccountable I became tired and sick,

Till rising and gliding out I wander'd off by myself,
In the mystical moist night-air, and from time to time,
Look'd up in perfect silence at the stars.[2]

* * *

Matthew asks his students to jot for a few minutes on Whitman's message and how it's conveyed. As his students write in response to the day's prompt, he walks around the room and applies the same strategies we discussed in Chapter 4. It's not long before a trend begins to emerge. Here's what a typical student writes:

Sample Student Work

Whitman's Message

Student:
Whitman's poem uses free verse to convey that the speaker gets bored at a lecture and leaves it.

Matthew pauses to think back to his exemplar. His students seem to have a grasp of the poem's literal meaning, but most haven't yet appreciated what makes it so powerful: Whitman's manipulation of line length, his playfulness with alliteration and cadence, his not-too-subtle nod toward spirituality in the natural world. A whole universe awaits his class in these eight lines.

We join the discussion that follows. What do you notice about the way it unfolds?

Sample Class Discussion

"When I Heard The Learn'd Astronomer"

Matthew: How does Whitman communicate this message? [Students talk with each other for 2 minutes.] OK. Let's share out. Steve, Tookah, then Faith.

Steve: I said there's a juxtaposition between academics and the mystical and the unknown. 'Cause I know it says "charts, diagrams, to add, divide and measure" and that's like, finite information. But later the "mystical moist night"—he pitched like a sense of the mystery and going deep into things—like philosophy.

Tookah: Also, the line lengths change, because in the beginning the lines were long but then they became shorter. It feels more repetitive and it's [the lecture is] draining him. At the beginning there's also repetition, but at the end it's like, more flowing.

Faith: I agree with Tookah. At the beginning the lines—each one is longer. The words are dragging out because he feels like it's [the lecture is] dragging out. But when you go to the bottom it's like that because he feels relieved and at peace.

Matthew: Who can connect what Faith and Tookah are saying about line length with what Steve said about a mystical connection? Turn and talk, and then we'll share out.

In this brief excerpt of the discussion, a number of things stand out. For one, the students pick up quickly on the fact that Whitman's poem has two halves—let's call them the "I'm bored at a lecture" half and the "I'm transcendent out in nature" half. They've also begun to surface some key takeaways: Steve names the juxtaposition early, while Faith and Tookah find Whitman's line length intriguing and push the discussion in that direction.

On the surface, it appears Matthew has done very little, stepping aside to let students lead. And it works. But we know that just opening the floor to students won't always yield gold. How often has discussion petered out? Or have a few outspoken students dominated the conversation while the rest nodded, smiled, or remained poker-faced? Matthew knows that, like Whitman's speaker, learning isn't something he can lecture to his students—they need to go out and find it for themselves. But he also knows he can set up his conversation in favor of discovery. How?

For English teachers, great class discourse is the art of saying less while receiving more. When it succeeds, student don't just clock the time—they melt the clock.[3]

Core Idea

Great discourse doesn't clock the time; it melts the clock.

That joyfulness might feel like reason enough to invest time here, but there's plenty of research to support the power of strong conversations. A 2003 study, for example, indicated that high academic standards and discussion-based approaches correlated positively with spring performance—even when controlling for initial literacy levels, race, ethnicity, gender, and socioeconomic status.[4] The study's conclusion highlights a simple truth: great discourse is a tonic for the intellect. When you change the way students talk about reading, you'll change the way they think about it.

Core Idea

Change the way students talk about reading,
and you'll change the way they think about it.

But what, specifically, does high-quality talk entail? And how do we build a classroom like Matthew's, where it happens regularly—even predictably?

The next two chapters will address these questions:

- Chapter 5—Set the Stage for Discourse (Create the Conditions)
- Chapter 6—Build Habits of Discourse (Model and Teach the Habits)

Set the Stage for Discourse

"Writing and reading can only be intimately interrelated by floating both on a sea of talk."

—James Britton, *Writing and Reading in the Classroom*[1]

Consider this scene: a new teacher goes to observe the best teacher in the school—a true veteran—to see how she runs student discourse. Our new teacher arrives with notebook and pen in hand and has a camera handy to record the conversation. Class begins, discussion starts, and it looks like her mentor does. . . nothing?

Great discourse often feels magical to the observer, but there are no tricks at play. Skilled teachers know it takes loads of preparation for a discussion to run like clockwork. (Clocks, after all, are full of finely calibrated pieces—most of them hidden from view!) If we want our class conversations to reflect the excellence of student thought, we can copy some of the behind-the-scenes moves that make intellectual conversations—discourse like the kind we just saw in Matthew's class—look so effortless. Before we do, let's define what we mean by discourse.

DEFINE DISCOURSE

Our brains are wired for speech; it's the primary way we create and communicate meaning.[2] Still, it can be challenging to describe what we mean when we talk about discourse. Take this definition from a recent academic study:

> Classroom discussion is often defined by contrast with teacher monologues or Initiation-Response-Evaluation sequences, rather than by specifying its own defining features. . . . A feature of good discussions is high student engagement, as indicated by attentive listening and eagerness to contribute. Good classroom discussions differ from traditional classroom interactions in the participation structure: The ratio of student to teacher talk is high, and students have rights to respond directly to one another. High-quality discussions are also differentiated, though, from many engaged and participatory interactions by the degree of focus: In good discussions, claims, warrants, and conclusions are related to a topic or question.[3]

This is a strong definition: it lists so many wonderful features that we want to see and hear in a class discussion. But it falls flat in one area. If we were to check all the boxes in this description, would we be certain students had learned? Not necessarily. It's possible to have a highly engaging, student-led discussion that doesn't change learning outcomes. Students can be enthusiastic, playful, and curious in discourse and still not get any better at the *discipline* of literary study. And while we want our conversations to buzz with energy and student voice, it's insufficient if student talk doesn't push understanding forward.

So we've added an additional, essential feature to our definition of discourse—that it can shift our understanding. When we change what we say, we are, at a deeper level, changing what we think. And when we allow students to nudge each other—or when we do some gentle nudging ourselves—we elevate understanding. Talk *becomes* discourse when we expand its purpose: to change what and how students think about what they've read.

Core Idea

Discourse is talk that changes what and how we think.

Using this definition means that even when our students talk frequently and freely, what they say is not necessarily discourse. Take the worst moments of talk radio or cable news. Although the hosts and their guests argue opposing viewpoints, we can't call their exchanges discourse. The goal of this type of conversation is to avoid concessions. Each person is more focused on defending their own stance than listening to what the other person has to say. Discourse, on the other hand, involves a willingness to consider new information and incorporate it into our worldview. But conversations like that won't happen in our classrooms by chance. We need to plan for them.

GET READY TO LISTEN

Hollywood icon Viola Davis has amassed an impressive résumé across stage and screen. Julliard trained and winner of a Best Supporting Actress Oscar for the film *Fences*, she is perhaps most well known for her portrayal of lawyer Annalise Keating in the TV mystery drama *How to Get Away with Murder*. Does Davis prepare meticulously? Yes. Know her script cold? You bet. Yet when asked about the most important part of making her acting work, she has a surprising secret. Here it is, in her own words:

> One of the things I do when I collaborate is: whatever the actor gives me, I use. I don't go home and prepare a performance and then come to the set and use that performance that I prepared at home. . . . When I go onstage, I prepare myself for the fact that the actor may give me something completely different. Because what has happened in the past—and I see it with other actors—they'll tell another actor how to act. And the reason why they do that is because they've already planned what they want to do. That's not how it works: you've got to say yes to your partner.[4]

What's most striking about Davis's process is where she directs her focus: not on the script—but on her partner. Although she learns her lines, Davis doesn't try to control the outcome of the performance. Instead, she leaves herself open to whatever her partner gives her, listening with intent so she can respond to what she receives. Davis's philosophy applies well to classroom discourse. When we plan for discourse, our goal is not to control what will happen. It's to know the content well enough that we can focus our attention on what students say. We learn the lesson so we can listen.

> ## Core Idea
>
> We don't prep for discourse to help us speak, we prep for it to help us listen.

How can we listen and respond like Viola Davis? The answer lies in how we prepare ourselves for class.

FIND THE PRODUCTIVE STRUGGLE

Let's unpack Matthew's planning process for "When I Heard the Learn'd Astronomer." (See Figure 5.1.) He followed the steps we discussed in Chapter 3 and first read the poem to identify the major points of value. Next, he crafted a prompt and an exemplar response, sparring with several academic analyses to revise his exemplar. His work looked like this:

Sample Teacher Work

Matthew's Preparation for Whitman

Figure 5.1

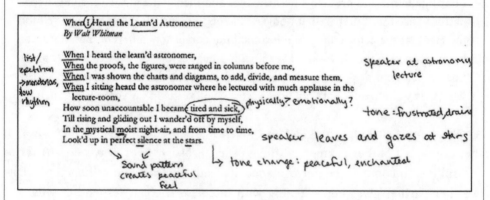

Matthew's prompt:
How do Whitman's structure and language choices help convey his theme?

Matthew's exemplar:
Whitman's careful choices in this text underscore the poem's themes around the power of experiential learning. His language highlights the change in mood

from bored to transcendent. For example, in the second half of his poem, Whitman shifts from list making to linked, assonant diction. He connects "rising" "gliding" "time" and "silence" to emphasize the freedom his speaker feels away from the lecture hall and out in nature. Through this shift, Whitman alters the emotional atmosphere of the poem from listless to enchanted and peaceful. Whitman's poetic form also reflects this theme concretely. In the poem's first half, the poet uses repetition to illustrate the monotony of the astronomer's lecture. In the early lines of the poem, when the speaker is inside, each line begins with the word "When" (1–4). This repetition shows how controlled and unoriginal this setting is by forcing the speaker to limit his language. It is only after the speaker leaves the lecture that he uses the more varied language that concludes the poem. Likewise, the line length implicitly supports the theme of the text. The initial lines of the poem grow in length as the speaker grows increasingly exasperated with the lecture. It is only in line 5, as the speaker decides to venture outside, that the lines become measured and equal, reflecting the tranquility that the speaker encounters in the natural world. Through this physical shaping of the text, Whitman again emphasizes a common theme in his work: describing the natural world cannot come close to what is learned— intellectually and spiritually—by experiencing it firsthand.

Productive Struggle(s) → line length, structure, cadence

Most of Matthew's process will feel familiar by now, but an additional component likely caught your eye. A note at the bottom reads: "Productive Struggles → line length, structure, cadence." What's productive struggle?

In Chapter 3, we discussed the importance of identifying the key points of value in a text: what we want students to take away from what they read. Matthew knows that students will easily spot the poem's use of free verse, and their schema will help them note other important features, like the poem's Transcendental elements and the speaker's preference for experiential learning (a common topic in Whitman's work). But other elements of the poem will probably challenge students, and these fall under the umbrella of craft: how Whitman uses line length and cadence to drive his message home. Matthew highlighted these exact areas for productive struggle—the place where he wants his class to spend time grappling.[5]

Matthew's move is subtle but remarkable. He hasn't just figured out the big ideas of the poem, he's also anticipated where he believes students will struggle as they think about them. But he doesn't want them to avoid the struggle; in fact, he plans to lead them right toward it. Why?

Consider how we grow in other disciplines, like weightlifting or learning a second language. Olympic weightlifters don't build muscle or reach the pinnacle of their sport by lifting weights that are comfortable. Rather, they consistently do something called "progressive overload": adding more weight/resistance to grow larger muscles and build more strength. Likewise, you don't increase fluency in a language by memorizing a vocabulary list or repeating "Hello, how are you?" a thousand times. You improve the most when you struggle to listen and speak—not drowning, but vigorously treading water. In both cases, you don't avoid the struggle—you just make it productive.

Great teachers follow this same premise when they plan for discourse. Instead of removing the struggle for students, they embrace it—productively.

Core Idea

The magic of discourse lies in productive struggle.

We know that too much struggle frustrates students, and too little bores them; hence the value of the "zone of proximal development," the space between what a student can do on their own and what they can do with support.[6] Great teaching promotes struggle and then provides the structures to make it productive. The place for that to happen is in discourse.

Planners like Matthew use the following questions to help them identify the struggle(s) they want for the class discourse:

- What is the most sophisticated thinking that students need to do to understand this text in its fullness?

- What did I do naturally/intuitively when reading this text to be able to produce that level of thinking? What moves might students not be able to do?

  ○ What knowledge gap might block student understanding?

  ○ What skill gap(s) might block student understanding?

These questions are designed to remind you of your goals and the experience of a student who will need to struggle to reach them. Without planning, we run the risk of underwhelming students with low expectations or overwhelming them with unstructured challenge.

Proper planning keeps the challenge productive. Let's see how.

ACTIVATE OR DROP KNOWLEDGE

As we learned in Chapter 2, students need background knowledge to understand complex texts. For example, imagine you're teaching a lesson on Shakespeare's *Romeo and Juliet*. Students are preparing to dive into Juliet's "O Romeo, Romeo" speech, and you are excited to see what they will find in the text. You've planned an exemplar response and identified an area in the text for productive struggle. And yet when you monitor student work and start discussion, you uncover a common misunderstanding.

"Juliet starts off confused," a student says. "She says, "wherefore art thou, Romeo? It's like she's looking for him, but she can't find him. And then she gets more frustrated as she goes on." Several other students nod.

Despite all your preparation, here's a problem you didn't see. Students have misinterpreted the meaning of "wherefore," and this error has derailed their reading. There is also little way for students to infer the meaning of "wherefore" by looking at it in context. Only knowledge can bridge the gap.

"Wherefore" you write on the board. You turn to your students. "In Shakespearean English, 'wherefore' means 'why.'"

"Oh!" several students say. The text has just transformed.

In class conversations, a small bit of knowledge can go a long way. Discourse soars on the wings of schema.

Core Idea

Discourse soars on the wings of schema.

Background knowledge is key to keeping discourse aloft. After all, if students don't know what they're talking about, how can they say what matters?

There are several methods we can use to make sure that students have the background knowledge necessary to talk about the big ideas: supplying a resource, frontloading knowledge, "dropping" knowledge, or activating strategies midstream. Here is a brief overview of each.

Supply (or Create) a Resource

Visual anchors in the classroom can help our students activate prior knowledge (or refresh themselves when they get rusty). Word walls, for example, help students access recent or important vocabulary. Academic signage can remind students of key concepts or essential questions. Jotting an idea on the whiteboard (either as ephemera or in a more long-term "parking lot" space) can help students quickly access the big "aha" moments from your instruction. (See Figures 5.2 and 5.3.)

Figure 5.2 This poster was designed to provide a fast reference for the literary history students would use in a 10th-grade class.

Source: © Uncommon Schools. Used with permission.

Figure 5.3 Creating word walls can be a simple as listing key terminology or vocabulary for students to reference in class.

Source: © Uncommon Schools. Used with permission.

Not every class resource needs to be tacked to a wall. You can create a glossary of key terms for students to keep at their desks. Or you can take the advice of our colleague Doug Lemov, who recommends providing students with knowledge organizers—lists of key unit dates, ideas, and facts—to help them hold on to critical schema.[7] Steve *still* keeps a copy of his high school reading and writing handbook, which he used as a trusted resource throughout his college days.[8] (If you wish, you can use the handbook in the online appendix as the foundation of your class's own!)

However you approach it, having easy access to key schema about vocabulary, a text, or literature in general allows students to fill in the gaps that can quickly become chasms in class.

With the right resource on hand, all you need to do is call on students to use it.

Frontload Knowledge

Sometimes students already have the knowledge they need, they just need to be reminded to use it. Middle school English teachers Michelle Wallace and Hadley Westman are preparing each of their classes for the day's lesson. What strikes you about their approaches? (Note that these transcripts focus just on what teachers say. To hear student responses, watch each clip.)

WATCH Clip 9—Michelle Wallace launches a structure analysis

http://www.wiley.com/go/lal

> ## Sample Class Discussion
>
> ### Structure and Theme in Poetry
>
> **Michelle:** You're familiar with structure because in 7th grade you studied poetry. So, how do poets utilize structure to communicate their themes? Turn and talk.

WATCH Clip 10: Hadley Westman—Reading Edna St. Vincent Millay

http://www.wiley.com/go/lal

> ## Sample Class Discussion
>
> ### Preparing for Poetry
>
> **Hadley:** Based on our focuses, how should we annotate this poem? What kinds of things should we be looking for?
>
> **Hadley:** What kinds of language and structure do we usually focus on when we read poetry?
>
> **Hadley:** Perfect. That's what we should be looking at for structure [number of stanzas, line breaks]. How about language?

Michelle and Hadley both guide students to unpack what they need to think about as they read. Michelle's students recall right away from a single prompt (with the additional benefit of highlighting the link to the previous year's learning and the arc of learning over time!) Hadley prompts for specifics to make sure her class is ready to read.

By "frontloading" schema at the start of class, both teachers make sure students are primed to apply the right conceptual framework to the text, a process that will support them as they read. Michael Smith, Deborah Appleman, and Jeffrey Wilhelm write about the practice of frontloading in *Uncommon Core*, arguing "The most important

Figure 5.4   Michelle prompts students to use what they know to tackle a new text.

Source: © Uncommon Schools. Used with permission.

time to teach is before reading—or writing—or learning anything new. . . . Frontloading *is* teaching, and it is the most powerful kind of teaching: instructional assistance that is proactive and prepares students for success."[9] Frontloading background knowledge leverages what researchers call the *primacy-recency* effect, which names the start of class as one of the most powerful moments to share key information with students.[10]

Drop Knowledge or Vocabulary

As we said in Chapter 2, the right knowledge, at the right time, is a powerful tool. And that means the start of a unit or lesson is not always the best moment to leverage schema. In fact, introducing the "aha" information too early can take away the very struggle that we want students to encounter. In those cases, or when we run into an unanticipated gap in student knowledge, we can "drop knowledge" in the moment.

To see what this looks like, let's visit Sarah Schrag's AP Language classroom. Her class is unpacking the same *Gatsby* library scene that we analyzed for *Fun Home* in Chapter 2. Students have already been discussing for a bit on their own. They've picked up on some of Gatsby's obvious traits, like his kindness and generosity, and are now beginning to discover his falseness and showmanship. Sarah wants students to use the library scene to complicate their reading of Gatsby's character. How does she deepen their analysis?

WATCH Clip 11: Sarah Schrag—Dropping Knowledge in The Great Gatsby

http://www.wiley.com/go/lal

Sample Class Discussion

The Great Gatsby

Sarah: Another quote, which you may not have understood because it has an archaic cultural reference. [*Gives page number. Students turn to page*]. We're in the library with Owl Eyes. "It's a triumph. What thoroughness! What realism! Knew when to stop too—didn't cut the pages." And what that means is that his books have words on them, but it used to be that older books were sealed. The first time you'd open them and read them, you had to cut open the pages. [*Pauses*] So, how does this add to the evidence we're bringing up so far?

There is a clear knowledge gap in Sarah's class: students don't know what unopened books are (we didn't, either!). Without this knowledge, the library scene lacks punch and, more importantly, significance. By defining unopened books, Sarah gives students the key they need to unlock the scene and pushes the productive struggle forward. If she'd done this at the start of class, she'd have put her finger on the scale, telling students exactly where to look and what to look for. By waiting, Sarah gives students knowledge right when it'll be most powerful—and she keeps them in the driver's seat.

Activate Strategy or Knowledge Midstream

Vy Graham's students are stuck. They're reading Adrienne Rich's poem "Aunt Jennifer's Tigers" and can't figure out which object in the poem—the needle or the wedding ring (or both)—is a symbol. How does Vy address the issue?

WATCH Clip 12: Vy Graham—Connect to Strategy

http://www.wiley.com/go/lal

We've already discussed the power of adding background knowledge into discourse, but it's important to name that it's a particularly powerful technique when discussion has stalled. In this case, Vy wasn't sure if students would catch the symbol or not. She hoped they would but was prepared when they didn't.

Instead of defining a symbol for students, Vy wants them to perseverate a bit. For a 7th grader, knowing how to discern whether something might or might not be symbolic is valuable analytical knowledge. So, Vy asks her class to think back to their study of John Steinbeck's *The Pearl* and how they identified symbolism then. Students share the features that made them consider the pearl a symbol, namely its repeated appearance and the unexpected imagery that Steinbeck uses to describe it. (In the text, the pearl shows reflections of characters' dreams for the future—so it's certainly atypical as far as gemstones go!) Working from this student-created definition, Vy asks students to reexamine the two objects in Rich's poem and choose the one that best fits their definition. By connecting back to previously taught material, Vy helps students make their knowledge of strategies transferable and far more useful for the long haul.

Teachers aren't the only ones who activate knowledge or strategy—if you do these moves regularly, you'll find that your students will also adopt these habits. In this snippet of discourse from Danny Murray's class, you'll see Rilwan activate knowledge in his reference to the work of academic and activist bell hooks.

Sample Class Discussion

The Women of Brewster Place

Rilwan: And, when we read bell hooks's reading, a power feminist is someone who, at the expense of other women's freedom and other women's power, they take over, they use that power to acknowledge themselves and make themselves more powerful. She empowers herself, that's the feminist part, but she uses it at the expense of other people which makes her a power feminist rather than a womanist or a feminist.

WATCH Clip 13: Danny Murray—Connect to Background Knowledge

http://www.wiley.com/go/lal

Rilwan connects to schema about power feminists to fuel the class debate about whether the character Etta is a feminist—without a single intervention from his teacher. Intellectual tension like this is a beautiful thing: it can encourage students to question their beliefs or adjust to new ones.

Activating schema highlights for students that no text exists in a vacuum, and how we can bring deeper understanding to bear when we know what other writers have said. The more we know about the world of ideas, the richer our conversation.

These short classroom visits have shown us the power of activating or providing student knowledge in discourse. Watch how Matthew puts that all together in his plan to teach "When I Heard the Learn'd Astronomer":

Sample Teacher Work

Matthew's Plan for Activating Knowledge in "When I Heard the Learn'd Astronomer"

Prompt: How do Whitman's structure and language choices help convey his theme?

- Do Now:
  - What do you know about free verse poetry?
  - What have we learned about Walt Whitman's style and topics so far this year?
- Vocabulary (on poster):
  - cadence, repetition, assonance, line length, anaphora

This simple plan for how to embed or activate knowledge can make all the difference in class. We can choose from a number of options: shift a Do Now, suggest a reading to assign, or just determine which terms to add or highlight on the class's word wall. Even though these resources may seem invisible once class discussion is in full swing, they make all the difference. With adequate knowledge, students can more confidently access a text without getting tripped up. That allows us to focus on what we can do to get the discourse started on the right foot.

LAUNCH THE DISCOURSE CYCLE

Let's say you're preparing to teach a close reading of Frederick Douglass's speech "What to the Slave Is the 4th of July?" and you want students to analyze how Douglass crafts his prose. A former enslaved person and nineteenth-century abolitionist, Douglass was (and is) well known for his skills in oratory. If you've read his speech before, you know it's challenging—and commonly taught in AP-level classes. An excerpt from his speech is the focus of this close reading lesson:

Excerpt—"What to the Slave Is the 4th of July?"

Directions: Read the following excerpt of a speech Frederick Douglass gave in 1852 to the Rochester Ladies' Anti-Slavery Society.

Source: © U.S. Library of Congress.

Fellow citizens, pardon me, and allow me to ask, why am I called upon to speak here today? What have I or those I represent to do with your national independence? Are the great principles of political freedom and of natural justice, embodied in that Declaration of Independence, extended to us? And am I, therefore, called upon to bring our humble offering to the national altar, and to confess the benefits, and express devout gratitude for the blessings resulting from your independence to us?

But such is not the state of the case. I say it with a sad sense of the disparity between us. I am not included within the pale of this glorious anniversary! Your high independence only reveals the immeasurable distance between us. The blessings in which you, this day, rejoice, are not enjoyed in common. The rich inheritance of justice, liberty, prosperity and independence, bequeathed by your fathers, is shared by you, not by me. The sunlight that brought light and healing to you, has brought stripes and death to me. This Fourth of July is yours, not mine. You may rejoice, I must mourn. To drag a man in fetters into the grand illuminated temple of liberty, and call upon him to join you in joyous anthems, were inhuman mockery and sacrilegious irony. Do you mean, citizens, to mock me, by asking me to speak today?. . .

What to the American slave is your Fourth of July? I answer, a day that reveals to him more than all other days of the year, the gross injustice and cruelty to which he is the constant victim. To him your celebration is a sham; your boasted liberty an unholy license; your national greatness, swelling vanity; your sounds of rejoicing are empty and heartless; your shouts of liberty and equality, hollow mock; your prayers and hymns, your sermons and thanksgivings, with all your religious parade and solemnity, are to him mere bombast, fraud, deception, impiety, and hypocrisy—a thin veil to cover up crimes which would disgrace a nation of savages. There is not a nation of the earth guilty of practices more shocking and bloody than are the people of these United States at this very hour.

Let's imagine that at this point in your yearly curriculum, not only do you want students to identify Douglass's message but also how he uses repetition and juxtaposition to enhance it. Your next step is to determine how you'll begin the class conversation.

Start Broad

Below is a list of three potential questions we could use to spark discussion. Which one sets up students for the most productive, generative discourse?

Stop and Jot—Start with the Right Question

Pathway 1: "Find evidence of juxtaposition and explain how it supports Douglass's argument."

Pathway 2: "Who is Douglass's audience—what is their race—and when is he speaking? How do they likely feel about the 4th of July, and how is Douglass's view potentially surprising?"

Pathway 3: "What does Douglass want his audience to feel (and how is he creating that feeling)?"

Which pathway would create the most productive, generative discourse?

_____

_____

_____

_____

Vy faced the same challenge. Let's see which she chose.

 WATCH Clip 14: Vy Graham—Starting with a Broad, High Rigor Question

 http://www.wiley.com/go/lal

What made Vy choose the third prompt? It invited students to do most of the thinking.

What would've happened if Vy had chosen differently? Pathway 1 would have led students straight to juxtaposition—they wouldn't have had to identify the technique for themselves. And while Douglass's use of juxtaposition is essential to his claim, students in Vy's class were able to pick up on even more literary elements. Pathway 2, meanwhile, is over-scaffolded, leaving students with little work to do on their own. The danger here is clear: providing too many supports leaves students with little to think about. If you want students to digest big ideas, don't force-feed them. Set the table and let them eat.

> ### Core Idea
> Don't force-feed your students; simply set the table.

Let's revisit the clip we just watched, this time from the perspective of a student. Notice what they say:

> ## Sample Class Discussion
>
> ### "What to the Slave Is the 4th of July?"
>
> **Joseph:** "What does Douglass want his audience to feel and how is he creating that feeling?"
>
> [Vy cues students to write independently and then turn and talk to share out responses. This dialogue comes from the start of discourse.]
>
> **Allen:** I think the technique used in paragraph 2 might be sarcasm or juxtaposition. . . It says, "You may rejoice. I must mourn. To drag in man in fetters to the grand illuminated temple of liberty and call upon him to join you in joyous anthems." And I think that this might show that even though the white people are enjoying the holiday, Blacks aren't really celebrating it that much because they are not the ones with the freedom, and the whites really are.
>
> **Aaliyah:** I partially agree with you when you say that . . . but I think that it's juxtaposition [not sarcasm] because he's basically contrasting the perspectives and how they are feeling towards the holiday. [There's more evidence] it's juxtaposition when it says: "The sunlight that brought life and healing to you has brought stripes and death to me." . . . So it's showing his perspective on the Fourth of July and what happened during this time because he was still oppressed.
>
> **Fayonna**: Aaliyah, I agree with you that he uses juxtaposition of the audience's perspective and his perspective. And I also think he uses a metaphor because in paragraph 2 he says that: "The sunlight that has brought life and healing to you has brought stripes and death to me." The metaphor emphasizes, like Aaliyah said, two different perspectives of how African Americans are not free but the white people are. Also he uses a rhetorical question at the end of the paragraph. It says, "Do you mean, citizens, to mock me by asking me to speak today?" That also shows that white people have freedom and he feels that he is being mocked because they asked him to speak on a day when he doesn't have freedom."

Students are in the beginning stages of cracking the text. They've picked up on Douglass's use of literary techniques, like juxtaposition and metaphor, and have started to mine the second paragraph for additional evidence to support their analysis. While they have successfully zoomed in on Douglass's craft, they haven't yet zoomed out to connect those techniques to how Douglass wants the audience to feel. Yet this is precisely the point: the students are engaged in productive struggle, freely speculating about possibilities and not worrying about whether or not they are "right."[11]

As she listens, Vy monitors how well students navigate the struggle on their own. That's not to say that Vy never pushes into discourse—she does, especially if students get stuck and are unable to help each other. (We'll talk more about that in the next chapter.) But Vy lets students get as far as they can on their own before she intervenes. By starting broad, she signals that the intellectual responsibility rests with her students. And what's more, she does it in a way that involves them all.

Follow a Cycle

Let's linger in Vy's classroom for a moment longer. Here's a play-by-play of what we see in the clip:

Play-by-Play: How Vy Graham Launches Discourse

1. **Individually Write**—Students answer the high-level prompt about Frederick Douglass's speech.

2. **Turn & Talk**—Students share their ideas with a peer.

3. **Cold Call**—The teacher cold calls a student to begin sharing. (This can also be done as a "warm call," giving a student a heads-up that you'd like to hear them share first.)

4. **Volley**—Students share and build on each other's responses with minimal intervention from the teacher.

What do you notice? Before large group discussion begins, every student has had the chance to grapple with the prompt on their own, and then with a partner. From there, talk bounces like a beach ball, with each speaker adding new information or thinking to keep discourse in motion.[12] Think about the impact of this cycle: at the start of discourse, every student has already had a chance to write and speak.

Without an opening writing prompt or turn and talk, only the most eager students are likely to speak. Meanwhile, other students get comfortable with sitting back and not engaging, and in the worst of cases, learning to depend on others' analysis before attempting their own. But when students have a chance to share ideas with a peer, they enter the larger discourse with additional confidence and the knowledge that they've already field tested their thinking. Students who find the text challenging get something extra: an additional opportunity to process with a peer.

Launching discourse this way is the first step in increasing student talk. Once it's up and running, we step out of the way.

MAXIMIZE STUDENT TALK

Two barriers consistently keep our students from talking: time (too little of it!) and teacher talk (too much of it!).[13] As teachers, we have the power to change both—and the responsibility to do so. If we don't provide students the space to speak regularly, how can we expect them to sustain discourse on their own? Teachers like Matthew have tapped into some powerful ways to maximize student voice in discourse by minimizing their own.

Strategically Call Students

Matthew's students have consistently struggled to connect poetic elements, like cadence and line length, to a deeper understanding of a poem's theme. Here's the sort of plan he can craft for discourse to tackle this challenge head on. What strikes you about it?

Sample Teacher Work:

**Matthew's Plan for Discourse in
"When I Heard the Learn'd Astronomer"**

Prompt: How do Whitman's structure and language choices
help convey his theme?

Anticipated Responses (in order of decreasing sophistication)

Exemplar Response [seen earlier in this chapter]:
Whitman's language highlights the shift in mood from bored to transcendent. For example, in the second half of his poem, Whitman shifts from list making to linked, assonant diction. He connects "rising" "gliding" "time" and "silence" to emphasize the freedom his speaker feels away from the lecture hall and out in nature. In the early lines of the poem, when the speaker is inside, each line begins with the word "When" (1–4). This repetition shows how controlled and unoriginal this setting is by forcing the speaker to limit his language. Likewise, the line length implicitly supports the theme: the initial lines of the poem grow

---

in length as the speaker grows increasingly exasperated with the lecture. It is only in line 5, as the speaker decides to venture outside, that the lines become measured and equal, reflecting the tranquility that the speaker encounters in the natural world.

Almost-There Response:
Whitman's structure shifts mid-poem. He moves from repetition and long lines to much shorter, measured lines. He shifts from "sick and tired" to "rising, gliding." This relates to how his speaker feels, demonstrating his sense of freedom in nature.

Partially-There Response:
Whitman's opening tone is bored, which is seen in the line "sick and tired" of all the passive learning.

Further-Off Response:
Whitman's poem is in free verse, which gives the text a sense of freedom and conveys his themes.

Matthew has done more than simply write an ideal response: he has thought about his students and what partial answers might be. What's the power of that? Anticipating the gaps allows Matthew to plan for them. There are two ways for him to close the gap: activate knowledge (as we discussed earlier) or activate the class, which we'll discuss now.

Let's return to the dialogue you read earlier from Matthew's classroom. What do you notice about whom Matthew calls on and when?

Sample Class Discussion

"When I Heard the Learn'd Astronomer"

Matthew: So most of us—almost 100% of us—have something like this [holds up paper]. That the tone at the beginning of this poem is bored. Prove it to me. Tookah, start us off.

Tookah: The tone in the beginning is bored. He says he became "tired and sick." And then that shows that he's tired of all of the passive learning he's doing in the classroom.

Matthew: Build on that—Iyana.

Iyana: The connotation of sick means that you're not able to do many things; there's like a loss of life. So if he's saying. . . that he's bored in the class to the extent that they're doing the same thing over and over—he's sick and tired of recycling the same knowledge over and over again, so his tone is lifeless.

Matthew: Iyana is suggesting something quite interesting, that the speaker is *more* than bored. What does that mean?

Amira: He's more than bored. Sick, like Iyana said, has this connotation of a loss of life. It shows his experience is lifeless. And also—usually we say, "sick and tired," but he uses "tired and sick" to convey a more charged meaning of sick—that "sick" is more powerful.

Daré: I also want to add that when you're bored with something, you can always kind of come back to it. Like you could have a boring English class [Mr. McCluskey: "Never!"] . . . but that doesn't mean that you're all of a sudden going to just like leave school or just drop out. . . . But when something is draining you and you have a loss of life—we see that he actually had to leave. . . which supports that he was more than bored.

Matthew's discourse doesn't start with a student who has a perfect answer—and that wasn't a mistake. Matthew had monitored student written responses prior to launching discourse (following the write/turn-and-talk/cold call cycle). He knew Tookah's answer was on the right track but could be pushed by her peers, so he called on her first. Why didn't he start with someone who was closer?

Matthew's decision was strategic. Calling first on a student who is partially there or further off begins discourse in a place that most students can access. It allows the class to build on each other and make their own discoveries, without Matthew's input.

It's tempting to start discussions with raised hands (usually students with the most developed answers), but that often allows those students to dominate the conversation and leaves the rest of class out of it. With strategic calling, Matthew avoids this pitfall and sets up his class to bridge confusion together. His moves demonstrate a powerful concept: most of the time, students can sort out questions on their own—when we let them. Strategic calling lets students be the teachers.

Core Idea

Don't be the sage on the stage when there's wisdom in the room.

Matthew follows some basic core principles with strategic calling:

- **Start with a student who has a response that's partially there or further off.** This gives all students access at the start of the discourse and the opportunity to participate.

- **Ask students with the same level answers** to do the initial evaluation/response. Resist the temptation to immediately go to your strongest responder and let students close the gaps themselves.

- **Call on students with stronger initial responses** when conversation stalls and you need to push it forward.

- **Call on students with weaker initial responses** when you want to check for student understanding and see what they are grasping.

No single voice, or level, dominates the conversation—discourse is a group effort. Although Matthew facilitates, student voices fill the air.

Leverage "Universal" Prompts

With strategic calling, students do most of the talking, which allows Matthew to facilitate without jumping in. Let's step back into Matthew's class to see how he participates as students are digging into "When I Heard the Learn'd Astronomer." Here's the video for the transcript you read earlier:

WATCH Clip 15: Matthew McCluskey—Students Analyze Tone in "When I Heard the Learn'd Astronomer"

http://www.wiley.com/go/lal

Let's focus now on what Matthew does. We've bolded his prompts to highlight his moves during discourse:

Sample Class Discussion

"When I Heard the Learn'd Astronomer"

Matthew: So most of us—almost 100% of us—have something like this [holds up paper]. That the tone at the beginning of this poem is bored. **Prove it to me.** Tookah, start us off.

Tookah: The tone in the beginning is bored. He says he became "tired and sick." And then that shows that he's tired of all of the passive learning he's doing in the classroom.

Matthew: Build on that—Iyana.

Iyana: The connotation of sick means that you're not able to do many things; there's like a loss of life. So if he's saying. . . that he's bored in the class to the extent that they're doing the same thing over and over—he's sick and tired of recycling the same knowledge over and over again, so his tone is lifeless.

Matthew: Iyana is suggesting something quite interesting, that the speaker is *more* than bored. **What does that mean?**

Amira: He's more than bored. Sick, like Iyana said, has this connotation of a loss of life. It shows his experience is lifeless. And also—usually we say, "sick and tired," but he uses "tired and sick" to convey a more charged meaning of sick—that "sick" is more powerful.

Daré: I also want to add that when you're bored with something, you can always kind of come back to it. Like you could have a boring English class [Mr. McCluskey: "Never!"] . . . but that doesn't mean that you're all of a sudden going to just like leave school or just drop out. . . . But when something is draining you and you have a loss of life—we see that he actually had to leave. . . which supports that he was more than bored.

Matthew deliberately uses short prompts ("build" or "prove it") that could be applied to any text. These universal prompts are a go-to in his playbook, because they can be reused all the time. They keep his voice minimal and remind us that most of the time, the best way for us to lead students is to stay out of their way. If you want to maximize student talk, minimize your own.

Core Idea

To maximize student talk, minimize your own.

Here's a set of some of the most common universal prompts we hear in classrooms. Feel free to use or revise it.

Universal Prompts for Discourse

- "Build."
- "Elaborate."
- "Agree/Disagree."
- "Prove it." / "Evidence?"
- "So what?"

CONCLUSION

Together, the moves in this chapter provide everything you need to start discussion right. You've targeted a productive struggle, activated the necessary knowledge, and launched the conversation in a way that maximizes student voice. What's left after a strong start? Helping your class to keep it going.

Stop and Jot—My Takeaways

So far, what are your top takeaways for your classroom?

_____

_____

_____

_____

Chapter 6

Build Habits of Discourse

"Ah, love may be strong, but a habit is stronger."
—Peter S. Beagle, *The Last Unicorn*

When he's writing a book, author Haruki Marukami is a creature of habit. Every day he wakes up at 4 a.m. and writes for 5–6 hours. In the afternoon, he chooses between a 10-kilometer run or a 1500-meter swim. At night, he relaxes by reading a book and listening to music. At 9 p.m., he goes to bed.[1] Other well-known authors boast different habits—writing longhand, while standing or while walking—but the common denominator is the way they practice their craft. They don't wait for the muse or the right moment to begin. Instead, these authors write well because they write daily. It is the habit, then, that creates the space for great works to be written.

Great discourse, like great writing, is the product of daily practice. It is made up of specific, concrete moves we want students to make when they talk, ways of speaking that we model and teach until they become more than good technique. Once internalized, these moves become habit: a conversational grammar that unites students' expectations of themselves and each other.

BUILD HABITS OF DISCOURSE 101—CREATE CONVERSATION

"The Jury each formed a different view / (Long before the Indictment was read), / And they all spoke at once, so that none of them knew / One word that the others had said."
—Lewis Carroll, *"The Hunting of the Snark"*

How many of us have presided over classes (or meetings!) that function just like the jury from the above epigraph—where students trumpet their views to an audience of peers who are mainly concerned with making their own point, regardless of what anyone else has said? When students don't listen to each other, it's just a short few steps to Carrollinian nonsense.

Eric Diamon's 6th graders show us another way. In this clip, students are discussing *Esperanza Rising* by Pam Muñoz Ryan. The novel follows Esperanza, a Mexican girl who is forced to leave her childhood of privilege for the labor camps of 1930s California. Take a moment to watch. What do you notice about the way students interact with one another?

 WATCH Clip 16: Eric Diamon—Students Discuss Esperanza Rising

 http://www.wiley.com/go/lal

Sample Class Discussion

Esperanza Rising

Rasheemah: [reads prompt] Esperanza will never be able to change to be a person who works hard and is kind to everyone. One for agree, two for disagree.

[Students vote].

Rasheemah: Jahne, you can go first because you're the only one [who agrees].

Jahne: I said I agree because in a lot of the chapters, she still doesn't realize she's poor now. . . . We see that she's not changing at all. And the evidence that I have is when they get to the cabin where they're going to be living, she says they're living like horses, and that she's going to try to change. That doesn't show that she's actually changing.

Darryl: When she tries to ask her friend for help. . . to learn how to do chores. Does that show how's she going to change or how's she going to stay the same?

Jahne: That might show she's going to change, but that's only one point in the story. In every other chapter we've read so far, she hasn't been changing at all.

Darryl: So does that mean progress or that she's not going to change?

Jahne: [Pauses, smiles] Progress.

Rasheemah: I hear Jahne saying that Esperanza will never be able to change because she still believes she's living a rich life, but I disagree. I'd like to say that Esperanza is already beginning to change; she's holding onto Silvia's, Isabel's friend's hand even though she knows it's dirty. She realizes she's going to be dirty too living in this place. Like Darryl said, she even wants to learn how to clean. But Jahne, you do have a point. She only wants to learn how to clean so she doesn't make a fool of herself. . . .

Let's start with the most striking fact—students are leading the discourse *by themselves*. They speak in turn, respond to each other with care, and signal careful listening by giving each other credit for earlier responses. Their agreements and disagreements are rooted in the text, and when students critique a classmate's reading, they do so with measured neutrality. Neither magic nor luck explains these remarkable abilities—habits of discourse do.

Think back to what happens when Eric cues his class to begin—a buzz of talk about the book erupts. Student habits (active listening, speaking in turn, and projecting one's voice) make up a shared set of ground rules. They free students to think more deeply about what they've read, as well as what to do when they want to say something about it. They also prevent a cacophony of peers who just want to be heard but forget their role is to listen, too. Below is a detailed list of Eric's expectations. Watch the clip again to see how students have internalized these habits to keep conversation in motion.[2]

Habits of Discourse 101 Create Conversation		
Core Habit	**Ideal Student Actions**	**Teacher Talk Moves**
Project	• Speak audibly and make eye contact with classmates, not just the teacher.	• Put hand to ear or move to opposite side of the room. • "Please Project" or "Strong voice" • "Speak to your peers."

Habits of Discourse 101 Create Conversation		
Share in turn	• Speak in turn. • Invite others in.	• "Give her a chance to finish her point." • "One voice at a time." • "We haven't heard from everyone yet. Would someone who hasn't spoken yet like a chance?"
Speak as an intellectual	• Use classmates' names. • Use complete sentences. • Address question succinctly.	• "With whom do you agree?" • "Speak in complete sentences." • "Interesting! Let's pause to invite an additional voice into our conversation."
Listen as an intellectual	• Make eye contact with the speaker. • Nod or affirm nonverbally. • Turn to page if speaker references it (pause to give time to turn to page).	• Gesture at students, make eye contact with speaker, and/or hands down. • Model affirmations. • "Destiny, give the class a moment to find the page and confirm that everyone is with you."
Take notes as an intellectual	• Write down/summarize key information. • Evaluate the arguments. • Annotate diagrams.	• Model or select a student to model strong note-taking. • "If you are not currently speaking, you should be listening and taking notes." • Provide time at the end for key takeaways to be recorded. • Share exemplary student notes for students to see a model.

Habits of Discourse 101 Create Conversation		
Build & Critique	**Agree with all or parts of ideas and elaborate:** • "I agree that. . . I would add. . ." • "Mark's point is right, but/and I think there is better/additional evidence for it. . ."	• "Build." • "Agree or disagree?"
	Disagree: • "Actually, there is evidence in the text that refutes that view." • "Respectfully, I have a different view."	• "Agree or disagree?" • "Is there evidence in the text that refutes that view?"
	Examine evidence in a different way: • "I actually viewed that text differently."	• "Is there another way we can view this evidence?"

Together, these habits are the 101 course for creating conversation. Introduce and practice these moves at the start of the academic year, and they'll keep student voices at the center of your classroom all year long. But these habits—designed to help create authentic conversation—are just a start. Once they're in place, you can graduate to the 201 level. It's here that you'll develop the habits that help students drive the conversation to new and more complex places.

BUILD HABITS OF DISCOURSE 201—DEEPEN DISCOURSE

Revoice

Students in Danny Murray's African American literature elective are reading Gloria Naylor's *The Women of Brewster Place*, a novel about seven women who live in a housing development in an unnamed city. Students are debating whether Etta, one of the novel's principal characters, is a womanist. Womanism's definition can vary, but students in Danny's class know it as social theory similar to feminism that centers around the experiences and concerns of Black women.[3] You've already watched this discussion as part of our discussion on activating strategies and schema (Chapter 5, Clip 13). We invite you to look again through a different lens and pay careful attention to how the discourse unfolds. Aminah and Damiano share their opinions of Etta. What does Danny ask the class to do after they both share out?

WATCH Clip 17: Danny Murray—Revoice in The Women of Brewster Place

http://www.wiley.com/go/lal

Sample Class Discussion

The Women of Brewster Place

Aminah: Women didn't feel like they were living their full lives because they weren't seen as equal to men. Because she's looking—because he sees her as having this full-fledged life it shows her. . . her just walking with her head up high and having that equality that other women don't have.

Damiano: I remember when we were going over the definition of womanism and I'm pretty sure we touched on the topic of women of color helping other women of color, uplifting each other, and I'd like to draw attention to page 74 at the end of the chapter. I feel like this specific moment when Etta knew she could confide in Maddie, it highlighted womanism.

Danny: So before we hear from our dissenters, those who believe she's not a womanist, let's practice revoicing. One person who'd like to disagree, can you first revoice the pro-womanist perspective as a way to challenge their stance? We'll go hands down from here. And then I'd like the same thing to happen for those who are stuck in between—to revoice those who believe she is not a womanist. We'll open the floor.

Danny asks the students who disagree with Aminah and Damiano's stance to revoice their argument before offering an opposing one. What does Danny mean by revoicing? By asking students to paraphrase (or revoice) what they hear, Danny is asking them to filter someone else's argument through their own thought process. Revoicing is a powerful instructional tool, and like many of the techniques we'll show you, it's supported by research.[4]

Let's jump back into the conversation.

> ## Sample Class Discussion
>
> ### *The Women of Brewster Place*
>
> **Bangale:** Rilwan is saying she wants to gain power over other women. I feel like that's not true. I feel like she kind of set an example for the women she's getting in front of, they just don't agree with her, so it seems as if she wants to be better than them, but I feel like she has no choice because they're already against her.
>
> **Rilwan:** Bangale, I have a question. When I mentioned in the past about her going to Reverend Woods. . . to become over the pastor's woman and the wives and all the other women. She's using those women; she's putting them down. She wants to become above them, and that directly refutes your point.
>
> **Danny:** So what are they debating about? Could someone revoice? What's the real tension?
>
> **Simon:** Rilwan, he's suggesting that instead of Etta being considered a feminist, a womanist, or not either, she's a power feminist and she's trying to use men at the expense of women to gain an advantage over them or empower herself, but Bangale is saying that's not what she's doing. She's being empowered by other women and she's not using men in the way that Rilwan is saying. Am I interpreting what you're saying correctly, Bangale?

With Danny's simple prompt, he not only includes more voices in the debate, but he strengthens the habit of active listening, something that Bangale and Rilwan are already demonstrating. Revoicing accomplishes many things at once:

- Clarifies Simon's own understanding of the two readings of Etta
- Establishes a common understanding for the class
- Provides an entry point for anyone—teacher or student—to complicate or build on the current readings of the character

This technique encourages students to grapple with each other's ideas, not simply provide their thoughts in isolation.

In the end, revoicing creates a special type of dialogue, where I am dependent upon your ideas to express my own. If I can revoice your argument, I've truly listened to it. After all, you can't respond to what you haven't heard.

"Excellence, then, is not an act, but a habit." That line—somewhat famous—is a paraphrase by philosopher Will Durant, but it's almost always attributed to Aristotle.[5] Why? Because Durant understood Aristotle's points so well he could voice them himself—in language that's resonant to the modern ear. There are few better ways to show you are attending to someone's ideas than revoicing them.

Press for Reasoning

Come with us to Rue Ratray's 6th-grade class. His students are reading Lois Lowry's *The Giver*, a dystopian novel that follows Jonas, a young boy that comes of age in a society governed by sameness. His father cares for the young infants born in the community and has been assigned to euthanize a baby named Gabriel for failing to meet growth metrics.

Rue has chosen to center discourse around a close reading of Jonas's father's dialogue and what this indicates about his character. In the transcript that follows, you'll see Rue add a habit of discourse. As you read, consider: How does Rue help his students build stronger arguments?

Sample Class Discussion

The Giver

D.T.: When I read the text, I thought that Jonas's father didn't give much thought into kind of. . . killing the baby and he acted fine with it.

Rue: Why?

D.T.: He acted fine with it because he didn't, he was talking to the baby like he talked to Jonas.

Rue: But why? What in here is telling you that?

D.T.: When it, on the last sentence it says, "a shrimp" and he acted like it's fine, this always happens.

Rue: But why?

D.T.: Because "shrimp" is italicized.

Rue: So?

D.T.: So that's saying that he's talking to the baby in kind of, like, in a baby voice.

Rue relies on prompts like "But why?" and "So?" to push students to provide more evidence for their claims. At the start of this exchange, D.T. gives little text-based evidence for her argument. Rue presses for more reasoning and asks, "What in here [the text] is telling you that?," a prompt that directs D.T. back to *The Giver*. She zooms in on the father's use of the word "shrimp" and interprets its italicization as the father speaking to Gabriel in a baby voice.

Prompts like "Why?" or "How do you know?" push students to build defensible arguments. Similar to what we've seen in the revoicing clips, students can also use this habit to challenge each other. After all, a claim without evidence is just an opinion.

> ## Core Idea
>
> A claim without evidence is just an opinion.

Revoicing and pressing for reasoning allow students to communicate and defend what they *already* think. But there are times when you want discourse to help students form *new* ideas. So what do you do if the discourse doesn't stir up a fresh debate? You provoke it yourself.

Problematize

Let's return to Danny's class for a few more minutes, this time to a moment earlier in the period—before that great intellection tension. Students at this point have settled on the notion that Etta is dependent on others—not a feminist or womanist. As you watch, take note of how John, then Danny, spark a debate:

WATCH Clip 18: Danny Murray—Problematizing in Class

http://www.wiley.com/go/lal

Sample Class Discussion

The Women of Brewster Place

[Lengthy class debate about whether Etta is a womanist—most say no. Then John jumps in:]

John: I'd like to play devil's advocate. I feel as though Naylor is showing how Etta is a womanist because she doesn't depend on men. At the scene where they were leaving, it states, "Etta got out of the car unassisted and didn't bother to turn and watch the tail light as it pulled off. . .She had asked him to leave her at the corner because there was no point in having to make a U-turn in the dead-end street, and was less than a hundred yards to the door." So, she shows how she doesn't depend on a man, she doesn't need a man to drive her and stop her right at the door. She was unassisted at the car. She did it herself, she walked home, basically, herself, and she didn't even turn back to look at the man who did all that for her, because she didn't really care about it.

Danny: So here's the tension that I'm hearing in our first set of comments. . . On one hand, Etta can be described as independent. On the other side of the spectrum, she is dependent and seeking men, most notably Reverend Woods, as a way to validate herself and a way to find more societal standard. . . So John's question is a good one. Is Etta a womanist? Why or why not? Let's turn and talk.

[Students discuss in pairs.]

Danny: All right. Hands up [if] she is a womanist.

[Collection of hands go up.]

Danny: Hands down. Hands up [if] she is not a womanist.

[Another set of hands go up.]

Danny: [looking at unraised hands]. People who didn't vote—what's your stance?

Ahnad: Can it be both?

Danny: Oh! There's a third option. Hands up [if] she's simultaneously a womanist and not womanist.

[A new set of hands go up.]

Playing devil's advocate—or problematizing—is a powerful way to deepen the substance of the discussion. You invite students to challenge their own assumptions and see the world in all its multivalence, complexity, and nuance. The strategy ignites debate. Who doesn't want to respond to a devil's advocate? It's a technique as old as

Socrates's famous debates with his students—and undoubtedly goes back further than that. Sometimes students do this on their own (as John does) but teachers can do so just as well (as Danny encourages with his class vote). Problematizing in a discussion can be as simple as making a claim and saying, "Agree or disagree?" One thing is clear, though: if you want a lively debate, don't be afraid to instigate it.

Core Idea

If you want a lively debate, instigate it.

Problematizing is one way to go deeper. You can also push for sophistication.

Sophisticate

Let's return to Hadley Westman's classroom. (See Figure 6.1.) In this clip, she is teaching her 7th graders Julia Alvarez's *In the Time of the Butterflies*. Students are discussing one of the book's climaxes, when Minerva Mirabal slaps dictator Rafael Trujillo at the Discovery Day dance. As you might imagine, slapping the country's dictator does not bode well for Minerva or her family. Hadley's instruction is focused on helping her

Figure 6.1 Hadley prompts students to push for sophistication in their analysis.

Source: © Uncommon Schools. Used with permission.

students understand the motif of rain in this section of the novel, which Alvarez uses to suggest both chaos and—later on—catharsis. Her students have registered that the language of "slapping rain" echoes the physical slap the dictator has received, but they can't go much further yet. As you watch, consider: How does Hadley push student analysis?

WATCH Clip 19: Hadley Westman—Zoom in and Zoom out In the Time of Butterflies

http://www.wiley.com/go/lal

Sample Class Discussion

In the Time of Butterflies

Revival: I would like to include the moment when Minerva slapped him because she is showing the power that Minerva has, or had. . . and then it said, "The slapping sheets of the rain." And you know that when something is slapping down hard, it's really powerful or really heavy.

Hadley: Why would she [Alvarez] use that word?

Revival: Because she [Minerva] just slapped the president.

Hadley: So it seems obvious, but what's interesting is that she doesn't use the word when she does slap the president, she uses the word when it starts raining. So what's she trying to connect here?

Saniyah: I think she's trying to connect what she really does to the dictator and the power of the rain, because on page 93 it was talking about how the rain was more severe than ever and now the rain is slapping down: it's knocking down everything, and it's destroying everything.

Hadley: So this motif is linked to what?

Michael: This motif is linked to chaos and how in the beginning it was talking about how hurricanes usually bring chaos, and right now after the event happened, everyone's scattered around, stuff is falling over, and it already is chaos.

Hadley: Build, Francia. You're the only one who hasn't talked yet.

When people talk about disciplinary literacy, it's often around the ways that historians or scientists process text. But the critical study of language is a discipline, too, and it hinges on careful attention to word choice and text construction. Consider Hadley's prompts. As we mentioned in Chapter 2, zooming in and out is a powerful way for

Hadley's students to think about analysis. And just as Hadley wants students to zoom in and out on important diction while reading, she pushes them to do the same in discourse, to unpack the phrase "slapping sheets of rain" for its connotations and symbolism. Had Hadley not stepped in, her students would have had a perfectly pleasant talk—it just wouldn't have made them better readers.

Zooming in and out is a great way to add sophistication to a discussion, but it's not the only way to do it. Let's return to Sarah Schrag's discussion of *The Great Gatsby*. As you'll recall, discourse centers around the early party scene where we first meet Gatsby and his dubious library. In Chapter 5, we saw Sarah drop knowledge to help add nuance to her class's views, but this clip comes from earlier in class, when students were struggling to see Gatsby as anything more than sociable. Sarah wants her students to notice that there's more to the character than the gregarious, easygoing partier her students described initially. As you watch, notice how Sarah prompts her students to reread the text.

WATCH Clip 20: Sarah Schrag—Narrow the Focus on Jay Gatsby

http://www.wiley.com/go/lal

Sample Class Discussion

The Great Gatsby

Nashyne: Despite his [Gatsby's] wealth, he's a humble, kind, welcoming person.

Sarah: So he's humble, he's kind, he's welcoming. I think that there is a part of that in this chapter and the evidence you've pulled out has been really good. But there's another side to him too that I don't think we're pulling out yet. So go back to somewhere between 45 and 48 and see if you see anything that complicates that picture.

[Independent reading—Sarah reviews student annotations.]

Sarah: Talk with your partner about how to complicate this picture.

[Students turn and talk.]

Sarah: A lot of you pulled information from the second half of the paragraph, some of the things that we are suspicious of: his elaborate formality of speech, he's picking his words with care. But take another look at the first half of that paragraph. What does that add to our analysis of him? Take 30 seconds to review that first half.

In this case, Sarah wants to see if students pick up on the significance of the uncut pages on their own, so she provides students first with a broad chunk of pages. When they still don't get it, she directs them to an even shorter passage. Why? To narrow the focus of their attention. Grappling with a text in increasingly smaller segments is a great way to build the skill of identifying strong evidence. Not only does Sarah's approach keep the cognitive lift on students, but it also keeps them from using her analysis in place of their own. As we've seen in Chapter 2, Sarah monitors student understanding so she can meet her class at their point of struggle. When students don't include the unopened books in their turn and talks, Sarah knows that she will need to drop knowledge to bring greater significance to the library scene.

Together, Hadley and Sarah's moves comprise powerful ways to add sophistication. You could also feign ignorance ("Wait! I don't understand. I thought Daisy *loved* Gatsby. . .") or even just give a hypothetical ("What if these characters were living in the '60s, not the '30s. . ."). These 201 habits invite students to step outside their current frame of thinking and try on another—and often that's all they need to discover something new. Here is a summary of all the 201 habits of discourse.

Habits of Discourse 201 Deepen Discourse		
Core Habit	**Ideal Student Actions**	**Teacher Talk Moves**
Activate or Drop Knowledge	• "X is. . ." • "I've heard of X. It's. . ." • "I'd like to connect Leon's interpretation to the article we read about the Harlem Renaissance."	• "I have some additional context that might be helpful here." • "Some us are confused by what X is, and I was too when I read this. I looked it up, and here's what I found." • "I'd like to give you some formal language for what you just named."
Revoice	• "What you're arguing is X." • "If I understand you correctly, then you're saying X?" • "Are you saying [paraphrase argument]?"	• "Could you revoice what Dawanna said before adding?" • "If I hear you correctly, you seem to be saying X. Is that correct?" • "Are you saying [paraphrase or re-work their argument to see if they still defend it]?"

Habits of Discourse 201 Deepen Discourse		
Core Habit	**Ideal Student Actions**	**Teacher Talk Moves**
Press for Reasoning	• "Why do you think [rephrase argument]?" • "What evidence supports your argument?" • "How do you know?" • "Could you walk me through your thought process?"	• "Could you explain how you came to that conclusion?" • "What's your evidence?" • "Why/why not?" • "How do you know?"
Problematize	• Name or provoke debate: *"It sounds like we're divided between X and Y. I think. . ."* • Name contradictions: *"Rene and Gabriel have opposite readings of X. I think. . ."* • Play devil's advocate: *"I'm going to play devil's advocate here. I think. . ."*	• Name or provoke the debate: *"Some of you say X. Some of you say Y. What do you think?"* • Name contradictions: *"These two ideas are contradictory. How can we make sense of this?"* • Play devil's advocate: *"Allow me to play devil's advocate. What if I argued. . ."* or *"Who can play devil's advocate?"*
Sophisticate	• Zoom in & out: *"I want to focus on X," "X is important because. . . .," "Y creates or makes Z in the text."* • Dive deeper into the text: *"Let's turn to page XX. Does it support or challenge our theory?"* • Apply within different or new context/perspective: *"What do you think ___ would think about X?"* • Give a hypothetical: *"What if. . ."*	• Zoom in: *"What connotations does this diction have?"* • Zoom out: *"So what?" "What's the consequence of that choice?"* • Narrow the focus: *"Given what you've said, what do you make of pages. . .?"* • Feign ignorance: *"I don't understand. I was thinking. . ."* • Apply within different or new context/perspective: *"What would ___ think about this?"* • Give a hypothetical: *"What if. . ."* or *"I have a theory I'd like your opinions on. . ."*

One quick note: whereas the 101 habits can be picked up quickly by students, the 201 habits take a bit more time—often requiring you to model and prepare. We'll talk more about how to roll out new habits in Chapter 8.

Discourse is the engine of learning. When the moves we've described work together, our students travel full speed ahead toward a greater analysis. But how will they mark their arrival? This final move ensures that discourse culminates in new understanding.

STAMP THE LEARNING

Picture it: the last few minutes of class after a lively debate. Students are writing their final analysis of the text. Tired, but satisfied, you sink into the chair with a satisfied grin. It vanishes once you read student exit tickets. Few write to the depth of what happened in the discussion. *How can this be?* you wonder aloud. *Weren't they in the same class as I was?*

Many of us have lived through some version of this scene. Although we thought the discussion went great, it seems as though students attended a different class. They didn't leverage the "wow" moments in their writing—they barely even registered them.

The world of filmmaking gives us a way to reedit that ending. Think back to some of your favorite movies. During pivotal scenes, directors focus our attention on what matters. The music crescendos, the lighting changes, and even the nature of time seems to shift—unspooling into slow motion or coming to a complete standstill. These moves work together to underscore the movie's big ideas. What if we had a way to do this in class?

Let's return to Matthew's lesson. When he taught "When I Heard the Learn'd Astronomer," his students initially breezed past the speaker's self-description as "tired and sick," noting only that he was vaguely bored. They weren't exploring the possibility that sitting in the lecture hall was somehow a draining experience. Matthew knows his students have previously struggled to consider the implications of diction, so he emphasizes the point once his class gets there. As you watch him teach, consider: How does Matthew make sure his students capture the big ideas? What does he mean by "stamping ideas"?

WATCH Clip 21: Matthew McCluskey—Stamps the Power of Analyzing Whitman's Diction

http://www.wiley.com/go/lal

Matthew "stamps" ideas when he asks students to voice key points of the lesson. As he does, he makes sure to call on a variety of students to check the understanding; this is especially helpful in making sure that students who are quieter or have struggled don't fall under the radar. But he doesn't stop there. Matthew also asks his students to get metacognitive. He wants them to think about how unpacking the connotations of the word "sick" enhanced their understanding. Now his students have a double takeaway: a key learning about the text, and a key learning about how they can read other texts.

Research tells us that reflection is a form of "retrieval practice" that builds student learning and helps them retain information.[6] As Matthew knows, it's not enough for his discussions to melt the clock. When big takeaways emerge, he needs to slow down time.

Matthew's instruction is a reminder that amazing discourse matters little if students don't learn from it. Call it an essential teaching from the Ferris Bueller School of Instruction: discourse moves pretty fast—if you don't stop and look around once in a while, you could miss it.[7]

CASE STUDY: PUTTING IT ALL TOGETHER

Admittedly, we introduced many moves for discourse in this chapter. You may feel overwhelmed to see them all together, but these are more easily accomplished than they seem. Let's put them together and see how to integrate them into our daily practice. In this case study, we use Saeed Jones's poem "Isaac, After Mount Moriah."[8] Jones is an award-winning poet[9] who takes a creative twist on the story of Abraham and Isaac found in the biblical book of Genesis. Take a moment to savor it before we begin.

> ### Isaac, After Mount Moriah
> by Saeed Jones
>
> Asleep on the roof when rain comes,
> water collects in the dips of his collarbone.
>
> Dirty haired boy, my rascal, my sacrifice. Never
> an easy dream. I watch him wrestle my shadow, shut eyelids
> trembling, one fist ready for me.
>
> Leave him a blanket, leave him alone.
>
> Night before, found him caked in dirt,
> sleeping in a ditch, wet black stones for pillows.
>
> What kind of father does he make me, this boy
> I find tangled in the hair of willows, curled fetal
> in the grove?

Once, I found him in a far field, the mountain's peak
like a blade above us both.

Source: © Saeed Jones. Used by permission of the author.

What a rich poem for unpacking! Let's apply all the steps we have discussed, starting with crafting a broad, rigorous prompt and an exemplar response. From there, we can consider where we want the productive struggle to occur. Here is a sample of each:

Prompt, Exemplar, and Productive Struggle

Prompt: How does Jones's language develop a theme of his poem?

Exemplar Response: Jones uses figurative language to suggest that the relationship between Abraham and Isaac was the true sacrifice made in the famous biblical account. For his part, Isaac is portrayed as traumatized by the near-slaughter. He is described—by the speaker, Abraham—as having been reduced to a shell of himself, wrestling with his father's shadow and "curled fetal / in the grove" (10–11). Jones's choice of "fetal" is telling, since this diction suggests Isaac's ultimate vulnerability and innocence. The Isaac of this text does not get his own lines, but rather is the reflection of Abraham's guilt. In the closing couplet, Abraham describes the peak of Mount Moriah as being "like a blade above us both" (13). His simile is carefully chosen; it alludes to the climax of the biblical story, the moment when Abraham has raised his knife to murder his son, only to be stayed by an interceding angel. In this telling, however, the blade hovers over *both* people, and Abraham includes himself in the sacrifice. Jones provides readers with an Abraham who holds himself culpable for the death of his relationship with his son. Ultimately, the poem suggests that while Isaac lived, his relationship with Abraham did not—calling into question the true lesson of the Bible's famous story.

Productive Struggle(s): *Jones's imagery and diction, particularly language around the relationship between Isaac and Abraham; the implications of Jones's closing couplet for the themes in the text*

With these elements defined, we create a discourse map aligned to where our students are right now. The map below assumes that students are already familiar with metaphor, simile, and imagery. Review it and consider: What's included? What's the value of thinking through these elements before class?

Discourse Planning Template

Background knowledge:

- The binding of Isaac is one of the foundational narratives of the Old Testament (Gen: 22–19). Abraham is tested by God, who asks Abraham to sacrifice his son, Isaac, on a mountain in the region of Moriah. Abraham gets so far as to raise the knife for the sacrifice, but an angel stays his hand, saying that he has proven his devotion to God and will be blessed for it. In the Bible, there are no scenes of Abraham and Isaac ever speaking again.

Literary Terms:

- **Allusion** is an indirect reference to another idea, work of art, or text
- **Intertextuality** (n.)—the way one text's meaning is shaped by another's. (In this case, there is an intertextual discourse between Jones's poem and the Bible.)

Vocab:

- **Rascal** (n.)—a mischievous person (often used as a term of affection)
- **Curled Fetal**—the fetal position is the body position held during prenatal development

Ideal Answer

Jones's imagery establishes Abraham's deep regret for having been willing to sacrifice his son (e.g. "curled fetal," "wet black stones for pillows," water collecting in Isaac's collarbone). His closing simile ("a blade above us both") suggests Abraham feels judged for this himself, or at least that it was his relationship that was ultimately sacrificed.

Almost There

This poem is about Abraham's lasting regret that the relationship between him and Isaac has deteriorated. Abraham sees Isaac as a victim, using multiple pieces of imagery ("curled fetal," "wet black stones for pillows," water collecting in Isaac's collarbone) to show that Abraham knows he has wronged and truly harmed Isaac. *[a defensible reading that attends to language; the response doesn't investigate the final image, though, or the intertextuality between the poem and the biblical story]*

Partially There

Jones's text uses imagery to show that Abraham and Isaac don't get along. *[a generally defensible understanding of the text, but one that does not capture the specific relationship between the two characters; response does not rely on specific imagery to make its case; there is no discussion of intertextuality]*

Further Off
Abraham and Isaac hate each other, because Abraham has abandoned Isaac and left him to suffer. *[limited understanding of the poem's narrative]*
Problematize/Sophisticate Prompts
What imagery does Abraham use to describe Isaac, and what does that suggest to you about how he feels toward his son?

- Given what we know about the biblical allusion, let's zoom in and out on the final couplet. How do they connect to the biblical story?
  - Follow-up: The angel tells Abraham that he has passed God's test. In Jones's poem, what do you think Abraham feels? Would he agree? Do you?

In one simple page, you've put it all together—the end goal of discourse, a draft of anticipated responses, and the questions you need to push the conversation forward. Consider the power of this preparation. You won't need to brainstorm prompts on the fly because you've already thought of an "almost there" answer and where it might miss the mark. And you'll know "partially there" and "further off" answers when you hear them, so you'll be ready to leverage your students to bridge those gaps themselves.

Planning in this way frees us to listen—deeply and with care—to what our kids are saying. It also gives us the confidence to pivot when it best serves the class. (You can find a copy of this planning template in the *Reading and Writing Handbook* in the online appendix.)

A Word on. . . Hands-Down Discourse

Socratic Seminar—a protocol in which students do almost all of the talking—is a great place to solidify habits of discourse. Students are often even more diligent about using them when they know a teacher is unlikely to jump in. You can rebrand all class conversations as "mini-Socratics" or "hands-down" discussion and begin asking students to respond to each other without raising their hands. We didn't invent this idea—many educators run classrooms where students don't need to be called on. However, while hands-down discussion seems natural, this protocol takes practice and familiarity.

As a middle school teacher, Sean Reap found success by starting small. He asked students for a 2- to 4-minute hands-down talk and set a timer. During this time, he stepped back, listened, and coached. Students received

(continued)

(continued from previous page)

feedback at every turn, from the content of their conversation to the quality of their discourse. At the end, Sean filled out a discourse rubric (or gave informal feedback) to keep the class metacognitive about how they spoke and responded to each other as a whole. Here's a sample. What value does a rubric like this add to instruction?

Academic Discourse Rubric				
	4	**3**	**2**	**1**
Participation Adjust this category based on the amount of time provided for discourse.	80–100% of students participated. Students made an effort to invite quieter peers in by asking them questions.	70–80% of students participated (6–9 students/30 did not participate)	60–70% of students participated (9–12 students/30 did not participate)	50% or fewer students participated (15+ students/30 did not participate)
Academic Register Academic register includes: • strong, clear projection • use of classmates' names • speakers directly addressing peers and their ideas, not the teacher • overall high energy • no inappropriate responses (giggling, etc.)	All or nearly all comments demonstrated appropriate academic register in all areas. Discussion was thoughtful and academic. Energy was high and it was easy to hear all students.	Most comments (90%) demonstrated appropriate academic register in all areas. One area may have been weaker than the others. Energy was mostly high (80% of students). It was easy to hear most students.	Some comments (70%) demonstrated appropriate academic register in all areas OR 1–2 areas were distracting during the discussion. Energy was low (<80% deep engagement). Many students spoke too softly.	Fewer than 50% of comments demonstrated appropriate academic register. Discussion sounded informal and lacked urgency. Energy was poor.

Analytical Skill Goals include:	All or nearly all comments meet analytical skill goals (see left).	Most comments (80%) met analytical skill goals.	Some comments (60%) met analytical skill goals.	Discussion lacked analytical skill from most participants.
• comments reference specific sections of the text and offer analysis, not just summary • comments connect to previous points • comments take risks by analyzing diction, suggesting new evidence, playing devil's advocate, providing new perspective • students challenge peers to clarify or support their thinking	Students led most of the discourse, questioning each other when appropriate or offering the class questions to consider. Nearly all comments contained text references OR analyzed material being discussed in a new way.	Students led a good chunk of the discourse, pushing for deep analysis of the questions the teacher posed. Most comments contained text references. A few comments simply repeated other ideas.	More often than not, the teacher led the discourse. Many comments were surface-level comments, or students' comments did not build on each other's ideas.	The teacher led almost all of the discourse. Most comments were surface-level comments and did not build on each other's ideas. There were few and/or vague references to the text.
Habits of Discourse Answers include:	All comments demonstrated academic English or self-correction for it.	Most comments demonstrated academic English.	Some comments demonstrated academic English.	Few comments contained strong language or discourse habits.
• use of complete sentences with academic grammar • sophisticated vocabulary and precise literary terms • use of Habits of Academic Discourse (as identified on our class chart/poster)	At least 70% of comments contained particularly notable vocabulary <u>and</u> 80% of students regularly used habits of discourse.	At least 50% of comments contained particularly notable vocabulary <u>and</u> 75% of students regularly used habits of discourse.	At least 50% of comments contained particularly notable language and/or discourse habits.	

(continued)

(continued from previous page)

Giving students real-time feedback helps them monitor their own progress and build the habits of mind that they need to facilitate discourse on their own. As their leadership grows, a rubric like this makes us less likely to dominate the conversation, and more available to listen to what students have to say.

Facilitating quality class discourse can feel a lot like teaching reading. At first glance, it appears automatic. It's anything but. Real growth comes when we break down the process into tiny moves that students practice until they become habit. When we teach these habits of discourse in class, we both spotlight our students' voices and ensure that class conversations leave them more prepared, confident, and excited about literature than they were beforehand. The following one-pager puts together the key ideas we've discussed. You can also find a printable version in the *Reading and Writing Handbook* in the online appendix.

Literacy Discourse: One-Pager

This one-pager maps out the key components of a discussion-based ELA class.

	Facilitate Discourse
Activate	**Activate Knowledge (prior to and during discourse, as needed)** • **Use a word wall and/or resource/text:** *"Use your notes. Turn to ___"* • **Recall:** *"Think back to ___. What do we already know about ___?"* • **Drop knowledge/vocab:** *"Some additional context is. . . How does this support/shift our thinking?"*
Launch	**Launch the Discourse Cycle** • **Start with your prioritized high-rigor question** • **Follow the sequence:** Everybody Writes, Turn & Talk, Cold Call, Volley (multiple students speak before the teacher does)

Maximize	**Maximize Student Talking and Thinking**
	Let students drive 95% of the discourse:
	
	• **Strategically call on students:**
	  ○ Call on students who are 'further off' and 'partially there' first.
	  ○ Call on students who are 'almost there' to push the group forward.
	  ○ Call on originally incorrect students to stamp new understanding.
	
	• **Use universal prompts (students and teachers):**
	  ○ Revoice (student or teacher)—prompt students to strategically paraphrase other students' reasoning.
	    • Teacher: *"If I hear you correctly, you seem to be saying X. Is that correct?"*
	    • Student: *"Are you really saying [paraphrase or rework their argument to see if they still defend it]?"*
	  ○ Press for Reasoning (student or teacher)—justify your answer with evidence, key terms, vocab
	    • *"Why/why not?"; "How do you know?"; "Prove it."; "What text evidence supports this idea?"*
	  ○ Open up the debate (teacher):
	    • *"Evaluate." "Build." "Agree/Disagree."*
	
	• **(When needed) Teach Habits of Discourse:**
	  ○ Roll out, model or give reminder of a specific habit prior to launching discourse.
	    • See online handbook for guidance and a list and examples of various habits.
	  ○ Prompt/praise students to use habits of discussion with each other.

	Facilitate Discourse

Deepen	**Deepen and Stretch It**
	When you have an 'almost there' response, use your scripted prompt(s) to push the class:
	
	• **Drop new knowledge:** *"[new knowledge]. How does this connect to. . .?"*
	
	• **Problematize** (create tension)
	   ○ Name the debate: *"Some of you say X. Some of you say Y. What do you think?"*
	   ○ Provoke debate: *"[Name] would say this [name alternative argument]. How would you respond?"*
	   ○ Highlight contradictions: *"These two ideas are contradictory. How can we make sense of this?"*
	   ○ Play devil's advocate: *"I disagree. I actually think. . ."* or *"Who can play devil's advocate?"*
	   ○ Feign ignorance: *"I don't understand. I was thinking. . ."*
	
	• **Sophisticate** (add complexity)
	   ○ Zoom in/Zoom out: *"What do we associate with __? What's the effect of this choice?"*
	   ○ Narrow the focus: *"Let's test our hypothesis against pages _-_. Review and see if they support or challenge our view."*
	   ○ Apply within different or new context/perspective: *"What's another way we could think about this?" "What would ___ think about this?"*
	   ○ Give a hypothetical: *"What if. . ."*

Stamp	**Stamp in Student Voice**
	
	• **Stamp the Content and/or Purpose**
	   ○ *"Stamp this for us—what do we need to remember about ___?," "How has our thinking changed?"*
	   ○ *"Why does this matter?," "What does this enable us to do?"*
	
	• **Stamp the Skill**
	   ○ *"What steps did we take to ___?," "How did we ___?"*

Stop and Jot—My Takeaways

So far, what are your top takeaways for your classroom?

_____

_____

_____

_____

Conclusion

Discourse brings learning to a crescendo, shifting the focus of class directly to our students—where it belongs. In many ways these can be the most memorable moments of class: when asked to picture an English classroom, most of us likely imagine some type of lively and passionate discussion.

But sound cannot travel in a vacuum. The culture you establish within the classroom will determine if your students' ideas resonate or fall flat. Our final section, then, addresses the conditions for success: How can you create a culture of literacy? And, given what's hopefully become a long list of ideas for your class, where do you begin?

THERE AND BACK AGAIN—PART 3 SUMMARY

Key Takeaways

- Great discourse doesn't clock the time; it melts the clock.
- Change the way students talk about reading, and you'll change the way they think about it.
- Discourse is talk that changes what and how we think.
- We don't prep for discourse to help us speak, we prep for it to help us listen.
- The magic of discourse lies in productive struggle.
- Discourse soars on the wings of schema.
- Don't force-feed your students; simply set the table.
- Don't be the sage on the stage when there's wisdom in the room.
- To maximize student talk, minimize your own.
- You can't respond to what you haven't heard.
- A claim without evidence is just an opinion.
- If you want a lively debate, instigate it.
- Don't just melt the clock. When big takeaways emerge, slow down time.

Self-Assessment

A summary of key techniques from the chapter are listed here. Take a moment to self-assess your classroom or school; we'll return to these ideas in Chapter 8.

Part 3: What Will I Hear When Students "Get It"?	
• **Find the Productive Struggle:** Before class, I name the productive struggle I want students to have, and I have a plan to respond to multiple levels of student response.	___/4
• **Launch the Discourse Cycle:** I start with a broad, open-ended question, ask students to write, and give them time to share their thinking with a peer before we discuss.	___/4
• **Create and Make Meaningful Conversation (Habits of Discourse 101):** ○ Students routinely share, critique, listen to, and take notes on each other's ideas. ○ Students do 90% of the talking during class discussions; I use short "universal" prompts to keep their voices front and center. ○ I strategically call on students to allow them to resolve most of their own questions without teacher intervention. ○ Students consistently revoice peers' thinking and defend their own with evidence and reasoning.	___/8
• **Deepen Discourse and Stamp It (Habits of Discourse 201):** ○ I model and ask students to use prompts that problematize class thinking, connect to others' ideas, and add sophistication to the conversation. ○ Stamp the Learning: When big ideas occur, students capture the major take aways in their own words and writing.	___/8
Score:	___/24

Planning for Action

- Which resources from Part 3 will you use to adjust your instruction? (All of these are available in the online *Reading and Writing Handbook* in print-ready format—download and print at will!)

  - Habits of Discourse 101: Create Conversation (*Handbook* p. 20)

  - Habits of Discourse 201: Deepen Discourse (*Handbook* p. 21)

  - Academic Discourse Rubric (*Handbook* p. 22)

  - Discourse Planning Template (*Handbook* p. 23)

  - Discourse Planning Example (*Handbook* p. 24)

  - Literacy Discourse One-Pager (*Handbook* p. 25)

  - Literacy Discourse One-Pager, with Remote Teaching Adaptations (*Handbook* pp. 26–27)

- How will you modify these resources to meet the needs of your class(es)?

_____

_____

_____

_____

Action	Date

Part **4**

How Do I Build It?

"A voice had begun to sing. It was very far away and Digory found it hard to decide from what direction it was coming. Sometimes it seemed to come from all directions at once. Sometimes he almost thought it was coming out of the earth beneath them. Its lower notes were deep enough to be the voice of the earth herself. There were no words. It was hardly a tune. But it was, beyond comparison, the most beautiful sound he had ever heard."

—C.S. Lewis, *The Magician's Nephew*

At first glance, Clinton Hill Middle School in Newark, New Jersey, looks like a typical school. Students arrive most mornings a bit bleary-eyed, and after breakfast in the cafeteria, they shoulder their multicolored backpacks and set off for class. But lean in and look a little more closely. You'll start to see the small details that tell a different story.

Peering into a classroom, you see students eagerly at work with heads bent over their writing. A few early finishers catch your eye. Each one has picked up the book from the corner of their desk: it's one they've chosen, and it's been waiting for them all class

209

Figure P4.1 Students at Clinton Hill Middle School always have an independent book ready for quiet moments—for when they've finished an assignment early or are waiting in line to enter their next class. As a result of this and many other initiatives, Principal Jody Jones and her team have built a strong culture of literacy.

Source: © Uncommon Schools. Used with permission.

(Figure P4.1). Deeply engrossed, they read until the teacher calls everyone together. It's time to transition. Doors swing open. A teacher strides into the hallway followed by a line of students. The first one cradles a book—*The Hate U Give*. Behind him is a student intent on the last few pages of *Harry Potter and the Prisoner of Azkaban*. Behind her stands a student who is riveted by *The Poet X*. As more students stream past, you begin to lose track of the titles—so many students have books in their hands.

You stand alone in the now empty hallway. Words are everywhere: images of book covers pepper the wall alongside reading trackers, posters of famous authors like Maya Angelou, and an advertisement for a story competition. You ask a student what's on today's schedule, and he mentions a whole-school discussion of *Lucky Broken Girl*. And, he adds, the spelling bee is last period. You should come![1]

Clinton Hill is no ordinary middle school: it is a haven for readers. And Clinton Hill's success isn't just reflected in its cheerful, engaged students and reading-centric culture. On the 2019 New Jersey Student Learning Assessment (a close mirror of the PARCC test), Clinton Hill's students averaged 80% proficiency. That's 17 percentage points higher than the state average and 8 points higher than the average for non-economically-disadvantaged students—especially impressive considering 80% of students at Clinton Hill qualify for free- or reduced-price lunch. What's the secret behind their success?

While there is magic at work at Clinton Hill, that magic is replicable. So let's investigate how Clinton Hill makes powerful literacy instruction come alive—by building a culture of reading for students and a strong implementation plan for teachers. Here's how we'll do it:

- Chapter 7—How Do I Create a Culture Where Reading Thrives? (Building Blocks of a Culture of Literacy)

- Chapter 8—How Do I Get Started? (Tools and Resources for Change)

How Do I Create a Culture Where Reading Thrives?

We opened Part 4 with an epigraph from our favorite scene in C.S. Lewis's *The Magician's Nephew,* when the lion Aslan sings the world into existence with a trembling, beautiful song. There's singing at Clinton Hill too: in a culture that reminds students—at every minute and at every turn—that reading is part of their community's identity. In some cases, students already know the melodies. But when they don't, or when they forget their song, the culture at Clinton Hill is there to sing it back to them.

Core Idea

A culture of reading isn't just a song you sing to your students.
It's one they sing to you.

Researchers note that when students develop a "reading self-concept"—a sense that being a reader is part of who they are—a virtuous cycle of growth begins. In fact, says cognitive scientist Daniel Willingham, this type of self-concept may be even more important than how students feel about reading:

> If "reader" is part of your self-concept, it will occur to you as a viable activity more often. "What will I do on that two-hour train trip?" I could bring my iPod. Oh, I should bring a book, too." And of course, the more you read, the more "reader" becomes cemented as part of your self-concept.[1]

As English teachers, we have a huge opportunity to foster this belief in our students. Researcher Peter Johnston points out in *Choice Words* that "the way we interact with children and arrange for them to interact shows them what kind of people we think they are and gives them opportunities to practice being those kinds of people. We provide them with what James Gee calls an 'identity kit.'"[2] And while any student might develop a reading self-concept on their own, we have the power to build a culture that reinforces it at every turn. How? By both expanding their world and calling them home.

EXPAND THEIR WORLD: READ BROADLY AND OFTEN

Think back to this chapter's opening. Students filled every free minute with reading—before class, after completing an activity, even waiting in line in the hall. It would be hard *not* to fall in love with reading in this environment—or at least to get enough practice that reading feels second nature. Strong independent reading programs like Clinton Hill's build broad background knowledge and motivate students to see themselves as readers.[3] What's more, independent reading programs show students that reading is what intellectuals *do:* they read things they're interested in—and then they think about them.

Get a Book in Their Hands: Access and Choice with Independent Reading

In middle and high school, you don't need to add extra time into your day to make space for an independent reading program. While we've seen that work well in many schools, we've also seen successful schools ask students to do most of their reading on their own. What do all these schools share in common? The following two components:[4]

- **Get the books in their hands:** Offer students a variety of genres to choose from; these can include high-interest texts and new topics for exploration. If your school has a library, perfect. If not, consider using a site like DonorsChoose to help build one in your classroom. Talk to your department chair about getting digital library cards for your students. Most libraries will allow them to check out eBooks and audiobooks through their mobile devices. You'll need to develop clear routines and procedures around how to find, check out, and return books, but once these are in place, most students can independently manage the process. One thought: rather than organizing the library purely by reading level, we recommend following Achieve the Core's guidance in its Book Basket Project. By creating topic "baskets" first, then ordering books by complexity within each basket, you'll allow students to read a text set of increasing difficulty on a single topic, a huge boon to their broader background knowledge and vocabulary development.[5] (Check out this endnote for where to find free materials from Achieve the Core.[6])

- **Let them choose what they read:** There's a place in curricula for shared experience with texts, but independent reading is a great opportunity for choice. Professors Richard Allington and Rachel Gabriel write, "The research base on student-selected reading is robust and conclusive: Students read more, understand more, and are more likely to continue reading when they have the opportunity to choose what they read."[7] Get to know your students as readers and people by surveying their interests at the start of the year. Use that data to recommend titles and have them report back to you what they liked and disliked.

School offers a fantastic launch pad for students to build a sense of independence through choice. And with a few simple shifts to our instruction, we can enhance what they take away from what they read.

Give Them Productive Time: Honor Independent Reading

The research on the impact of independent reading time is mixed.[8] Why? Time with a book doesn't help every student become a better reader—teaching and guiding them does. The best independent reading programs are never totally "independent." They're opportunities for us to coach students as they develop their own reading instincts and tastes. Here's how to honor that:

- **Offer support:** Take time to confer with students on their chosen text, goals, and struggles. What you learn can inform student grouping and future instruction. If you can't do this in person, consider making it an assignment you review.

- **Be authentic:** Post-reading activities such as reading journals, book reviews, book talks, or small-group discourse add accountability and support a culture of independent reading. One of the best accountability structures for independent reading is the most authentic—book club discourse. Let students form mini book clubs where they can choose and discuss a shared text.

Independent reading broadens students' horizons, helping sate a curiosity to discover the world beyond your walls. But a strong reading culture isn't just about looking outward. If we want students to fall in love with literacy, we'll also need some powerful ways to call them home.

CALL THEM HOME: REMIND STUDENTS OF READING'S GIFTS

"We don't turn to story to escape reality. We turn to story to navigate reality."
—Lisa Cron, *author of Wired for Story, at TedxFurmanU*[9]

Not every student immediately embraces reading. In those cases, our job is to show them why we turn to literature in the first place. This charge can be awe-inspiring—and challenging. For many of us, the study of humanities taps into something visceral, humming just below the surface. How do we put all of those feelings into words, let alone actions? Fortunately, we're not the first to navigate this challenge. That means we can learn a bit from the moves of teachers whose students have consistently fallen in love with reading, year after year.

Create Peak Moments

Chip and Dan Heath, authors of *The Power of Moments*, encourage us to think about how a typical family remembers a trip to Disney World. In the moment, they'll note the long lines, a child's temper tantrum, and the overpriced food. But months later they're likely to recall eating ice cream, riding Space Mountain, or touring the Haunted House. Remarkably, the highlights far outweigh the negative moments, even though they represent only a tiny fraction of the time (Figure 7.1). As the Heaths share, experiences are "mostly forgettable and occasionally remarkable." People remember the ride, not the line.[10]

> ### Core Idea
> People remember the ride, not the line.

Figure 7.1 Space Mountain is remembered for the thrills, not the lines.

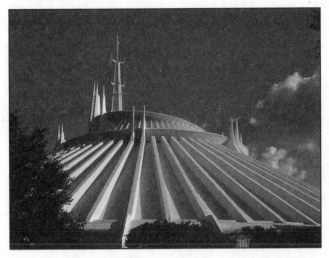

Source: Photograph by Benjamin D. Esham, courtesy of Wikimedia Commons.

The Heath brothers advise managers to spend less time "fixing potholes" and more time "building peaks" for their teams. That advice feels right at home in our schools.

Think of peak moments as the intellectual holidays of your school calendar, events that cement and celebrate the identity you've worked so hard to build. These moments are most effective when spread throughout the year, and they don't need to be grand in scale—a rich Socratic Seminar or class trial might be exactly what students need. (If you think back to your own schooling, those might be some of your favorite memories.)

Big or small, peak moments pack cumulative punch. When Steve taught at Washington Park High, his department started with a school poetry festival. Open mic nights followed soon after. And any time students published anything, Steve's principal made sure the community celebrated by making time for everyone to read it together. (If you've ever published a newspaper or literary magazine, you know there is *nothing* like watching the whole school read and discuss it.) A morning book club for student advisories was the next step. With the ground now fertile for an independent reading program, the school created a reading space with ample access to books. Slowly and steadily, peak moments reshaped the culture of reading at Washington Park.

We share this story to illuminate a simple truth: culture builds over time. The easiest place to start is your own classroom. Create a case for peak moments by making your instruction the first high point. If there's one thing that can sway an administrator or district to invest in new ideas, it's successful, happy students. Grow from there.[11] To help you brainstorm, we've compiled the following list of popular peak moments in the middle and high schools we've visited. Use it to spar and generate further ideas.

Ideas for Whole School Peak Literacy Moments

Initiative	Description
Writing Oscars	• Students submit their best writing piece of the year in a category (e.g. narrative, analytical, poetry, persuasive) and judges (e.g. teachers, alumni, students, etc.) vote on a grade-level winner for each category. • Celebrate in a Writing Oscars ceremony with trophies, decorations, refreshments, and dressy attire.
Word Wizards	• During whole-school gatherings, student leaders in costume ("The Word Wizards") reveal the word of the week. • Highlight the word of the week throughout the school in hallway signage and during class instruction across subject areas. Celebrate students when they use the word verbally and in writing. • In subsequent weeks, student volunteers creatively share the ways that they've used the word that week (e.g. skit, song, visual presentation) and the new word is introduced.
Whole School Reads	• Whole grades or the whole school (all adults included) commit to reading the same book. This culminates in 1 or 2 whole-community discussions or a presentation and then discussion in small advisory groups.
Flash Fiction Challenges	• Students submit 2-sentence narratives or haikus around a topic (scary stories, autobiographies, science fiction); there is a reading and awards for the winners.

Get Caught Reading	• Share images of teachers and students reading in their free time. List the books that teachers are currently reading and student recommendations in a central place at school.
Power Speaking Extravaganza	• Students prepare and practice to deliver a speech/spoken word, poem, or dramatic excerpt. During the event, student names are chosen out of a hat to perform on stage the piece they have been preparing. This means that all students need to be prepped and ready to go with their piece. In the weeks leading up to the PSE, students have multiple opportunities to prepare, practice, and get feedback on their delivery during advisory time.
Independent Reading Celebrations	• Hold a whole-school celebration of independent reading—(e.g. "Reading Royalty"): ○ Tracking words read or number of pages read by advisory/homeroom ○ Tracking number of levels grown • Incentives include design-your-own reading T-shirt contest, celebration during whole-school gatherings, field trips, dances, "principal for a day," and others.
Pajama Party/ Read-a-thon	• Students come to school in cozy pajamas and independently read a book of their choice for an extended time (Friday block, whole-school meeting time, etc.). Rooms have pillows, blankets, beanbags, or other comfortable seating arrangements, and snacks are provided.
Poetry Slam	• Students learn about slam poetry and then write their own. Create classroom competitions where two winners per homeroom are selected and those students rehearse with English teacher coaches to be ready for the big day. • Homeroom-level winners perform their poems in front of the whole school at a special morning meeting dedicated to the poetry slam. • Older students can judge the competition and the winner receives swag from the literary magazine and gets published for the whole high school to see.

Spelling Bee	• Class and whole-school competition that culminates with winners being sent as representatives to the local Scripps National Spelling Bee competition.
Battle of the Books	• Provide a list of 25 books and a time frame. If students read at least 15, they can participate in "Battle of the Books," a school comprehension competition in mixed-grade teams.
Author Visits	• Partner with organizations like the Dodge Poetry Festival to bring guest authors to speak at school. Schools have successfully hosted authors in person and by video conference, as well as invited acting troupes (e.g. having a local company do a scene presentation and talk-back on a play students have read).
Book Raffles	• Raffle off the opportunity to be the first reader of new books in your IR library. Build buzz around new texts!

Peak moments maintain vitality in a culture of literacy. But we don't have to wait for a peak moment to feel a little joy—we can build a classroom space that radiates with it daily.

Design a Room That Sings

Steve can remember sitting in his 8th-grade Spanish class and looking around the room. Various trinkets and memorabilia hung down from the ceiling and colorful bulletin boards lined the walls. Spanish words announced themselves everywhere. "Wow," he recalls thinking. "Ms. Zippler *really* loves Spanish." Maybe this class would be more interesting than he first thought.

Room design sends many messages to our students. It signals our interests, beliefs, and values, just as Steve experienced. And it can say even more. If you build your walls to teach about English, students will develop the habit of consulting this reference in the same way they might consult a literary terms glossary or dictionary. Walls talk. Make what they say matter.

Core Idea

Walls talk. Make what they say matter.

When we publicly post information, we create a joyful space and normalize the process of seeking help when needed. Both explicitly and implicitly, room design influences student learning, and that's why it's so important we get it right. Here are guidelines to help you intentionally design your class space:

Instruction Front, Inspiration Everywhere: Post your instructional signage (e.g. elements of characterization, common literary terms, vocabulary word walls, etc.) toward the front of the room. A word wall that kids have to turn around to see is a word wall that is unlikely to be used. Post your inspirational signage (e.g. posters of books and authors) on the sides and toward the back, so students can see them as they enter class. (See Figure 7.2.) Make intentional decisions

Figure 7.2 Rebecca Lord Gomez's 8th-grade English classroom at Vailsburg Middle School shouts "I love English." It also helps students learn it. Notice the classroom signage at the front of class, and student work displays and the fully stocked classroom library toward the back.

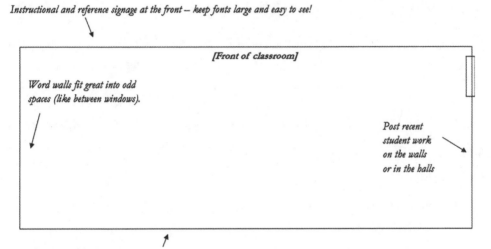

Instructional and reference signage at the front — keep fonts large and easy to see!

Word walls fit great into odd spaces (like between windows).

[Front of classroom]

Post recent student work on the walls or in the halls

Inspirational signage in the back — inspire students as they enter. If you display author images, be sure they are inclusive — so all your students can see the "big tent" of literature.

Source: © Stephen Chiger.

about the works and authors featured on the walls. An inclusive classroom space, like an inclusive curriculum, reflects a diverse array of writers—especially those whose voices have been historically marginalized. Seeing (and reading) authors who are Black, indigenous, people of color, disabled, and LGBTQ+ expands the traditional canon and invites more students to participate in the great, global conversation.

Custom Build—Mass-market posters can be great for inspirational signage, but less so for posters designed to teach. It's far better to create posters that reiterate the lessons that *you* teach. To help you get started, we've included a set of posters in the online appendix, all aligned to the material in this book.

Go Big—Resist the temptation to cram volumes of text onto your wall charts. Focus on the key concepts and highest-level details and put them in large font. Here's the test: go to the back of the room and see if you can read the signage without squinting. Posters that kids cannot read are just wallpaper.

Grow your signage with your students—We know that schema is a powerful driver of student talk and comprehension, but it's also a big challenge. Even with our handbook close by and a daily lesson plan, how do we make sure our students have a running record of the class's big ideas? To answer, we can visit the classroom of MK Pope and Zachary Roach. Their 10th-grade classes are reading *The Adventures of Huckleberry Finn*. In the text, each character and scene functions as part of Twain's satire of the antebellum South. To help their students, MK and Zachary have done something powerful to capture knowledge and build momentum. What do you notice about their signage—how does it support discourse?

MK and Zachary's (Figure 7.3) signage allows students to refresh their understanding of past takeaways. (Based on the chart, students are about halfway through the book.) When they need to refresh students on their past analysis, all they need to do is point to the wall. The signage grows and develops as the class reaches new takeaways, making it a meaningful record of evolving understanding. (At the far right of the image, you'll note that they have new class vocabulary posted, too. Students are literally surrounded by growing resources.)

Stop and Jot

How does MK and Zachary's signage (shown in Figure 7.3) support discourse?

Figure 7.3 When MK or Zachary needs to refresh students on their analysis, all they need to do is point to the wall.

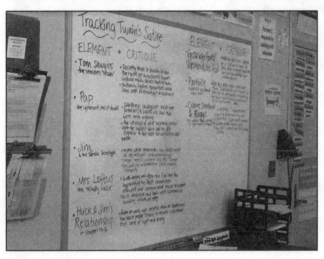

Source: © Stephen Chiger.

_____

_____

Let bulletin boards teach, not just speak—Few students are likely to leaf through the 20 essays stapled to a bulletin board or page through a vocabulary quiz to see precisely which questions each student aced. Why should they? Bulletin boards should be a showcase of students' intellectual prowess and curiosity, not a ragtag assortment of minor assignments. The most effective boards we've seen showcase student thinking, and they do it with a focus. For example, if you want to emphasize great analysis, choose a section from the students' work and physically highlight it. (See Figure 7.4.)

Figure 7.4 This bulletin board physically highlights student analysis, so that passersby can learn from exemplars in the class's recent focus.

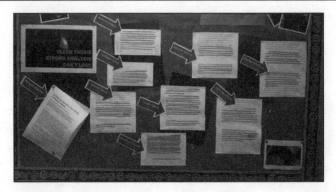

Source: © Stephen Chiger.

Students won't read a whole paper in the hallway, but they might stop to read two sentences deemed wall-worthy. And when you create these displays, highlight students, too! Use photos of your students or enlarge their names to show who is on the board and why. Students appreciate being honored for their work in front of their peers, especially as part of a class culture that values intellectualism.

Everything we do in our classrooms sends a message to our students: about our priorities, about what we love, and about what we hope they'll love too. When that message rings out loud and clear, we've created a resonant culture of reading.

So far, we've discussed large moves you can make: the power of independent reading, peak moments, and classroom space design. These are the big pillars of a reading culture. But small moments can move mountains too. Conducted daily, these have just as much potential—maybe more—to shape your classroom community.

Savor the Text

"There's something about hearing someone's voice—whether it's your own or not—shape the words of a book, bring the story into being with sounds that crackle, slide, dip, or sometimes even pop. Why else would many people, young and old alike, love so fiercely the story that is sung to them, more than the one they take in with their eyes? Why do so many of us choose and fiercely defend our right

to hear a story? Maybe it awakens in us some ancient, deep memory, when the written word was hardly a dream, and tales were told by firesides in houses gilded by twilight, person to person."

—*Sharanya Sharma*[12]

In the *Odyssey*, that most famous of Greek epics, Odysseus is so eager to hear the call of the Sirens that he instructs his crew to stuff their ears with wax and tie him to the mast of his ship so he can listen to their song. (See Figure 7.5.) Many a shipwreck owed its fate to sailors who, enthralled by the Sirens' enchanting tune, crashed their ships onto the rocks. Today, the human voice is no less alluring. Perhaps that's why National Public Radio speaks of "driveway moments," those times when listeners are so captivated by a story that they simply cannot leave their parked cars. While a bit less perilous than the call of the Sirens, the principle behind both remains the same: there is power in the lilt and cadence of the human voice, an incantation that can animate stories and verse well beyond what's on the page.[13]

For most of us, reading is a silent activity. But some pieces of writing—this section's epigraph, for example—demand to be read aloud. Not only does this hone a student's ear for complex language, it also builds their ability to appreciate these moments of

Figure 7.5 Odysseus and the Sirens, eponymous vase of the Siren Painter, ca. 480–470 BC.

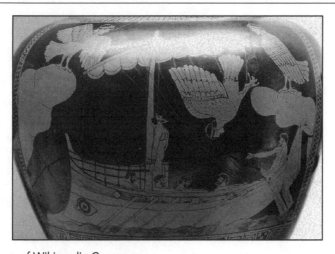

Source: Courtesy of Wikimedia Commons.

beauty in a text. Consider this clip from Reggie McCrimmon's 6th-grade classroom. Reggie knows that reading aloud can model fluency for his students, but the move he's making in this clip is primarily cultural.

WATCH Clip 22: Reggie McCrimmon—Savoring *The Giver*

http://www.wiley.com/go/lal

The Giver is a story that simply begs to be read aloud, quite appropriately as it speaks to seeing the world in color vs. black-and-white. By reading to his class, Reggie brings the book alive, demonstrating a love for the written word that he shares with his students.

When reading aloud, aim to share—or invite students to share—a paragraph or a page. Sharing a section of text that feels cadent or powerful elevates the role that reading and writing play in our lives and welcomes students to this experience. For whole-class novel instruction, an extended reading is rarely necessary and likely won't be helpful considering the other goals of your lesson. But, if you can, aim to read a paragraph or two aloud when you come to a beautiful moment. Go ahead, savor the text. Your students will, too.

Savoring the text allows literature to speak *to* us. Its corollary, talking and writing about that literature, comes *from* us—an extension of our drive to grapple with the world and contribute a verse. It's a force we can expand and accelerate—by centering student voice.

CALL THEM HOME: CENTER STUDENT VOICE

"If I can instill confidence in them, a sense of self, then hopefully it will give them the tools they need to face the real world."

—TJ Klune, *The House in the Cerulean Sea*

In class, the voices that matter most are those of our students—both orally and in writing. When our instruction prioritizes that, we send a profound message about who they are and the role they might play in the world. In recent years, calls have increased for schools to consider how students' literacy experience shapes and honors them as people—and to value that aspect of our curriculum at the same level we would knowledge building or skill acquisition. As researcher Gholdy Muhammad reminds us, "Teachers cannot get to skills or content-learning standards until students see and know themselves in the curriculum designed for them."[14] That's why this next section is critical: middle and high school are key periods when students deepen their sense of identity and voice, and there is much we can do to center and elevate it along the way.

Voice Lesson #1: Make It Personal

Julie Miller's AP Language class has just analyzed the rhetoric of two speeches: one by Dr. Martin Luther King, Jr., the other by Malcolm X. As you watch this clip of her instruction, ask yourself: How does Julie's questioning change the way students engage with the text?

WATCH Clip 23: Julie Miller—Engaging with the Text as People

http://www.wiley.com/go/lal

Sample Class Discussion

The Speeches of MLK Jr and Malcolm X

Julie: You guys have done a really nice job here of not only figuring out differences in messages and differences in devices, but stamping the most important point—why their strategies differ and how different strategies appeal to different audience types. Which of these compelled you most? . . .If you were living during this time and you heard both of these speeches. . .where would you have landed?

Justice: I would have sided with Malcolm X because, when you talk about, if he were to bring up the past and how we were oppressed, how we've been so treated wrongly, and bring up the idea of how, when America wants something, they had the Civil War and they actually used violence. I would have did the same thing, I would have looked at MLK and said, "You're advocating for a peaceful movement, but what have you gained, what progress have you made?" And you would see that there was still segregation and oppression so, I would automatically side with Malcolm X. I feel like MLK is sugar-coating his meaning so that white people, so he can appeal to white people, but that's not who is being oppressed.

Melik: Are we just hearing it or reading it too?

Julie: Hmm. What's the difference?

Melik: Because hearing it, people hear the debates on the news all the time, like speeches, but they don't really move you as much until you actually read it and see the words that were used.

Julie: Would one of them be more compelling in print versus out loud?

Think of the power of the question Julie asks: "If you lived during this time and you heard both of these speeches, which would have compelled you?"[15] The class time she has spent on rhetorical analysis creates a platform from which students can respond more deeply to the text from a personal perspective. This connection supplements analysis rather than replaces it; they are mutually reinforcing. Making it personal both increases engagement and respects students as intellectuals capable of wrestling with Dr. King, Malcolm X, or anyone else. As we've watched teachers provoke and challenge their classes, we've seen a variety of question types that help students connect and reflect:

Prompts to Connect and Reflect

- **Do you agree** with X? What would you do in this situation?
- **What if** X had made the opposite decision here?
- **How would** author Y **respond** to this?
- How could this **connect** to [recent events]?
- **What's your theory** on this? What's author X getting at?
- Is this text **convincing/compelling** to you? Why?

Questions that provoke and challenge can also be used to pique student interest throughout the lesson—beginning, middle, or end. For example, you might invite students to evaluate *Othello's* Iago by asking, "Which would you rather have: a false friend or an openly hostile enemy?" Linking the day's objective to authentic student views bridges students' experiences to a text, builds motivation, encourages deeper critical thinking, and even leads to better knowledge retention.[16]

Class debate is one way to make it personal; another way is a quiet reflection or more intimate response. Starting at the middle school level, students will find that the works they read are tackling social issues in increasingly complex and important ways. These books not only reflect a slice of our students' and our own reality, they also challenge us to examine our beliefs about the world. Reading these stories responsibly means giving students some space to process as they read, and so the middle school teachers we work with save time for regular journaling. This is purely time for students to think and respond to text—not for a grade, not even necessarily to share—but so that they can process what they are reading and respond to it from their own perspective.[17] Consider the following reading journal images:

✍ 🗨 📖 *Anticipation Guide* 📖 🗨 ✍
Intersectional Feminism

Directions: Read each statement and circle whether you *agree* or *disagree*. There are no right or wrong answers!

Opinnionaire	Before Reading	After Reading
1. Feminism is a movement that is by and for women, solely concerned with gaining equal rights (e.g. voting, pay) for them.	*strongly agree* *agree* *disagree* *strongly disagree*	*strongly agree* *agree* *disagree* *strongly disagree*
2. As a movement, feminism has always fought for the rights of all women.	*strongly agree* *agree* *disagree* *strongly disagree*	*strongly agree* *agree* *disagree* *strongly disagree*
3. Despite issues in the past, U.S. society is now in a place where men and women are for the most part treated equally.	*strongly agree* *agree* *disagree* *strongly disagree*	*strongly agree* *agree* *disagree* *strongly disagree*
4. At birth, everyone is assigned a gender, either male or female.	*strongly agree* *agree* *disagree* *strongly disagree*	*strongly agree* *agree* *disagree* *strongly disagree*
5. Boys and girls naturally like different things (e.g. video games, the color blue v. the color pink).	*strongly agree* *agree* *disagree* *strongly disagree*	*strongly agree* *agree* *disagree* *strongly disagree*
6. Writing fiction is often an act of resistance, protest or even rebellion.	*strongly agree* *agree* *disagree* *strongly disagree*	*strongly agree* *agree* *disagree* *strongly disagree*
7. Reading fiction is often an act of resistance, protest or even rebellion.	*strongly agree* *agree* *disagree* *strongly disagree*	*strongly agree* *agree* *disagree* *strongly disagree*

Before Reading Challenge: Explain your opinion for statement #_____ *(choose one)*.

_____

_____

_____

_____

_____

Reflection Journal: My Response to the *feminism unit*

Use this space to reflect on our unit. You may consider reflecting on:

- What resonated with you as you were reading? What questions do you have about what you have read? What are you still thinking about after reading?

- Have you had a similar experience to something our characters faced? How did you feel and/or respond? Or, how would you feel/respond in a similar situation?

- What do you think about a decision or action a character has made? Evaluate.

- Intersectionality is the idea that we must take into account people's overlapping identities (race, class, gender, religion, ethnicity, etc.) in order to understand the complexity of the oppression they face and work to overcome it, because people can be disadvantaged by multiple sources of prejudice. What connections do you see between what we've been reading and other fights for equality and justice?

- If you were to share one idea from our texts with a younger sibling/cousin/friend, what would you share? Did anything surprise you? What are you taking to heart?

- How does this text further your understanding of the 8th Grade Essential Question: *What types of oppression appear in our society? What are some ways we can respond to them?*

- How does this text further your understanding of the novel big idea statements (page 13)?

After Reading Reflection: Compare your answers <u>after</u> our unit and related materials with your answers from <u>before</u> reading the novel.

Which statement(s) have you changed your mind about? Why?

_____
_____
_____
_____
_____
_____
_____
_____
_____
_____
_____
_____
_____
_____
_____

Which statement(s) have you strengthened your opinion on? Why?

_____
_____
_____
_____
_____
_____
_____
_____
_____
_____
_____
_____

Momma's a little to serious
She doesn't like fun
Fun.

↳ Everyone was having
fun while mama
went to
focus on
the big
change

↳ Byron going to
Alabama

Thats a
little harsh

Oh that would
be fun! Maybe
you should write
the scene 😊
(great journal
option)

I wanted to see how
his classmete's will
react to his hairstyle

IF I were
Kenny I would cry of
tears of Joy that Byron is
Leaving

Even if Byron is the
worst brother ever he
can be nice sometimes

Hopefully, byron will
Learn to be king & good
when he get back from
Alabama.

Developed by middle school teacher Erin Dillane, these pages combine a few best practices: students reflect before they read, while reading, and afterward, to consider how the experience has changed them. Students journal in any format that feels right to them and they don't have to share. But if they do choose to share, they'll get a response from Erin in the form of a sticky note that responds to their ideas without evaluation or assessment. Journaling is a beautiful opportunity to build voice. It gives students a safe opportunity to respond to what they read, either for a caring audience or in the sanctity of their own private thoughts.

Books sing in the here and now, inviting students into conversation with the authors they encounter. If you want a person to connect with a text, make the connection personal.

Core Idea

Connection makes it personal; personal makes it memorable.

It's important to keep in mind that creating a personal connection for students isn't as simple as adding a few techniques to supplement your curriculum—it cuts right at the heart of what books you choose and how you teach them. Review our discussion of curricular complexity (Chapter 1) or thematic schema (Chapter 2) for additional ways to foreground this connection.

Voice Lesson #2: Give Forward-looking Feedback

Think back to your own experience writing for school. What was the written feedback that you received from teachers or professors that was most valuable to you?

If you're like us, you might remember the teachers who took time to write you detailed notes with feedback for you to implement. They were invested in your ideas, so when you impressed them, it really meant something. They saw you already as a writer, and in doing so they made you a better and more confident one.

This same experience can be said of any great coach. The best coaches see the greatness in you and push you to get better, sometimes even beyond what you originally thought you were capable of doing.

In *Culturally Responsive Teaching and the Brain*, Zaretta Hammond speaks to the power of acknowledging the challenge of a task and affirming your support for students. Although her focus is culturally diverse learners, this is great advice for any learner. She reminds us that, "contrary to what we may think, simply giving feedback doesn't initiate change. It has to be accepted as valid and actionable by the learner. . . Part of our role as an ally is to offer emotional support as well as tools. You have to be able to be in conversation with students who are trying to stretch themselves."[18] Borrowing language from researcher Judith Kleinfeld, Hammond speaks of effective teachers as being warm demanders: they earn the right to demand great student work by developing rapport and relationships.[19]

Core Idea

Students respect your ideas when you respect theirs.

Written feedback can build students' sense of confidence as intellectuals, inviting them into conversation with an intellectual mentor who sees their brilliance. With that in mind, here are two ways to make your feedback more impactful:

- **Reinforce strengths:** Students are sometimes unaware of what makes their writing effective. Narrating the positive names what worked and encourages students to continue using these techniques.[20]

- **Bite-size actions:** If you've read Paul's *Leverage Leadership,* you know the power of providing bite-sized, concrete action steps. Give clear next steps to set up students for success. ("Use at least two pieces of text evidence to support each major claim you make.") When students have a sense of their goals for a piece, there is a tangible positive impact on student learning.[21] Teachers can leverage the power of this process by delivering targeted feedback. It's easier and more effective to give notes on one or two aspects of student writing than on all of it.

For English class, this may sound like, "I noticed how carefully you're choosing evidence that links to your claim! As a writer, I think your next challenge lies in making that connection even clearer. After your evidence, try revising your sentences so they answer the 'so what?' for the quotes you've chosen. You've got this!"

For some of us, changing how we deliver feedback requires a paradigm shift from seeing our comments as evaluation to part of an ongoing conversation with our students. But imagine what's gained in a class where students receive and even relish this sort of commentary.

A Word on. . . Writing Conferences

As a former writing teacher, Zaretta Hammond creates frameworks that translate quite well to coaching student work in conferences. The following framework is largely based on her work, as well as that of Peter Johnston.

	Confer with Students (small groups or 1:1)

Writing Conferences	• Notice what's working and affirm your partnership.
	  ○ *"I know you've been really making strides with your. . ."*
	  ○ Ask the student: "What part are you feeling good about, and where can we partner?"
	
	• Acknowledge the challenge of the task and affirm for the student your belief in their ability to succeed.
	  ○ Reference past success for this student or for other students in similar situations.
	
	• Deliver bite-sized feedback, affirming the student as a writer.
	  ○ *"As a writer, one thing you might try is revising your thesis to make a how or why claim."*
	  ○ *"I think, as a writer, you're ready to add some more detail to your climax. One way would be to add some of your protagonist's thoughts."*
	
	• Create a space for the student to react.
	  ○ *"What do you think about this idea?" "Are you up for trying this?"*
	
	• Ask the student to roll back the gap you found and the next steps.
	  ○ *"So summarize for me. What's our challenge and how will we approach it?"*
	
	• Affirm your belief in the student and how you'll follow up.
	  ○ *"I'll look for this when I review your work, but if you'd like to talk about this further, we could meet at [time and place]."*

Voice Lesson #3: Encourage Curiosity and Risk Taking

"Trust thyself: every heart vibrates to that iron string."

—Ralph Waldo Emerson

Risk taking isn't just for skydivers. In the best English classes, students are free to be inquisitive, unconventional, daring—and even wrong.

Core Idea

No risk, no reward. When we grapple, we grow.

We've seen teachers use the methods below to build bolder readers. Note the connection to our discussion of discourse in Part 3.

- **Coach questioning and curiosity:** A favorite classroom poster of ours reads simply "Questions are the Oxygen of Intellect." It reminds us that questioning is essential, not ancillary, to learning. To cultivate this mindset, you might incorporate question generation into the daily routine by asking students to draft meaningful questions about the text as homework. Often, these can be incorporated directly into the day's lesson. As E.E. Cummings reminds us, "Always the beautiful answer who asks a more beautiful question."[22]

- **Encourage different perspectives:** There is rarely one "right" answer in English class, and it's important we signal this to our students by the way we consider their ideas and hypotheses. (See the box "An Exemplar, Not The Exemplar" in Chapter 3 for more on that.)

- **Praise and model risk taking:** Whether in feedback or class discourse, pausing to note, "That's a bold claim we haven't heard yet; let's think about it" sends a message that you value this type of thinking in class. What's more, you can model it any time your class gets stuck in groupthink by using the 201 Habits of Discourse from Chapter 6. For example: "You might be right, but I'd like to play devil's advocate for the sake of our discourse. . ."

Encouraging curiosity means accepting that learning is typically a messy, generative process. After all, some of the most joyful moments of class happen when students take us down a pathway we didn't expect. So let's enjoy the ride.

CONCLUSION

A popular adage in the business world is that culture eats strategy for breakfast.[23] This quip fits well for our purposes in class. Culture is the bridge between who we are and how we wish to see ourselves. It's the hidden curriculum of any great English coursework, and it matters as much as anything else you teach.

The culture we create shapes what our students think and do as readers. When we embed independence, curiosity, and risk-taking into our class community, we let students direct their own journey as readers. In the scope of their lives, our role may be small. But if we can build a place where they can fall in love with texts, it may be enough.

Stop and Jot—My Takeaways

So far, what are your top takeaways for your classroom?

_____

_____

_____

_____

Self-Assessment

Following is the final section of the rubric, which focuses on the keys to creating culture. Where do you stand in this section? In Chapter 8, we'll talk about how to put all your reflections together and translate them into action.

Part 4: How Do I Create a Culture Where Reading Thrives?	

• **Expand Their World:**
 	
  ○ Whether before, during, or after the school day, I provide opportunities for students to choose their own books to read independently.
 	
  ○ I confer with students about their independent reading and I hold them accountable to doing it with quizzes, book reviews, book talks, or small-group discourse.
	___/8

• **Call Them Home—Remind Students of Reading's Gifts:**
 	
  ○ Multiple peak literacy moments (e.g. class competitions, poetry festivals) are planned throughout the year.
 	
  ○ I post my instructional signage where it's accessible during instruction. My inspirational signage invites all students into the great, global conversation.
 	
  ○ My students and I choose intentional passages to read aloud to savor the beauty of the written word.
	___/6

• **Call Them Home—Center Student Voice:**
 	
  ○ Students have time to respond to/reflect on the texts personally through writing and/or discourse.
 	
  ○ My feedback to student writing reinforces student strengths, gives them specific next steps, and affirms their ownership of their own growth.
 	
  ○ Students take risks and ask questions.
	___/10

Score:	___/24

Chapter **8**

How Do I Get Started?

> *"Gryphon added 'Come, let's hear some of YOUR adventures.'*
> *"'I could tell you my adventures—beginning from this morning,' said Alice a little*
> *timidly; 'but it's no use going back to yesterday, because I was a different person then.'"*
> —Lewis Carroll, *Alice's Adventures in Wonderland*

Imagine your classroom a few months from now: Where do you want it to be? *Love and Literacy* gives you the tools to get there. Now it's time to map the journey. Of all the resources provided, which would be most useful in your classroom? How do you adapt these approaches to your school or district? And how do you keep from doing too much at once?

Consider this chapter the "do it yourself" guide to get you started.

ASSESS THE STATE OF LITERACY IN YOUR CLASSROOM

Just as we wrote in Chapter 1, assessment is the starting point for instruction, not the end. To determine where to start, we have to assess where we are.

At the end of each part of this book, we've given you a partial rubric to evaluate your classroom or school against the ideas we described. Here, we've consolidated all of them into the full implementation rubric listed below. You will notice that not all sections are weighted equally (e.g. having a complexity curriculum carries more weight than teaching annotation techniques). This is intentional: it reflects the areas to prioritize when you can't do it all.

To start, take a moment to fill out the rubric for your classroom: Where do you currently stand? (If it's easier, you can find a version that prints on a single page available in the online appendix. Visit http://www.wiley.com/go/lal to download.)

Love & Literacy Implementation Rubric

Part 1: What's My Dream for Kids?	
• **Create a Complexity Curriculum:** My curriculum deliberately sequences texts so they increase in quantitative, qualitative, and task complexity over time. Across the year, students read a diverse set of perspectives, genres, and experiences, including those far different from their own experience.	__/12
• **Build Background Knowledge:** From my teaching, students receive the schema necessary to access texts.	__/8
• **Read for Claim:** My students find the claims and sub-claims in narrative and non-narrative texts.	__/6
• **Read for Analysis:** My students use consistent methodologies (e.g. MR. CUF, NEZZ) to analyze, discuss, and write about author's craft.	__/6
Score:	__/32

Part 2: What Will I See When Students Get It?	
• **Spar with an Exemplar:** I analyze the texts I teach to generate an exemplar class product before teaching. My exemplar includes potential evidence that students might use, the ideal analysis for that evidence, and any additional ideas uncovered during sparring with others.	__/6
• **Teach Students to Talk to Their Texts:** When students read, they underline key claims and create brief margin notes around them. With shorter texts, students jot an overall claim or theme note after reading.	__/6
• **Honor and Monitor Independent Practice** ○ 90% of my students use work time for purposeful, independent practice. I provide clear, what-to-do guidance and feedback to ensure they use this time effectively. ○ I reach every student at least once a day during independent practice. I mark up their papers, give them written or oral feedback, and I collect data to guide my instruction.	__/8
Score:	__/20

Part 3: What Will I Hear When Students Get It?	
• **Find the Productive Struggle:** Before class, I name the productive struggle I want students to have, and I have a plan to respond to multiple levels of student response.	__/4

- **Launch the Discourse Cycle:** I start with a broad, open-ended question, ask students to write, and give them time to share their thinking with a peer before we discuss. __/4
- **Create and Make Meaningful Conversation (Habits of Discourse 101):** __/8
  - Students routinely share, critique, listen to, and take notes on each other's ideas.
  - Students do 90% of the talking during class discussions; I use short "universal" prompts to keep their voices front and center.
  - I strategically call on students to allow them to resolve most of their own questions without teacher intervention.
  - Students consistently revoice peers' thinking and defend their own with evidence and reasoning.
- **Deepen Discourse and Stamp It (Habits of Discourse 201):** __/8
  - I model and ask students to use prompts that problematize class thinking, connect to others' ideas, and add sophistication to the conversation.
  - Stamp the Learning: When big ideas occur, students capture the major takeaways in their own words and writing.

Score:	__/24

Part 4: How Do I Create a Culture Where Reading Thrives?

- **Expand Their World:** __/8
  - Whether before, during, or after the school day, I provide opportunities for students to choose their own books to read independently.
  - I confer with students about their independent reading and I hold them accountable to doing it with quizzes, book reviews, book talks, or small-group discourse.
- **Call Them Home—Remind Students of Reading's Gifts:** __/6
  - Multiple peak literacy moments (e.g. class competitions, poetry festivals) are planned throughout the year.
  - I post my instructional signage where it's accessible during instruction. My inspirational signage invites all students into the great, global conversation.
  - My students and I choose intentional passages to read aloud to savor the beauty of the written word.

• **Call Them Home—Center Student Voice:**	__/10
○ Students have time to respond to/reflect on the texts personally through writing and/or discourse.	
○ My feedback to student writing reinforces student strengths, gives them specific next steps, and affirms their ownership of their own growth.	
○ Students take risks and ask questions.	
Score:	__/24
Total Rubric Score:	__/100

So, how did you do? You may have only a few target areas, making it relatively easy to know what and where to prioritize. But what if you have many areas to tackle? The strategies and techniques in this book took teachers years to develop and hone. Where do you begin?

Use this simple principle to guide you: start with what matters most.

START WITH THE HIGHEST LEVERAGE AREA

All techniques are important, but some have a larger ripple effect than others. Here is how you could approach the challenge.

Imagine a 10th-grade English teacher, Amy. The school's curriculum hasn't been revised in years, and her incoming sophomores are used to facile analysis with below-grade-level texts. They have limited experience with non-narrative works or writing complex essays. They're also pretty reticent in class discussion, and few if any annotate while they read. In other words, Amy's scores are low throughout the rubric—even though many of the reasons are out of her direct control.

Amy scans the weighting on the rubric. A few categories immediately stand out because they are weighted more than others. But which should she choose?

In her case, Amy chooses "create a complexity curriculum" and "center student voice." She can work all she wants on improving students' ability to read for claim, monitoring their work, or fine-tuning discourse, but if students don't have to grapple with challenging texts, and if they cannot personally connect to class, their reading skills will stall.

Ultimately, every decision to improve your classroom is a choice between good actions. To help you prioritize, we've provided the following chart that gives priority levels to each part of the rubric/book:

Literacy Implementation Rubric
Priority Levels for Instruction and Culture

INSTRUCTION	CULTURE
Priority Level 1	**Priority Level 1**
• Create a Complexity Curriculum	• Call Them Home—Center Student Voice
Priority Level 2	**Priority Level 2**
• Build/Activate Background Knowledge • Read for Claim • Read for Analysis • Spar with Exemplars • Find the Productive Struggle • Honor Independent Practice ◦ Clear guidance, focused independent work time	• Call Them Home—Remind Students of Reading's Gifts • Expand Their World
Priority Level 3	**Priority Level 3**

• Monitor Independent Practice
  ◦ Talk to their texts (annotate)
  ◦ Don't circulate, monitor
• Launch the Discourse:
  ◦ Launch the discourse cycle
  ◦ Strategically call on students
  ◦ Universal prompts
• Habits of Discourse:
  ◦ 101—Create conversation
  ◦ 201—Deepen discourse	

The Level 1 priorities are big (you don't set up a classroom overnight!) and are most easily addressed before or at the launch of the school year. Level 2 priorities are easier to implement at any time with the right rollout, though they are easiest and most powerful in the first quarter of the year. Level 3 are the beautiful things you get to do when you have the right foundation in place.

MAKE AN IMPLEMENTATION PLAN

A day in the life of a schoolteacher can be pretty hectic: the average teacher has between 1,200 and 1,500 exchanges with students per day![1] And even when you leave the classroom, there are family phone calls, meetings, work to review, and endless other tasks. How do you launch anything new with so much going on? It takes tight planning.

Here is an example of an implementation plan for a teacher who is focused on independent practice. What strikes you about it?

Sample Teacher Rollout Plan

Independent Practice

Month 1

Week 1:

- **Honor Independent Practice**
  - **Rollout:** Independent Work expectations
  - **Spiral Practice:** During independent practice, coach the class to stay engaged.

Week 2–3:

- **Honor Independent Practice**
  - ○ **Spiral Practice:** During independent practice, coach the class to stay engaged.
  - ○ **Respond to Data:** Course correct for any gaps noticed in independent practice.

Week 4:

- **Honor Independent Practice**
  - ○ **Assess:** Use the *Love and Literacy* rubric to assess the quality of independent practice.

Notice that the plan contemplates four major pieces: when to roll out a habit, how to continue practicing it, how to course correct, and how to assess how you did. It takes time—and some light project-planning—to build class expectations and norms until they are second nature. Excellence, as the saying goes, is not an act, but a habit.

Core Idea

Excellence is not an act, but a habit.

Of course, it's quite possible to roll out and assess multiple skills simultaneously, especially once you have some experience and comfort with the techniques in this book. Here is a slightly more complex plan that works on two areas—adding Reading for Claim to Honor Independent Practice.

Sample Teacher Rollout Plan

Independent Practice and Reading for Claim

Month 1
Week 1: • **Read for Claim/Teach Students to Talk to Their Texts** ○ **Rollout:** Reading for Claim (annotating for sub-claims and shifts). ○ **Spiral Practice:** Monitor student annotations for sub-claims and shifts. • **Honor Independent Practice** ○ **Rollout:** Independent work expectations. ○ **Spiral Practice:** Narrate the positive and prompt students during work time.
Week 2 –3: • **Read for Claim/Teach Students to Talk to Their Texts** ○ **Spiral Practice:** Monitor student annotations for sub-claims, shifts, and endnotes. ○ **Respond to Data:** Mini-lesson—reteach 1 skill (e.g. missing notes around claim shifts or vague endnotes). • **Honor Independent Practice** ○ **Spiral Practice:** Narrate the positive and prompt students during work time. ○ **Respond to Data:** Reteach any aspect of practice that fewer than 80% of students use.
Week 4: • **Read for Claim/Teach Students to Talk to Their Texts** ○ **Assess:** Use the *Love and Literacy* rubric to assess reading and annotating for claim. • **Honor Independent Practice** ○ **Assess:** Use the *Love and Literacy* rubric to assess independent practice.

Notice how this plan pairs complementary skills to introduce multiple moves across a month. If you did this for two consecutive months, you could hit four or more priority areas in one quarter. In every case, the plan follows the same flow as the first: roll out a skill, spiral practice, respond to data, and assess progress.

If you're newer to teaching or are still trying to establish your class culture, we recommend starting with one rollout at a time. If you are a more experienced teacher, or one or both areas are already developing, an approach like the second plan will allow you to move even faster. Take a moment to sketch out some initial ideas for the next month of school. You can change these later on.

Stop and Jot—My Takeaways

So far, what are your top takeaways for your classroom?

_____

_____

_____

_____

Next Month

Week 1: _____

_____

Week 2–3:_____

_____

Week 4:_____

_____

Once you have a plan, it's time to roll it out. Let's look at some examples.

BREAKING IT DOWN: THE ROLLOUT

Vy Graham (whom you may recall from Part 3) is a stickler about her rollouts. Investing in these has allowed her to grant substantial autonomy to her 7th graders. In this clip, she is looking to build precision in student language. What do you notice about what she says and does?

WATCH Clip 24: Vy Graham—Precision in Language (Poet vs. Speaker)

http://www.wiley.com/go/lal

Sample Class Discussion

Speaking With Precision About Poetry

Vy: Before we dive into discourse for the day, I want to roll out a new habit. Previously, when you spoke about poetry what you would often say is, "the text states," "in the text it says." As intellectuals, we want to make sure we're always using precise language. We pride ourselves in using accurate, precise vocabulary to develop and articulate our analysis. *[gestures to the board]* When we're talking about poetry and we're speaking about a narrator of a poem, we're always going to refer to the narrator as the speaker. Read the example. *[points to board]* In lines 5–7, the speaker argues that Aunt Jennifer is weighed down by her relationship with her husband. Now when we're talking about the author of the poem, we would refer to the author's name. *[points to board]* In lines 10–12, Rich uses a metaphor to highlight how oppressive the marriage is. Very often, students forget to differentiate between the narrator and the author. They are not always the same person. What are we going to do today to ensure that we are using precise language in our analysis of the poem? Turn and talk with your partner.

[Students turn and talk.]

Michael: Ms. Graham wants us to stop referring back to the text and start referring to the speaker and the author because we have to use precise language when referring to our evidence because we know that if we use precise language, we are getting stronger at analyzing poetry. . .

Vy: So when we're talking about the narrator of the poem, we are going to refer to that character as the speaker. When we're talking about the craft. . .we're talking about the author. So if I ask you to state a piece of evidence that referred to. . .how Aunt Jennifer spent her time sewing [images of] tigers, would you refer to that as the speaker or the author?

Yanni: I would refer to that as the speaker because you're not using the author's craft and we're talking about Aunt Jennifer and so the speaker would be their niece or nephew.

Vy: Beautiful. If I said that _____ used juxtaposition to convey Aunt Jennifer's strength, would we use the speaker or the author?

Apria: We would use the author because you're dealing with craft and techniques.

Vy: Let's stamp that key understanding. . . What do we have to remember about precise language?

Annika: When we're trying to use precise language, we need to remember to state the line that the evidence is in, and when we're pulling what the narrator says, we use "the speaker argues," but when we're talking about the craft used in the text, we say, "the author argues."

Paul first spoke about the power of the rollout in *Leverage Leadership 2.0*. Simply put: The way you launch your implementation dictates what follows. You never get a second chance at a first impression.

Core Idea

Sweat the rollout. You never get a second chance at a first impression.

Using the language from *Leverage Leadership 2.0*, Vy's rollout can be described as a simple series of moves: Hook, Frame, Model, Derief, and Practice. We see Vy hook students by calling them "intellectuals who pride themselves in using accurate and precise language" when speaking about poetry.[2] Her aspirational framing leads directly to the model. Using "Aunt Jennifer's Tigers" as the sample text, Vy models when the term "poet" or "speaker" is appropriate to analyze a work. She debriefs by checking for understanding and then quickly leads her students into a round of practice.

Rollouts can vary in length. Straightforward or familiar habits, such as the one Vy has introduced, can be introduced and practiced in 10 minutes. More complex habits, like reading for claim, could require a full class period—and a lot more follow-up. No matter the rollout's length, the bulk of it should be spent on practice. Like us, students learn best by doing.

An annotated map of this method follows. You'll see the hook, frame, model, and practice followed by a final section, "Monitor the Habit," which provides a clear cycle of moves to follow every time students have an authentic opportunity to practice.

How to Roll Out a Habit

	Hook
Roll Out the Habit	• **What/Why:** Explain what the habit is and why it is important. • **How:** Explain how the habit works.
	Frame and Model
	• **Frame:** Tell students what you want them to notice about the habit. Make it specific. • **Model:** Show students what the exemplar version of this habit looks like. This can be modeled in person, shown on video, or read about in a case study. • **Debrief (if needed):** Ask students to share what they noticed about the habit through the modeling.
	Practice
	• **Give students an immediate at-bat:** Move to a short, focused practice of the habit. • **Ask students to stamp in learning:** Ask students to share what they've learned about the habit by practicing it.
	Monitor the Habit

Monitor the Habit	• A habit develops from consistent, precise practice. Once you've introduced it, monitor the habit over time to make sure that the way it's practiced still meets your bar for excellence. Use the what-to-do-cycle every time students practice; it gives clarity to both teachers and students.
	• **What-To-Do Cycle:**
	  ○ **Give directions:** Tell students what you expect to see them say and do.
	  ○ **Look for engagement:** Stand in one spot to look for observable behaviors that indicate that students are meeting your expectations.
	  ○ **Narrate the positive:** Highlight one or two students who are using the habit.
	  ○ **Prompt students:** Gently prompt students who aren't using the habit. If more than 10% of students aren't using the habit, pause and restate your expectations, then cue students to restart.
	  ○ Repeat the cycle.

SCRIPT THE ROLLOUT

What does this look like concretely? In this section we've given you three sample scripts for rolling out a skill: Monitoring Independent Practice, Reading for Claim, and Revoicing. As you review, think about what makes these rollout lessons effective. What are students able to say or do by the end of each lesson?

Sample Rollout Script #1: Monitor Independent Practice

This is an independent practice rollout plan for middle school. In the upper grades, you might instead activate this habit through a short reminder, but make sure that follow up is thorough.

	Hook
Roll Out the Habit	• *Pre-Work: Create an Independent Practice poster that lists all the steps you want students to do during work time. Post this at the start of the lesson.* • "In this class, we only have 60 minutes to learn together. Just 60 minutes!" • **What/Why:** "Independent work time is your chance, every day, to put into practice what we've learned. It's your time to grow: sacred time just for you." • **How:** "Today I will show you how to make each minute multiply your knowledge."
	Frame and Model
	• **Frame:** "I will model for you what focused independent practice looks like. I'll play the student. X [student] will play the teacher. Note: What do I do after I'm given instructions?" *Give teacher script to student X.* • **Model:** *Write silently. Model a think-aloud.* "Hmm. I'm stuck. What can I do when I'm confused? That's right: I can refer to my resources—the anchor charts on the wall. Do any of them help me? Yes. I'll keep reading." *Mime reading silently. Then, continue think-aloud.* "Hmm. I'm stuck again. Let me look at my resources—do they help me? Not this time. So I'm going to raise my hand for help. The teacher cannot come right away, so I'll read my independent reading book [or move on to the next section] until they arrive." *Mime reading the independent reading book or continuing work.* • **Debrief (if needed):** "What did you notice about my actions?" *(Above responses).* "That's right. I made the most of the time I had."

	## Practice

	• **Give students an immediate at-bat:** "Today we're going to work on independent practice behaviors. Here is a 5-minute task for you to complete. Remember what to do if you are stuck:
	  ○ Use the signage at the front of the room for help.
	  ○ If you're still stuck, raise your hand.
	  ○ When waiting, or when you're done, read your independent reading book until the timer buzzes.
	The notes on the board list all these steps. Refer to it if you forget what to do next."

	## Monitor the Habit

Monitor the Habit	• **What-To-Do Cycle:**
	  ○ **Give directions:** "Ready? Let's begin: work silently until the timer goes off."
	  ○ **Look for engagement:** *Stand in a part of the room where you can see all students. Look and listen for expected student actions: pens/pencils moving, use of resources, raised hands, independent reading.*
	  ○ **Narrate the positive:** *Highlight one or two students who are using the habit, e.g.* "Marielle is referencing the Independent Practice poster to figure out what to do next."
	  ○ **Prompt students as needed:** *If one or two students aren't engaged, whisper prompt to them or lightly touch the student's desk to get their attention. If several students aren't engaging, pause the practice and restate your expectations to the class:* "Eyes on me. I've noticed that several students are not writing. Remember our key steps. It's important that everyone is learning. That's how we all grow as a class. If you are not sure of the answer, give it your best shot and we'll support each other." *Cue students to restart.*

Sample Rollout Script #2: Reading for Claim

This rollout is an introduction to identifying topic and sub-claims in an informational text. Feel free to use it with a short, grade-level-appropriate informational text. This rollout can also become a terrific knowledge building opportunity for your class.

Roll Out the Habit	**Hook**
	• "What do newspapers and advertisements have in common? They're both trying to sell us something."
	• **What/Why:** "Every text we read is making an argument about how we should see the world. As readers, our challenge is to identify the text's claim, or argument. Then we get to decide if we buy what they're selling."
	• **How:** "We read for claim by identifying the topic and reading for supporting sub-claims. At the end, we synthesize our annotations to determine the overall claim. The topic, plus the overall claim about the topic, form the central idea of any text."
	Frame and Model
	• *Make the text visible to the students: write on the whiteboard or use a transparency projector, document camera, or interactive display so students can see your annotations.*
	• **Frame:** "Today, I am going to show you how to read for claim, using the article 'Comparing Fourth Grade Literacy Skills Across the Nation.' As I read, watch what I ask myself and what I write in the margins to determine the author's claim."
	• **Model:** Exemplar Annotations [*You can use whatever text you have. This one is for a 5th-grade class*]
	○ "So, I'm going to start reading. First, I'll start with the title. I can see that the topic is reading skills of 4th graders, and the genre is journalism. I'll jot my topic and genre note next to the title."
	○ "Hmm. What am I noticing in this first paragraph? I see the phrase 'in other words.' I think that means this is a main idea. I'll underline the words that follow. Let me jot down a margin note. What is the main idea?" *Jot and say aloud*: "large difference btw wealthy/poor kids' reading lvls."
	○ *Read silently, make no notes.* "Wait a minute, I see the word 'however' in paragraph 3. I check my Reading for Claim one-pager, and I remember that 'however' is often used to reveal shifts in claim. So what's the shift? A large difference in reading levels across states. Let me write that down."

- *Read silently.* "Hmm. I'm noticing some charged, opinionated language in paragraph six: words like "urgent" and "must"—I bet there's a claim in here too." *Underline corresponding sentence.* "What must change? The gap between rich and poor reading levels is growing, change is urgent." *Jot the margin note and say aloud*: "Gap btwn rich and poor rdg lvls is growing; change=urgent"
- "I just finished the article. Now I'll review my annotations. So what idea do I see repeated? What are the main claims the text makes about this idea?"
- "Well, in my margin notes, I wrote about a big difference in student reading levels across states. And within states, there is a big gap between rich and poor students. The author emphasized that while progress is being made, it needs to happen more quickly."
- "Let me add up everything I've learned." *Jot end note*: "While many fourth graders struggle as readers, kids in certain states and kids from poor families struggle the most. Progress must be made because the gap is growing."
- **Debrief:** What did I notice to identify the claim?
  - Potential answers: *You identified transition words, you identified charged and opinionated language. You jotted notes by claims, but not by everything. You looked across your sub-claims to create an end claim.*
  - *Provide students with a one-pager on reading for claim. If you have your own, use that. Otherwise, ask students to review the one pager from the* Reading and Writing Handbook *(see the Online Appendix) and jot the top moves they need to make as readers.*

Practice

- **Give students an at-bat:** "Let's try it! Today, your challenge is to identify the argument in [a text I've chosen]. Here is what I'm looking for as you work.

  1) A clearly identified claim
  2) Annotations and margin notes that mark the shifts and sub-claims in the text.
  3) A final claim that connects the sub-claims and communicates the larger message."

- *Students work independently to annotate and read for claim.*
- *ID the 2–3 top claims in the text and monitor for these during work time. Give feedback as needed*: "As readers, we always look for claim shifts. I think you missed one in paragraph 4. Go back and see if you can find it and jot a note."

	• *At the end of independent work time, call students together to debrief. Choose a strong student example of annotations, sub-claims, and claims.* • "Class, what makes this a strong example of annotating and reading for claim?" • *Students revise their annotations and claims (as necessary) after the debrief.*
	Monitor the Habit

Monitor the Habit	• **What-To-Do Cycle [every time they read]:**
	  ◦ **Give directions:** "As you read, annotate for the topic and the sub-claims. Jot an end note that synthesizes the article's claim."
	  ◦ **Look for engagement:** *Look and listen for expected student actions: silent focus, students highlighting and annotating text, reference to resources as necessary.*
	  ◦ **Narrate the positive:** *Highlight when students use the strategy e.g.:* "Leon reviewed all of his annotations to identify the big picture of the article."
	  ◦ **Prompt students as needed:** *Name the gap and prompt students to provide the missing information.*
	    ◦ **Limited claim:** "Your final claim is incomplete because you haven't included the major sub-claim from paragraph __. Reread your annotations and add to your new understanding."
	    ◦ **Missing evidence:** "As readers, we always look for claim shifts. I think you missed one in paragraph 4. Go back and see if you can find it and jot a note."
	    ◦ **Summary, not Analysis:** "Why does the author want us to believe his claim? Add this understanding to your final claim."

Sample Rollout Script #3: Revoice

Revoicing sets the expectation that students build discourse by responding to one another's ideas. Introduce revoicing at the start of class, optimally on a day where there will be plenty of time to practice during discourse.

	Hook
	• **What/Why:** "We all feel respected when we feel heard. Today, we will learn a new move, called revoicing, that will help us become better listeners. To revoice, we paraphrase what someone else has said. Doing so signals that we value their thinking—even if we disagree. It also allows us to make sure we understand what was said before we respond." • **How:** "To revoice, paraphrase what someone else has said before adding your own thoughts."
	Frame and Model

Roll Out the Habit	• **Frame/Model:** "I'll model what this looks like. Pay attention to how I revoice Bianca's comment."
	   ○ "Bianca, can you share your response to the Do Now prompt?"
	   ○ *Bianca shares.*
	   ○ "Bianca, Do you mean that. . .? [correct] Then I agree with your argument that. . . and I think Stanza 2 provides further evidence of this when it says. . ."
	• **Debrief:** "What did I do to revoice?"
	   ○ Possible responses: *You paraphrased what Bianca said, and asked her if your revoicing was correct. You made sure your comment connected to hers by adding on to her thoughts or strengthening the argument.*
	• **Model:** "Although I revoiced and agreed with Bianca, you can also revoice to disagree or to check your understanding. Here's an example of how to clarify using revoicing."
	   ○ "Bianca, are you saying?. . . [incorrect]. No, oh—so what did you mean?"
	   ○ *Bianca explains.*
	• "Oh, okay. So that makes me think that. . ."
	• **Debrief the model:** *Ask students,* "What did I do to revoice here?"
	   ○ Possible responses: *You paraphrased what Bianca said and asked if it was correct. When she said it wasn't, you asked her to clarify what she meant.*

	Practice

	• **Give students an immediate at-bat:** "Let's practice revoicing. I will ask one of you to share your response to today's prompt. Then I will call on someone to revoice the comment before responding."
	   o *Do 3–5 rounds of practice, depending on how quickly students pick up the skill.*
	
	• **Ask students to stamp:** "When should we revoice?"
	   o Potential responses: *We should revoice prior to responding to someone else's statement. When we revoice, we should ask the other person if our paraphrasing is correct. We can revoice to agree, disagree, and build.*

	Monitor the Habit

Monitor the Habit	• **What-To-Do Cycle:**
	   o **Give directions:** "During discourse today, please revoice your classmate's thoughts before adding your own."
	
	   o **Look for engagement:** *Look and listen for expected student actions: one speaker at a time, active listening, paraphrasing of comments, asking if revoicing is correct, contribution of own thoughts.*
	
	   o **Narrate the positive:** *Highlight when students use the habit.* "Juana, that was a precise revoicing of Michael's claim. His interpretation is similar to your own."
	
	   o **Prompt students as needed:** *When students say 'I agree' or 'I disagree' but don't revoice, prompt with, 'What did __ say that you agree/disagree with? "Revoicing and making an irrelevant connection is also a common pitfall. Ask students, 'How does your claim connect to __'s?'"*

This framework can be adapted to almost every classroom practice you hope to build with your students. Feel free to use these scripts as they are or adapt them to the needs of your classroom or grade level. You can also write rollout plans for other habits using the template that follows.

Stop and Jot—Plan Your Habits Rollout

Now that you've reviewed these sample plans, it's time to make your own. The process will likely take more space than we can provide in this box, so we've included a blank planning template in the online *Reading and Writing Handbook*.

	Hook	
Roll Out the Habit	• **What/Why:** • **How:**	
	Frame, Model, Debrief	
	• **Frame:** • **Model:** • **Debrief the model:**	
	Practice	
	• **Give students an immediate at-bat:** • **Ask students to stamp:**	
	Monitor the Habit	

Monitor the Habit	• **What-To-Do Cycle:**
	  ○ **Give directions:**
	  ○ **Look for engagement:**
	  ○ **Narrate the positive:**
	  ○ **Prompt students as needed:**	

Now that you've put together a rollout, how do you think about it in the context of the school year?

CREATE A YEAR-LONG IMPLEMENTATION PLAN

A year-long implementation plan pulls together all the rollouts you'd like to do over the course of a school year. What do you notice about this sample?

Sample Yearly Implementation Plan

(NOTE: Within this plan, the numbers 1–4 represent each week of each month. For example, the "2" under September is the 2nd week in September.)

Month	Task
Before the School Year	☐ Create a Complexity Curriculum ☐ Culture: Classroom Set Up (Instructional and Inspirational Signage)
September	☐ 1- **School Begins:** Read for Claim, Call Them Home & Independent Practice—Rollout & Spiral Practice ☐ 2- Read for Claim, Call Them Home & Independent Practice—Spiral Practice & Monitor/Respond to data ☐ 3- Read for Claim, Call Them Home & Independent Practice—Spiral Practice & Monitor/Respond to data ☐ 4- Read for Claim, Call Them Home & Independent Practice—Assess
October	☐ 1- ☐ 2- Interim Assessment #1 & Analysis ☐ 3- Assessment response and reteach ☐ 4- Assessment response and reteach
November	☐ 1- Read for Analysis & Launch Discourse Cycle—Rollout & Spiral Practice ☐ 2- Read for Analysis & Launch Discourse Cycle—Spiral Practice & Monitor/Respond to data ☐ 3- Read for Analysis & Launch Discourse Cycle—Spiral Practice & Monitor/Respond to data ☐ 4- Read for Analysis & Launch Discourse Cycle—Assess
December	☐ 1- ☐ 2- Interim Assessment #2 & Analysis ☐ 3- Assessment response and reteach ☐ 4- Winter break

Month	Task
January	☐ 1- Assess all four areas on *Love and Literacy* rubric ☐ 2- Reteach any gap areas identified on the rubric ☐ 3- Spiral Practice & monitor/respond to data ☐ 4-
February	☐ 1- Habits of Discourse 101—Rollout & Spiral Practice ☐ 2- Habits of Discourse 101—Spiral Practice & Monitor/Respond to data ☐ 3- Habits of Discourse 101—Spiral Practice & Monitor/Respond to data ☐ 4- Habits of Discourse 101—Assess
March–June	☐ 1- (Continued implementation) ☐ 2- ☐ 3- ☐ 4-

In one document, you can see the summary of the rollout of each priority area, and they are appropriately spaced out for the launch of each quarter. You can see that the teacher avoids months where it is difficult to roll out new skills, such as assessment weeks and the ends of quarters. You'll also see that nothing new is launched after February: this time is best reserved to take stock of how the class has progressed before deciding any next moves.

With this tool, you could easily scale up (launch more initiatives) or down (launch fewer). Having a yearly plan allows you to see it all in one place and remain focused in the midst of the hectic nature of school life.

The rubric, implementation plan, and rollout scripts consolidate best teacher practices in a concrete, actionable way that can be adapted to fit a variety of classroom contexts. While the start of the year or moments after breaks can be optimal times to refresh class, these tools can be used at any time of the school year, so don't be afraid to try them out now, even if your school year has already begun.

A blank version of the yearly template can be found in the online *Reading and Writing Handbook*, or you could use your own planning system.

CONCLUSION

You've done it: you have the knowledge and tools to bring even more love—and life—to your literacy classroom. All that's left is to answer some of the most frequently asked questions we have received over the years. Turn to the next chapter for that guidance.

Stop and Jot—My Takeaways

So far, what are your top takeaways for your classroom?

_____

_____

_____

_____

Chapter **9**

Frequently Asked Questions

So far, we've walked through the process as it would ideally unfold. But we know the inspiration one feels in trainings and seminars can evaporate quickly amid the challenges of the real world. We'd be remiss if we didn't talk about the obstacles you may encounter when trying to implement change—and a few ways around them. Here are some of the most common questions we hear, along with our recommendations to help you remain true to your goals.

What do I do if I have a mandated curriculum and it is not diverse or complex?

We hear you: this is an incredibly frustrating and serious challenge. But it doesn't mean you're out of options. If you cannot immediately change the curriculum, add to it.

If a specific text you've been assigned to teach is not complex enough, build complexity by choosing rich, supplemental materials that deepen how students read the text and introduce counter narratives. We did this with the supplemental readings that we chose for the sample *To Kill a Mockingbird* unit in Chapter 2. The accompanying texts and resources enriched students' reading and prepared them for the challenge of the final task. If you're looking for where to start your search for supplemental materials, there are several resources in Tier It—Build Background Knowledge (again, in Chapter 2). Start there.

If your curriculum isn't diverse, you can supplement what's mandated to offer counternarratives and incorporate new voices. Reading Whitman's "I Hear America Singing"? Bring in Langston Hughes's "I, Too, Sing America" or Jimmy Santiago Baca's "Who Understands Me but Me." Reading Camus's *The Stranger*? Consider pairing it with all or part of Kamel Daoud's *The Meursault Investigation*. Teaching Greek myth? Bring in myths from non-Greco-Roman cultures, too. (And consider reading Madeline Miller's *Song of Achilles* or *Circe,* which revisit these myths from the perspectives of marginalized characters.) In the long term, though, this is an issue that demands your advocacy, so bring your concerns to your department chair and ask about the best way to make change. You can cite our discussion in Chapter 1 if it's helpful (see the section on curricular complexity). While this might be a difficult conversation, it is an imperative one. A curriculum that lacks diversity doesn't help students see—and see beyond—themselves. Instead it will continue to center some voices while marginalizing all others, meaning it won't be able to advance inclusivity at your school, no matter how well you teach it. As Audre Lorde reminds us, "The master's tools will never dismantle the master's house."[1]

I don't have a library of independent reading books. How do I create culture without one?

Choice is key to cultivating a love of reading in students. If you have no or few independent reading books in your library, see if your school has funds for purchase. You might also start searching for groups like First Book Marketplace, which offer books at discounts to schools serving students in low-income communities. It's also worth searching for online grants—there are a number dedicated to this purpose.

Another route is to set up your students with library cards. During the COVID-19 pandemic, many libraries shifted operations online, allowing students to apply for a card from a computer or their phone—and a number of apps now allow them to check out and read eBooks that way. While you'll want to collaborate with your school and parents about how to guide responsible book choices, it's an inexpensive way to get books in students' hands.

Another path is to try to raise the money yourself. Let's be clear: in the world our students deserve, you wouldn't have to do this. Nevertheless, many teachers—and we count ourselves among them—take matters into their own hands while we wait for the world (or at least those in charge of school funding formulas) to catch up. If you decide to raise funds, you can use websites like DonorsChoose and GoFundMe to create online fund-raising campaigns. Consider publicizing your campaign among your extended network (think: family, friends, colleagues, parents and guardians, etc.). Our networks often have untapped resources—such as extra books—they're happy to donate.

I don't write the lesson plans that I use. What should I do?

Using common lesson plans can be extremely helpful, but it can also be very challenging. There's simply no way another teacher can know your students—their needs, personalities, skills, and dreams—like you do. Depending on what your curriculum already includes, here are the most important areas to adjust when you teach a universal plan (we highlight which chapter to revisit for a refresher on each of these):

- **Match the Launch to the Need:** Activate the knowledge students need for this lesson. This can include dropping knowledge, introducing key terms and vocabulary, or connecting learning across units and time. (Chapters 2 & 5)

- **Connect to Students:** Lesson hooks are powerful opportunities for connection. Use them to link to your own experience or that of your students. (Chapter 7)

- **Use the Discourse Cycle:** Modify or create an opening prompt. Have students write in response to the prompt and turn and talk with a peer before launching whole-class discussion. (Chapter 5)

- **Let Students Lead Discourse:** Make substantive time for discourse. Coach students to talk to one another, not you, about the essential takeaways of the text. (Chapter 6)

- **Stamp the Learning:** End the lesson by asking students to verbalize and write down the major takeaways of the day's learning. (Chapter 6)

None of these moves force you to leave the common lesson—in fact, they enhance it. The bulk of the lesson remains the same, so these moves are unlikely to cause controversy.

It's mid-semester (or mid-March). Shouldn't I just wait for next semester (or next year) to launch these practices?

You're right that the best time to roll out a habit is the beginning of the year. But when you don't have that luxury, then the next best time to roll out habits is whenever you are ready. After all, most of us only get to teach our students for a single school year. Waiting until the next semester or year to roll out habits may mean we miss the opportunity to share these practices with the students we have now. For their sake, it's worth the effort to start as soon as you are able.

If you're doing a midyear or mid-semester rollout, keep the following in mind:

- **Make it short and sweet:** Present the rollout as a task that students can complete in just a day. Students may resist a midyear rollout if it's presented as time-consuming and arduous.

- **Refresh their memory:** If you're resetting a habit you established earlier in the year, remind students that they've already been introduced to it—now the focus is on perfecting it.

I feel all alone trying to do this in my school. How do I find a community?

Education can be so lonely, and trying to make change can be even more so! Staying motivated is much easier when working alongside someone who shares your goals. So where can you look for that community?

Search first among your school staff, even if that means going beyond your grade level. Is there another staff member who you think would also be invested in this type of change? If so, approach them and see if they would be willing to be a thought partner or partner-in-change.

You can also try expanding your network: attend workshops and meet like minded people who work in other schools, districts, and cities. Join listservs or Twitter chats where people are discussing the issues you care about. Find a blogger who inspires you. During the COVID-19 pandemic, teachers created Zoom communities to collaborate across schools and districts. One of the great lessons of literature is that even when we feel alone, we aren't. The larger your network, the easier it is to find someone who is just as eager as you are to push forward and try something new.

How do I adapt these techniques to serve readers in struggle? My students cannot handle such complexity.

At some point in our lives, all of us are readers in struggle. In today's world, sadly, there are so many factors that can cause this. Take your pick: the COVID-19 pandemic and lost instructional time, not having access to quality instruction and literature for years, lack of support with earlier struggles that morph into giant ones, learning disabilities, balancing learning across multiple languages, etc. It's reasonable to wonder: If we build a curriculum that prioritizes complexity, how do we not exacerbate the struggle?

The techniques in this book are designed to support all students, especially the most vulnerable in our care. While they may need intervention, our students in struggle don't need a separate or watered-down curriculum; doing so actually does them a disservice.[2] What makes special education teachers and anyone who supports a struggling reader effective is adjusting the teaching to meet the student (after all, this is the heart of any individualized education plan).

We've seen schools take a few steps that have made a difference, and we share them here in that spirit:

- **Frontload schema and model fluency:** If you're able to meet with small groups of students in advance of important lessons, double down on frontloading. Review key knowledge and vocabulary needed for class, and pre-read some of the texts with students, modeling fluency as you do. (You can also provide students with audio recordings of texts to listen to as they read.) This time before class is an incredible opportunity to give students a running head start.

- **Tier it:** In Chapter 2 we talked extensively about how to build student background knowledge—and thus reading accessibility—by tiering texts on the same topic with increasing levels of complexity. This is particularly powerful anywhere students are a few grade levels behind!

- **Make time to respond to student learning:** As teachers, we are bombarded daily with data on our students' progress. What we do with that information can make all the difference. The teachers we work with carve regular time to respond to learning gaps during their weekly instructional blocks. This can be as simple as adjusting a lesson's focus or adding an opening activity—or as detailed as reserving a full lesson or lessons for the work.

- **Invite students into the conversation:** Too often, the gap for a reader in struggle just gets larger because they sit back in class and don't participate. Change the game by inviting them in! Before whole-class discourse, provide students with extra time to think. Asking students to write first automatically does this, and you can also use turn-and-talks or small-group meetings to help students test and rehearse their thinking with a few peers, before sharing with the full group. Another technique is to give students a heads-up that you want to hear from them, a move Doug Lemov refers to as "warm calling." By way of example, imagine that you'd like to bring Jason into the conversation. Consider how these phrases might help do so:

  ○ "Let's hear from Sarah and Yasmin. Jason, I'm going to ask you to pick a side. . ."

  ○ "Go ahead, Charisma. Jason, I'll have you agree/disagree next."

  ○ [*during independent work*] "Jason, this is a terrific idea! Can you share it when discussion begins?"

  Modeling and creating a culture in which all voices are valued will go a long way. Phrases like, "I'm wondering if we can hear from someone who hasn't had a chance to share yet?" are a terrific way to highlight this value. Likewise, leaving notes to students on their homework ("This is a fascinating point! I hope you'll bring it up in class!") can surface student voice.

- **Strategic Seating:** As we discussed earlier in the text, a powerful move is to thoughtfully seat students so that each has a partner who can support them in class. If you are strategic in your seating, you'll be able to use a phrase like "Turn and talk—partner closest to the window shares first" knowing that you are actually asking partners who have struggled more recently to be the first speaker in the pairing. Just keep in mind that proficiency isn't fixed. Adjust your seating throughout the year to respond to students' needs. (Chapter 4)

- **Amplifying Relevance:** Students are far more willing to take risks and struggle with class material when it feels relevant to them. Take care to help students see the connection between class materials and their lives. Add thematic schema (Chapter 2) or use the techniques in Call Them Home: Make It Personal (Chapter 7) to help do this.

What if I'm teaching remotely? How do I adjust my instruction?

We've learned quite a bit about teaching remotely when we closed our schools in response to the Coronavirus pandemic. Many of our literacy practices worked well over video, but some needed tweaking. Here are our top takeaways:

- **Dream Digitally:** Switching to a remote curriculum doesn't affect what makes texts complex. It does, however, make a wider genre of stories available. Digital texts, like videos, virtual tours, social media, interactive fiction, and virtual demonstrations, are worthwhile additions to your class materials, assuming you can ensure equitable student access. Although written and digital texts convey information differently, remote instruction is a valuable opportunity to show students that reading strategies, such as reading for claim, can be used to analyze digital messages as well. If your curriculum invited students to productively struggle when class was in person (and it should!), it will pose new challenges for students working remotely. Message up front what students can do when they struggle on their own and make clear that this is natural. For example, our middle schools created extra video supports for students who got stuck when reading to help them grapple with the hardest part of each assignment.

- **See It Online:** While annotating takes a different form online, there are plenty of platforms (e.g., Actively Learn, Kami, and Owl Eyes) that allow students to annotate texts as they read. You can do the same in Google Docs using the comments feature. These platforms offer simple and immediate ways for teachers to review student work and give feedback.

- **Hear It Through Video Conference:** Managing discourse remotely will probably be the largest shift you'll need to make. While platforms like Zoom have allowed remote conversations to happen nationwide, these systems require additional habits to guide your class culture.

  - **Create a System to Manage Discourse:** Using the rollout systems mapped in this text, decide the culture you'd like to set for the following components:

    - How will students signal when they wish to speak? (e.g., via hand gestures, chat features, by un-muting?)

    - Will you ask your students to keep cameras on as part of class culture?

- What are your expectations for breakout rooms, which can be used for turn-and-talks?

- What will you use as your digital whiteboard? (e.g. a tech platform, the chat feature, a shared Google Doc, etc.)

○ **Save the Time for Talk:** Keep the bulk of your instructional time interactive: use it for discussion, analysis, and questions. If possible, consider using pre-recorded videos to introduce content. Students can pause, rewind, and play it back as needed. (This is especially helpful for students in struggle.) Scheduling interactive portions in each class every day raises overall student engagement and allows students to connect with people outside their home—an important academic and psychological benefit.

○ **Plan for Participation:** Videoconferencing can make engagement a greater challenge than it is in person. The following actions can encourage students to dive in:

- Before whole-class discourse, provide students with extra think time. Asking students to write before speaking automatically does this. In addition, you can use turn-and-talks or small-group meetings (via breakout rooms) to help students test and rehearse their thinking with a few peers before sharing with the full group. Once discourse begins, avoid calling only on raised hands—it's a surefire way to decrease engagement.

- Use strategies like warm calling (telling specific students they will be asked to answer a question) and batch calling (alerting the next four students in the order they will participate) to keep your class engaged. Keep a participation tracker so you can make sure you call on all students over time.

- If your videoconference platform offers an easy way to send messages, use it to have all students answer a question. Monitor responses for understanding and send individual messages to students to revise answers.

- Finally, model and create a discourse culture in which all voices are valued. Phrases like, "I'm wondering if we can hear from someone who hasn't had a chance to share yet" are a terrific way to highlight this value. Likewise, leaving notes to students on their homework ("This is a fascinating point! I hope you'll bring it up in class!") can go a long way to encouraging student voice.

- **Build Culture Online:** Creating inspiring, supportive learning communities is more challenging online—but that makes it even more important. In this context, students need to feel a personal connection to instruction more than ever, so use the Call Them Home techniques in Chapter 7 and the thematic schema described in Chapter 2 to help build that bridge. The shifts we've experienced—between remote to hybrid and sometimes back again—mean that we'll need to be more flexible than ever in our planning. It also means that the culture we build will be the glue holding our learning community together, even when we are physically apart.

- **Move Your IR Library Online:** There are a number of independent reading platforms that give students access to texts, including your local library. Many of them have now shifted services online to allow for greater ease of use.

- **Keep in Touch:** Find ways—whether by videoconference, phone, or message board—to stay connected with students. Synchronous instruction is powerful, but it's not always possible for all students; nevertheless, they need to know that they are in constant dialogue with you, their texts, and their peers.

- **See Them Where They Are:** Some students struggled to attend school when we switched to remote instruction. In those cases, we called students and their families to troubleshoot barriers to attendance. (Low-touch methods, like text and email, were largely unsuccessful here.) For example, when students struggled to find quiet working spaces at home, we worked with them to build an individualized plan, including having a buddy (e.g. a school staff member) to help the student make it through the day. But this is a challenge with no easy answer. We're still learning how to navigate it too.

Your decisions around remote instruction often depend on the technology platform you are using and what level of access your students have, but to help you get started, we've included a version of the discourse one-pager with suggested remote adaptations in the *Reading and Writing Handbook* available in this book's online appendix.

You don't have the students I have. They're simply unengaged. How will this really make a difference?

We've been fortunate enough to work with scores of teachers and schools, and we've found the following to be true regardless of the school: students will rise to the level of our expectations. What appears as a lack of engagement is often a cover for insecurity, frustration, or boredom. And that means we can do something about it.

The first step is to cut yourself some slack. The techniques in this book weren't developed overnight and can't be implemented overnight either. If you've read this far, you've already invested in improving your students' experience—count that as your first win.

Then, it's time for action. Survey your students about what's working and not working for them. Ask them their goals and what motivates them. Use the *Love and Literacy* rubric from Chapter 8 to assess where the class is and where it can grow.

Once you have your data, plan a reboot. (These are often great at the start of weeks, quarters, or right after a break.) Declare a new "Day One" that reflects both your and your students' aspirations. Tell them—directly if you can—that your high expectations apply both to them and to yourself, and that they come from a place of love.

Be vulnerable, be honest, and be prepared to hold the line on your new expectations. And with each small amount of progress, double the number of accolades you'd typically provide. It is no small work to shift student mindsets, but if you're a literacy teacher, you didn't sign up for small work, anyhow.

Conclusion: There and Back Again

Key Takeaways

- A culture of reading isn't just a song you sing to your students. It's one they sing to you.
- People remember the ride, not the line.
- Walls talk. Make what they say matter.
- Connection makes it personal; personal makes it memorable.
- Students respect your ideas when you respect theirs.
- No risk, no reward. When we grapple, we grow.
- Excellence is not an act, but a habit.
- Sweat the rollout. You never get a second chance at a first impression.

Planning for Action

- What resources from Part 4 will you use to adjust your instruction? (All of these are available in the online *Love & Literacy Reading and Writing Handbook* in print-ready format):

  ○ Ideas for Whole School Peak Literacy Moments (Handbook p. 28)

  ○ Classroom Signage that Teaches (Handbook pp. 29–30, with posters included)

  ○ Writing Conference Guidance (Handbook p. 31)

  ○ Love and Literacy Implementation Rubric (Handbook p. 32)

  ○ Love and Literacy Implementation Rubric Areas, Organized by Priority (Handbook p. 33)

  ○ Classroom Habits Rollout Guidance (Handbook p. 34)

  ○ Classroom Habits Planning Template (Handbook p. 35)

  ○ Sample Rollout Plan: Independent Practice (Handbook p. 36)

  ○ Sample Rollout Plan: Independent Practice and Reading for Claim (Handbook p. 36)

  ○ Weekly Implementation Rollout Planning Template (Handbook p. 37)

  ○ Yearly Implementation Rollout Planning Template (Handbook p. 38)

  ○ Sample Rollout Script 1: Monitor Independent Practice (Handbook p. 39)

  ○ Sample Rollout Script 2: Reading for Claim (Handbook pp. 40-1)

  ○ Sample Rollout Script 3: Revoice (Handbook p. 42)

- How will you modify these resources to meet the needs of your class(es)?

_____

_____

_____

_____

Action	Date

Closing: The Call to Love

"When love beckons to you, follow him / Though his ways are hard and steep."
—Khalil Gibran, *The Prophet*

English class doesn't spin without love: love of books, love of ideas, love of conversation, love of the written word. Perhaps that's why so many of us find a home here. But, in the end, teaching English isn't about language or literature. Not really.

It's about our students—and their incredible journey to make the humanities their own.

If you've ever experienced the magic of a great English class, you know what that feels like. Students diving headfirst into challenging texts. The chatter of voices in boisterous discourse. And perhaps even the declaration, "I know you're my boyfriend, but we're not talking until you've finished Chapter 7," before the sound of dial tone. (Yes, Steve's student Jasmine really said this to her boyfriend. A recent college graduate, Jasmine is now taking her passion out into the wider world.)

Imagine if that were the story of every child we taught.

The moves of the teachers in this book show us a pathway, as well as what we'll need to travel it: a complexity curriculum that challenges students to think about the big ideas; background knowledge to help students read with context; and strategies, such as reading for claim, that students can use to unlock levels of meaning in a text. We've seen that annotations and written responses, when read with care, reveal troves of valuable information. We've watched our peers facilitate powerful, student-led discourse centered around what matters most. And we've stepped back to remind ourselves that these moves are all powered by a rich culture of literacy, one that welcomes every student into the great, global conversation.

As an English teacher, you know that the path won't always be easy. You've seen your way through enough bleary-eyed, late-night grading sessions to understand what Robert Hayden called "love's austere and lonely offices."[1] Loving literacy means loving our vast, luminous world, and teaching literacy means sharing that love with others.

Being an English teacher means you are called to love.

And when that call comes, you answer.

Discussion Guide

We can find joy in reading books together. If you are teaching a class or doing a book study with this text, these questions could help facilitate discussion. Use as many or as few as you need—enjoy!

PART 1: WHAT'S MY DREAM FOR KIDS?

1. The debate over what matters most in an English classroom is as old as the discipline itself.[1] Where does complexity fit in the mix of grammar, vocabulary, reading comprehension, literary history, analysis, media literacy, argumentation, research skills, self-expression, career readiness, and multi-genre writing? Are these other points moot without it?

2. Many of us have a bias toward quantitative or qualitative measures of text complexity. Choose the one you are less comfortable with and make a case for it.

3. How would you respond to an educator who says that increasing text complexity will get in the way of students' love of reading? Do they have a point?

4. Literacy experts Kylene Beers and Robert Probst encourage students to consider the question "What did the author think I already knew?" as a way to defang the confrontation with their own gaps in background knowledge. Think back to a time you struggled to understand a book, painting, or other text because it assumed knowledge you did not have. How did it make you feel? Were you able to locate the knowledge you needed?

5. In *Before Reading*, Peter Rabinowitz argues that "intensive reading may well be a worthless skill for someone who has not already devoured a large and

heterogeneous collection of texts. Deep reading, in other words, can complement wide reading, but it cannot replace it." Do you agree or disagree with Rabinowitz? Why?

6. What are your takeaways for your own classroom?

PART 2: WHAT WILL I SEE WHEN STUDENTS "GET IT"?

1. The following quotation comes from HBO's adaptation of Michael Crichton's *Westworld*:

    'Mistakes' is the word you're too embarrassed to use. You ought not to be. You're a product of a trillion of them. Evolution forged the entirety of sentient life on this planet using only one tool: the mistake.

    How does this quotation connect to this chapter?

2. Edgar Allan Poe extolled the virtues of a well-annotated page, writing:

    The marginalia are deliberately penciled, because the mind of the reader wishes to unburden itself of a thought; . . . In the marginalia, too, we talk only to ourselves; we therefore talk freshly—boldly—originally—with abandonment—without conceit. . .[2]

    If we take Poe's words to heart, what is the value of annotation? What are the benefits of students and teachers sharing a common annotation language?

3. What are your takeaways for your own classroom?

PART 3: WHAT WILL I HEAR WHEN STUDENTS "GET IT"?

1. The ping-pong versus volleyball/beach ball metaphor is an easy way to visualize class conversations. Are yours more ping-pong (teacher-student-teacher-student) or volleyball (teacher-student-student-student)? What could change that?

2. Raymond Carver's story "What We Talk About When We Talk About Love" primarily describes a conversation between four characters around a table. At the end, the narrator says: "I could hear my heart beating. I could hear everyone's heart." Connect this quote to what you read in this chapter.

3. In Peter S. Beagle's *The Last Unicorn*, Prince Lír sings, "Ah, love may be strong, but a habit is stronger." Do you agree? Which habits from Chapter 6 do you think are most important to develop a powerful discourse culture?

4. Consider the remarks of literary scholar Kenneth Burke:

    > Imagine that you enter a parlor. You come late. When you arrive, others
    > have long preceded you, and they are engaged in a heated discussion, a
    > discussion too heated for them to pause and tell you exactly what it is
    > about. In fact, the discussion had already begun long before any of them
    > got there, so that no one present is qualified to retrace for you all the steps
    > that had gone before. You listen for a while, until you decide that you have
    > caught the tenor of the argument; then you put in your oar. . .[3]

    Think of your most tentative students, the ones less likely to put their oar in the
    conversation. What culture and habits do you want to have in your classroom to
    encourage them to jump into the waters?

PART 4: HOW DO I CREATE A CULTURE WHERE READING THRIVES?

1. There's a popular saying in the business world: "Culture eats strategy for break-
    fast." How does it apply to the literacy classroom? What are the takeaways for your
    own classroom?

2. In her famous essay "Total Effect and the Eighth Grade," author Flannery
    O'Connor argued that "no one asks the student if algebra pleases him or if he
    finds it satisfactory that some French verbs are irregular, but if he prefers Hersey
    to Hawthorne, his taste must prevail."[4] Spar with O'Connor: What value do you
    give student choice vs. assigned texts in a literacy classroom?

3. In their seminal text *Metaphors We Live By*, George Lakoff and Mark Johnson dis-
    cuss metaphors that undergird our culture, like "time is money." They challenge
    readers to consider the social implications of these metaphors. (For example, sup-
    pose the metaphor "argument is war," was replaced by "argument is dance.") We
    often think of our responses to student papers as feedback—a type of reaction.
    But what if we changed the metaphor and thought of our responses as dialogue—
    a type of conversation? How might that shift the kinds of comments we write on
    students' papers?

4. Books like *The Sense of an Ending* and *The Remains of the Day* play with the
    reliability of our memories. But knowing that our memories aren't reliable—
    that they prioritize peak moments—gives us opportunities when we build class

culture. How can you create peak moments to help shape how students feel about your class and curriculum?

5. Steve recalls that when he was in middle school, he would look at how his teachers designed their rooms to determine what they were passionate about. If one of your students did this in your classroom, what might they conclude?

6. As you get started, what thoughts do you have about your own classroom? What do you want to try this month? Use the template we provide to create a draft plan.

Endnotes

INTRODUCTION

1. See "National and State Average Scores," The Nation's Report Card. National Center for Education Statistics, accessed 04 Nov. 2019, www.nationsreportcard.gov/highlights/reading /2019/. See "Fast Facts," Institute of Education Sciences, National Center for Education Statistics, accessed 18 March 2020, nces.ed.gov/fastfacts/display.asp?id=147.

2. Musu-Gillette, L., de Brey, C., McFarland, J., Hussar, W., Sonnenberg, W., and Wilkinson-Flicker, S., *Status and Trends in the Education of Racial and Ethnic Groups 2017* (NCES 2017-051). US Department of Education, National Center for Education Statistics. Washington, DC, https://nces.ed.gov/pubs2017/2017051.pdf.

3. "Country Note: Key Findings from PISA 2015 for the United States," Programme for International Student Assessment, Organisation for Economic Co-Operation and Development, 2016, www.oecd.org/pisa/PISA-2015-United-States.pdf.

4. Dorn, Emma, et al., "COVID-19 and Student Learning in the United States: The Hurt Could Last a Lifetime," McKinsey & Company, 1 June 2020, www.mckinsey.com/industries /public-and-social-sector/our-insights/covid-19-and-student-learning-in-the-united-states -the-hurt-could-last-a-lifetime.

5. "District Summary," Newark Board of Education, accessed 5 Nov. 2019, www.nps.k12.nj.us /departments/data-research/district-summary/.

6. North Star Academy, where Beth taught, pitted themselves against the rest of the world on the PISA test in 2012. If they were a nation, their literacy scores would have placed them in the top 10 in the world. Friedman, Thomas L., "My Little (Global) School," *New York Times*, 2 Apr. 2013 www.nytimes.com/2013/04/03/opinion/friedman-my-little-global -school.html?ref=thomaslfriedman.

7. The notion that reading is some type of magic is so popular it comes close to what George Lakoff and Mark Johnson might term a conceptual metaphor—one that governs the way we see the world. To be sure, literature has always been unapologetically soaked in the mystical. Consider the "origin story" of Ray Bradbury, who said he was inspired to write

by a mysterious magician called Mr. Electrico, who claimed he knew the then-adolescent Bradbury in a past life and challenged him to live forever. Bradbury became a 12-year-old writer the next day. No one can prove Mr. Electrico existed, which feels just as it should be. See Lakoff, George, and Mark Johnson, *Metaphors We Live By*. University of Chicago Press, 1980. See also Weller, Sam, "The Education of a Young Magician," *Slate Magazine*, 6 June 2012, slate.com/culture/2012/06/ray-bradbury-the-author-of-fahrenheit-451-recalls-the-visit-to-the-circus-that-changed-his-life.html, and Moser, Whet, "Ray Bradbury and the Search for Mr. Electrico," *Chicago Magazine*, 6 June 2012, www.chicagomag.com/Chicago-Magazine/The-312/June-2012/Ray-Bradbury-and-the-Search-for-Mr-Electrico/.

8. Beth's instincts have generally been borne out by cognitive science. In *The Reading Mind* (2017), Daniel Willingham notes that our reading self-concept can help generate a virtuous cycle: we see ourselves as readers, and we read more often and have a better attitude toward reading as a result. The more we read, the better we read, and the more we enjoy the process, and that helps cement our self-concept as readers. In 2020, a meta-analysis of researching on reading achievement and motivation found them to be mutually reinforcing, with early reading achievement having the greater effect. The authors note: "From a theoretical standpoint, the current study provides evidence to suggest that reading performance may be driving the development of motivation over time, although motivation can further influence continued reading development." See Toste, J. R., et al., "A Meta-analytic Review of the Relations Between Motivation and Reading Achievement for K–12 Students," *Review of Educational Research* vol. 90, no. 3, 2020. doi.org/10.3102/0034654320919352. See Willingham, Daniel T., *The Reading Mind: A Cognitive Approach to Understanding How the Mind Reads*, Jossey-Bass, 2017.

PART 1 INTRODUCTION

1. Toomer, Jean. "Portrait in Georgia." Poets.org, Academy of American Poets, poets.org/poem/portrait-georgia. For commentary, see also Bloom, Harold (Ed.), *Toni Morrison's The Bluest Eye*, Bloom's Literary Criticism, 2009.

2. Hanh, Thich Nhat, *How to Love*, Parallax Press, 2014, p 10.

3. Carroll, Lewis, *Alice's Adventures in Wonderland & Through the Looking-Glass*, Bantam, 2006.

CHAPTER ONE

1. Bishop, Rudine Sims. "Mirrors, Windows, and Sliding Glass Doors," *Perspectives: Choosing and Using Books for the Classroom*, The Ohio State University, vol. 6. no.3, Summer 1990, https://scenicregional.org/wp-content/uploads/2017/08/Mirrors-Windows-and-Sliding-Glass-Doors.pdf. See also Grace Lin's wonderful talk, which uses this metaphor to make some of the points about curricular complexity we discuss in Chapter 1. Lin, Grace, "The

Windows and Mirrors of Your Child's Bookshelf," *YouTube*, TEDx Talks, 18 Mar. 2016, www.youtube.com/watch?v=_wQ8wiV3FVo.

2. Although US students have grown increasingly diverse, our teaching population has remained predominantly white. Consider that in 2015–2016, four out of five teachers in elementary and secondary schools were white, a number that was virtually unchanged from 2003–2004. That means there is a pervasive, looming risk of our nation generating curricula that favors white (not to mention cisgender, heterosexual, non-disabled) voices at the diminishment of others. To pursue an inclusive pedagogy, this is a vulnerability we need to confront. Especially if we're white and especially if those in our care are children of color, or indigenous, or LGBTQ. As one example, consider that in GLSEN's 2017 school climate survey, fewer than 20% of LGBTQ students reported that they'd been taught positive representations of LGBTQ people, events, or history at school. See "Spotlight A: Characteristics of Public School Teachers by Race/Ethnicity," *Status and Trends in the Education of Racial and Ethnic Groups*, National Center for Education Statistics, Feb. 2019, nces.ed.gov/programs /raceindicators/spotlight_a.asp. See also See Kosciw, Joseph G., et al., GLSEN, 2018, *The 2017 National School Climate Survey: The Experiences of Lesbian, Gay, Bisexual, Transgender, and Queer Youth in Our Nation's Schools.*

3. Whaley, Kayla, "Why We Need Diverse Authors in Children's Literature," *Brightly: Raise Kids Who Love To Read*, Penguin Random House, 3 Feb. 2019, www.readbrightly.com/why -we-need-diverse-authors-in-kids-ya-lit/.

4. In our view, reevaluating the canon is not about "canceling" cherished texts. It's about telling the whole story: whether that's by inviting in new voices or by surfacing racism, sexism, classism, ableism, and homophobia with the same intentionality we afford any other aspect of curriculum. See Ebarvia, Tricia, "Disrupting Your Texts: Why Simply Including Diverse Voices Is Not Enough." *Literacy Today*, 2019, pp. 40–41.

5. As notes #DisruptTexts cofounder Lorena Germán (who still teaches *Mockingbird*), "In my classroom, the book is not placed or kept on a book pedestal. We lift it up, look under its pages, between its characters, and expose its gaps." See Germán, Lorena, "Disrupting 'To Kill a Mockingbird." *#DisruptTexts*, 2018, disrupttexts.org/2018/05/13/disrupting-to-kill -a-mockingbird/.

6. Macaluso, Kati, and Michael A. Macaluso, "Challenging the Canonical Genre." *Teaching the Canon in 21st Century Classrooms: Challenging Genres*, Brill/Sense, 2019, pp. ix–xx. Critical Literacy Teaching Series. See also Applebee, Arthur N., *Tradition and Reform in the Teaching of English: A History*. Urbana, IL: National Council of Teachers of English, 1976.

7. This is a documented issue both within the industry and regarding the authors whom it publishes. See "Where Is the Diversity in Publishing? The 2019 Diversity Baseline Survey Results," *The Open Book Blog: A Blog on Race, Diversity, Education, and Children's Books*, Lee and Low Books, 20 Jan. 2020, blog.leeandlow.com/2020/01/28/2019diversitybaseline survey/. See also Corrie, Jalissa, "The Diversity Gap in Children's Book Publishing, 2018,"

The Open Book Blog: A Blog on Race, Diversity, Education, and Children's Books, Lee and Low Books, 10 May 2018, blog.leeandlow.com/2018/05/10/the-diversity-gap-in-childrens-book-publishing-2018/.

8. Viswanathan, Gauri, *Masks of Conquest: Literary Study and British Rule in India*, Columbia University Press, 2015.

9. Twitty, Michael W. "Black People Were Denied Vanilla Ice Cream in the Jim Crow South—Except on Independence Day," *The Guardian*, 4 July 2014, www.theguardian.com/commentisfree/2014/jul/04/black-people-vanilla-ice-cream-jim-crow-independence-day. Accessed 7 May 2017.

10. "Reading Between the Lines: What the ACT Reveals about College Readiness in Reading," American College Testing, *ACT*, 2006, http://www.act.org/content/dam/act/unsecured/documents/reading_summary.pdf. Accessed 09 Apr. 2017.

11. Wilkins, Chuck, et al., "How Prepared Are Students for College-Level Reading? Applying a Lexile®-based Approach," Washington, DC: U.S. DOE, Institute of Education Sciences, National Center for Education Evaluation and Regional Assistance, Regional Educational Laboratories Southwest, 2010, https://eric.ed.gov/?id=ED513585.

12. Weiner, Ross, and Susan Pimentel, "Practice What You Teach: Connecting Curriculum and Professional Learning in Schools," Aspen Institute Education and Society Program, Aspen Institute, 2 April 2017, www.aspeninstitute.org/publications/practice-teach-connecting-curriculum-professional-learning-schools/. Accessed 4 May 2017. PDF download.

13. Adams, Marilyn Jager, "Advancing Our Students Language and Literacy—The Challenge of Complex Texts," *The American Educator*, vol. 34, no. 4, Winter 2010–2011, pp. 3–11.

14. McTighe, Jay and Grant P. Wiggins, "What Makes a Question Essential?" *Essential Questions: Opening Doors to Student Understanding*, ASCD, 2013, pp. 1–16.

15. For example, Steve worked with a planner on a 10th-grade curriculum with the essential question: "Are people inherently good or inherently wicked?" This choice allowed them to investigate this debate across centuries: ranging from Plato's "The Ring of Gyges" to Shelley's *Frankenstein*. While this choice excluded some texts, it created an opportunity to invite in others.

16. If we used these texts, which definitely present some of the more grim aspects of society, it would be important to balance them with additional examples of citizens fighting back and overcoming corrupt or oppressive governments.

17. Rabinowitz, Peter J., *Before Reading: Narrative Conventions and the Politics of Interpretation*, Cornell University Press, 1987, p. 231.

18. So, for example, when *The New Yorker* calls Whitman's "Song of Myself" a "clear antecedent" to Claudia Rankine's "Citizen," students will know what that means, why it might matter, and be able to decide whether or not they agree. See Chiasson, Dan, "Color Codes: A Poet Examines Race in America," *The New Yorker*, Condé Nast, 20 Oct. 2014, www.newyorker.com/magazine/2014/10/27/color-codes.

19. In *Why Don't Students Like School?*, cognitive scientist Daniel Willingham writes, "For reading, students must know whatever information writers assume they know and hence leave out. . . we may still be distressed that much of what writers assume their readers know seems to be touchstones of the culture of dead white males. From the cognitive scientist's point of view, the only choice in that case is to try to persuade writers and editors at *The Washington Post, Chicago Tribune* and so on to assume different knowledge on the part of their readers" (47). See Willingham, Daniel T., *Why Don't Students Like School? A Cognitive Scientist Answers Questions About How the Mind Works and What It Means for the Classroom*, Jossey-Bass, 2010.

20. Liben, David, "Text Complexity," *The SAT® Suite and Classroom Practice: English Language Arts/Literacy*, edited by Jim Patterson, College Board, 2020, pp. 9–29. Common Core State Standards Initiative. Common Core State Standards for English Language Arts & Literacy in History/Social Studies, Science, and Technical Subjects. Appendix A: http://www.corestandards.org/assets/Appendix_A.pdf.2020.

21. Lexile isn't the only measure of quantitative text complexity, though it's the most commercially used. Other measures of quantitative complexity can focus on things such as information density, referential or global cohesion, or even degree of narrativity. These measures provide a critical starting point for assessing text complexity, but they are incomplete on their own. See Liben, David. "Text Complexity." *The SAT® Suite and Classroom Practice: English Language Arts/ Literacy*, edited by Jim Patterson, College Board, 2020, pp 9–29.

22. Hat tip to Sarah Nager, a former colleague who made this quip in one of our English trainings. She was right to do so. While there are other readability measures besides Lexile, these face similar critiques. Indeed, "readability measures are often criticized for excluding key aspects of what makes a text difficult (Hiebert & Pearson, 2014): the reader's familiarity with the topic and vocabulary, the concreteness of ideas and overall cohesiveness of a text, and the formality of language." See Lupo, Sarah M., et al., "Struggle Is Not a Bad Word: Misconceptions and Recommendations About Readers Struggling with Difficult Texts," *Journal of Adolescent and Adult Literacy*, vol. 62, no. 5, March/April 2019, pp. 551–560.

23. Common Core State Standards Initiative, *Common Core State Standards for English Language Arts & Literacy in History/Social Studies, Science, and Technical Subjects.* Appendix A: http://www.corestandards.org/assets/Appendix_A.pdf.2020.

24. Minot, Stephen, *Three Genres: The Writing of Poetry, Fiction, and Drama.* Prentice Hall, 2002.

25. Lemov, Doug, et al. "The Five Plagues of the Developing Reader," *Reading Reconsidered: A Practical Guide to Rigorous Literacy Instruction*, Jossey-Bass, 2016, pp. 29–44.

26. Wolpert-Gawron, Heather, "Engaging Teen Writers Through Authentic Tasks." *Educational Leadership*, ACSD, May 2019, www.ascd.org/publications/educational-leadership/may19/vol76/num08/Engaging-Teen-Writers-Through-Authentic-Tasks.aspx.

CHAPTER TWO

1. "The 100 Best Books of the 21st Century." *The Guardian*, Guardian News and Media, 21 Sept. 2019, www.theguardian.com/books/2019/sep/21/best-books-of-the-21st-century.

2. Chute, Hillary L. and Alison Bechdel, "An Interview with Alison Bechdel." *MFS Modern Fiction Studies*, vol. 52 no. 4, 2006, p. 1004–1013, *Project MUSE*, doi:10.1353/mfs.2007.0003.

3. It would be fair to argue that "getting" a text this way isn't the only purpose one might have for reading, and that "experiencing" a text can be just as valid. We agree. Our position, though, is that students are best served when they have the ability to do both.

4. Technically, *schema* refers to units of knowledge that can be categorized or interrelated. There is a large body of work around schema and schema theory in psychology and cognitive science.

5. Hirsch, E. D., "Reading-Comprehension Skills? What Are They Really?" *Education Week*, Editorial Projects in Education, 25 Apr. 2006, www.edweek.org/ew/articles/2006/04/26/33hirsch.h25.html.

6. Kant, Immanuel, *The Critique of Pure Reason*, Translated by John D. Meiklejohn, Project Gutenberg, E-Book 4280, 2003, http://gutenberg.org/ebooks/4280.

7. If you're a big fan of schema, then you probably already know about the 1988 "baseball study" on it. In it, 7th- and 8th-grade students with high prior knowledge about baseball were far more successful understanding a passage than stronger readers who did not. See: Recht, Donna R., and Lauren Leslie, "Effect of Prior Knowledge on Good and Poor Readers' Memory of Text," *Journal of Educational Psychology*, vol. 80, no. 1, 1988, pp. 16–20, doi:10.1037/0022-0663.80.1.16. For another example, read this oft-cited passage from a 1970s study on background knowledge. What mysterious procedure does it describe? *The procedure is actually quite simple. First you arrange things into different groups depending on their makeup. Of course, one pile may be sufficient depending on how much there is to do. If you have to go somewhere else due to lack of facilities that is the next step, otherwise you are pretty well set. It is important not to overdo any particular endeavor. That is, it is better to do too few things at once than too many. In the short run this may not seem important, but complications from doing too many can easily arise. A mistake can be expensive as well. The manipulation of the appropriate mechanisms should be self-explanatory, and we need not dwell on it here. At first the whole procedure will seem complicated. Soon, however, it will become just another facet of life. It is difficult to foresee any end to the necessity for this task in the immediate future, but then one never can tell.* Stumped? The answer is laundry. Go ahead, reread it. On the second reading, these seemingly vague instructions read crystal clear. That's the power of background knowledge. It illuminates what we read by giving us a framework to help process text. See Bransford, John D. and Marcia K. Johnson, "Contextual Prerequisites for Understanding: Some Investigations of Comprehension and Recall," *Journal of Verbal Learning and Verbal Behavior*, vol. 11, no. 6, 1972, pp. 717–726., doi:10.1016/s0022-5371(72)80006-9. In *Uncommon Core*, Michael Smith, Deborah Appleman, and Jeffrey Wilhelm cite this study to make the case for activating

prior knowledge during lesson launch, which we will discuss in Part 3. See also Smith, Michael W., et al., *Uncommon Core: Where the Authors of the Standards Go Wrong a\About Instruction—and How You Can Get It Right*, Corwin, 2014.

8. Willingham, Daniel T., *Raising Kids Who Read: What Parents and Teachers Can Do*, Jossey-Bass, 2015, p. 20.

9. This "Matthew Effect" has been used to describe both word knowledge and general schema. In short, it describes the virtuous (or vicious) cycle for children: the more you already know, the easier it is to learn more. Consider that "there's virtually no limit to how much learning we can remember as long as we relate it to what we already know. In fact, because new learning depends on prior learning, the more we learn, the more possible connections we create for future learning" (76). See Brown, Peter C., et al., *Make It Stick: The Science of Successful Learning*, The Belknap Press, 2014.

10. Lemov, Doug, "Knowledge Powers Reading," *Educational Leadership*, February 2017, vol 74, no. 5. pp. 10–16.

11. See Willingham, Daniel T., *Why Don't Students like School? A Cognitive Scientist Answers Questions about How the Mind Works and What It Means for the Classroom*, Jossey-Bass, 2010. As one additional example, in the earliest pages of *A Portrait of the Artist as Young Man*, Joyce shows adults singing "oh the wild rose blossoms" with a child, and then writes "oh the gween wothe botheth." English students may not immediately realize that what Joyce is doing is writing what it sounds like when the child sings the same song—but the tools they need to solve the puzzle are on the page, and the ideal teaching move is to try to get them to solve it themselves. *Animal Farm*, on the other hand, is easier to read but assumes a good deal of knowledge about twentieth-century geopolitics. Literacy experts Kylene Beers and Robert Probst encourage students to consider the question "What did the author think I already knew?" as a way to defang the confrontation with their own gaps in background knowledge. See Beers, Kylene, and Robert E. Probst, *Reading Nonfiction: Notice & Note Stances, Signposts, and Strategies*, Heinemann, 2016.

12. Lemov, Doug, "Bloom's Taxonomy—That Pyramid Is a Problem," *Teach Like a Champion: Doug Lemov's Field Notes*, Uncommon Schools/Wiley, 3 Apr. 2017, teachlikeachampion. com/blog/blooms-taxonomy-pyramid-problem/.

13. Christodoulou cites Hirsch, arguing that a better metaphor for thinking about background knowledge and comprehension is scrambled eggs: the egg white and yolk aren't getting separated anytime soon. See Christodoulou, Daisy, *Seven Myths About Education*, Routledge, 2014.

14. Adams, Marilyn Jager, "Advancing our Students' Language and Literacy—The Challenge of Complex Texts," *American Educator*, Winter 2010–2011, pp. 3–11.

15. Newton's quip itself is a rebranding of a metaphor attributed to Bernard of Chartres some 500 years prior. Shoulders of giants, indeed!

16. For a discussion of knowledge building and *Macbeth*, see: Chiger, Stephen, "Teach Background Knowledge? Yes! But What Type? Steve Chiger on 4 Kinds of Knowledge," *Teach*

Like a Champion: Doug Lemov's Field Notes, Uncommon Schools/Wiley, 1 May 2018, teachlikeachampion.com/blog/teach-background-knowledge-yes-type-steve-chiger -4-kinds-knowledge/.

17. Hat tip to our colleague Kelly Dowling, who refers to this as thematic schema.

18. This work is both promising and new. Even as we write this book, folks at the Johns Hopkins Institute for Education Policy are developing new tools to help English instructors evaluate how well their curriculum builds schema. See Pondiscio, Robert, "New 'Knowledge Mapping' Tool Evaluates English Language Arts Curricula," *Education Next*, Program on Education Policy and Governance, Harvard Kennedy School For Government, 14 Feb. 2019, www.educationnext.org/new-knowledge-mapping-tool-evaluates-english-language -arts-curricula/.

19. There are numerous sites for review. They include:

   - Newsela: https://newsela.com/

   - CommonLit: https://www.commonlit.org/

   - Smithsonian TweenTribune: https://www.tweentribune.com/

   - Actively Learn: https://www.activelylearn.com/

   - Student Achievement Partners: https://achievethecore.org/ (search for "text set")

   - Student Achievement Partners' Book Basket Project: https://achievethecore.org/ (search for "book basket")

   - Unbounded: https://www.unbounded.org/ (search "text set")

20. While this debate continues today, reignited by the publication of Lee's *Go Set a Watchman*, it was the subject of a number of law journal articles in the 1990s.

21. While the power of knowledge for reading isn't in dispute, researchers still question how much we should use, when and how. For a discussion of the dangers of relying exclusively on knowledge instruction, see Timothy Shanahan's blog post "Prior Knowledge, or He Isn't Going to Pick on the Baseball Study." In it, Shanahan writes: "That's where strategies come in. They let readers in on the secret that if you are intentional and strategic you can make sense of texts, even if you lack the background for them." See Shanahan, Timothy, "Prior Knowledge, or He Isn't Going to Pick the Baseball Study," *Shanahan on Literacy*, 14 Mar. 2020, shanahanonliteracy.com/blog/prior-knowledge-or-he-isnt-going-to-pick-on-the-baseball-study. Researcher Mark Seidenberg makes a separate but related point involving the intercedence of knowledge and basic reading skills. See Seidenberg, Mark, "Some Context on Context," *Reading Matters*, 10 Sept. 2020, https://seidenbergreading. net/2020/09/10/some-context-on-context/.

22. Pace, David, "Decoding the Reading of History: An Example of the Process," *New Directions for Teaching and Learning*, vol. 2004, no. 98, 2004, pp. 13–21.

23. Gholipour, Bahar, "Case Is Closed: Multivitamins Are a Waste of Money, Doctors Say," *LiveScience*, Future US, 16 Dec. 2013, www.livescience.com/42001-case-is-closed -multivitamins-are-a-waste-of-money-doctors-say.html.

24. That is, if you read enough detective novels, you'll know where to focus and where you can skim. Rabinowitz points to a humorous example, noting how Mark Twain, in *A Double-Barreled Detective Story*, played off his readers' assumption that they could "skim nature description in a nineteenth-century detective story." So, Twain wrote a description that is just a bunch of nonsense, crowned by the presence of a floating esophagus. (Yes, you read that correctly.) Twain, Rabinowitz reports, was surprised that no one could find it and had to resort to a footnote telling readers to read carefully so they'd get the joke (57). We know you're curious; so here's the passage: "It was a crisp and spicy morning in early October. The lilacs and laburnums, lit with the glory-fires of autumn, hung burning and flashing in the upper air, a fairy bridge provided by kind nature for the wingless wild things that have their home in the tree-tops and would visit together; the larch and the pomegranate flung their purple and yellow flames in brilliant broad splashes along the slanting sweep of woodland, the sensuous fragrance of innumerable deciduous flowers rose upon the swooning atmosphere, far in the empty sky a solitary oesophagus slept upon motionless wing; everywhere brooded stillness, serenity, and the peace of God." See Rabinowitz, Peter J., *Before Reading: Narrative Conventions and the Politics of Interpretation*, Cornell University Press, 1987.

25. Arieh-Lerer, Shon, and Daniel Hubbard, "Lucy, You Got Some Splainin' to Do," *Slate Magazine*, Slate Group, 12 Dec. 2016, www.slate.com/articles/video/brow_beat/2016/12/all_sitcoms_from_i_love_lucy_to_seinfeld_to_arrested_development_use_the.html.

26. Wilhelm, Jeffrey D., and Michael W. Smith, *Diving Deep into Nonfiction: Transferable Tools for Reading Any Nonfiction Text: Grades 6–12*. Corwin, 2017.

27. Johnston, Peter, and Peter Afflerbach. "The Process of Constructing Main Ideas from Text," *Cognition and Instruction*, vol. 2, no. 3/4, 1985, pp. 207–232, doi:10.1207/s1532690xci0203&4_2. In 2017, the topic-comment strategy—along with the notion of "readers rules of notice" was expanded on by Jeffrey Wilhelm and Michael Smith using mechanisms that inspired and informed the ones you see in this book. See Wilhelm, Jeffrey D., and Michael W. Smith, *Diving Deep into Nonfiction: Transferable Tools for Reading Any Nonfiction Text: Grades 6–12*, Corwin, 2017.

28. When written as sentences, direct claims often use key phrases like "in other words" or "similarly" to signal that the author is consolidating or recapitulating a previous point.

29. Beers, Kylene, and Robert E. Probst, *Reading Nonfiction: Notice & Note Stances, Signposts, and Strategies*, Heinemann, 2016.

30. "Beast Mode" is a term that comes from the career of American football player Marshawn Lynch. The phrase characterizes his all-in approach to overcoming challenges on the field.

31. Tantalus is a king from Greek mythology who was punished in a particularly terrible way: he was condemned to stand in Hades in a pool of water, just under the branches of a fruit tree. When he reached for the branches they would shift away, and when he tried to scoop up water, it would recede. Thus, Tantalus was always hungry and thirsty, with nourishment just outside of reach. The word "tantalize" takes its meaning from his terrible fate.

32. See Coleridge, Samuel T., *Biographia Literaria*, New York: American Book Exchange, 1881, p. 145. Hat tip to Thomas Newkirk, in whose *The Art of Slow Reading* we first encountered

this gem of a quote along with a discussion of the value of "teaching by contrast." See Newkirk, Thomas, *The Art of Slow Reading: Six Time-Honored Practices for Engagement*, Heinemann, 2012.

33. Lemov, Driggs and Woolway write about this briefly in *Reading Reconsidered*, referring to it as sensitivity analysis. In their example, a teacher asks students to consider why Lois Lowry has Jonas's father refer to a baby as a "shrimp" (as opposed to "little guy"). See Lemov, Doug, et al., *Reading Reconsidered: A Practical Guide to Rigorous Literacy Instruction*, Jossey-Bass, 2016, pp. 29–44.

34. Perhaps one of the things that makes this type of analysis so powerful is that our brains are built for it. In *Reader, Come Home,* researcher Maryanne Wolf writes, "Our words contain and momentarily activate whole repositories of associated meanings, and feelings, even when the exact meaning in a given context is specified. . . every word can elicit an entire history of meanings, myriad connections, associations, and long-stored emotions. . . the reading brain activates in a half a second something akin to the daily efforts of poets and writes to find the perfect word, the mot juste" (33). Essentially, our minds do the same gymnastics as great writers when they weigh the possible meanings and connotations of words—in milliseconds! No wonder literary analysis can feel so rewarding—it taps into something deep and instinctive in our consciousness. See Wolf, Maryanne, *Reader, Come Home: The Reading Brain in a Digital World*, Harper, 2018.

35. One benefit of zooming in comes in terms of vocabulary acquisition. While many first think of *breadth* of word knowledge when discussing vocabulary, student skill is also bolstered by understanding *depth* of words—why an author might have chosen one word over another. See Liben, David, "The Importance of Vocabulary and Knowledge in Comprehension," *The SAT® Suite and Classroom Practice: English Language Arts/Literacy*, edited by Jim Patterson, College Board, 2020, pp. 53–69.

36. The poem is called "Identity" and it's terrific.

37. It's easy here to fall into the trap of authorial intent, simply relying on asking students what the author's purpose is. Although speculating on the author's purpose is certainly one way to look at craft, it isn't the only way. Sometimes zooming out will sound like students discussing the effect a craft move has on them as a reader, or on the text or chapter as a whole. Regardless of your take on authorial intent, zoom-outs should allow students to flexibly answer not just the "why" but the "so what" when they discuss evidence. As Neil Gaiman reminds us in his introduction to *Fahrenheit 451*, "An author's opinions of what a story is about are always valid and are always true: the author was there, after all, when the book was written. She came up with each word and knows why she used that word instead of another. But an author is a creature of her time, and even she cannot see everything that her book is about." See Gaiman, Neil, Introduction. *Fahrenheit 451*, by Ray Bradbury, Simon & Schuster, 2012, pp. xi–xvi.

38. Author Junot Díaz's treatment of women has been called out as part of the #metoo movement. In Mike's class, students study and discuss this controversy along with *Oscar Wao's* exploration of toxic masculinity.

PART 1 CONCLUSION

1. This isn't just aspirational thinking, it's actively being studied by cognitive scientists. According to Annie Murphy Paul, "The brain, it seems, does not make much of a distinction between reading about an experience and encountering it in real life; in each case, the same neurological regions are stimulated. . . . Reading great literature, it has long been averred, enlarges and improves us as human beings. Brain science shows this claim is truer than we imagined." See Paul, Annie Murphy. "Your Brain on Fiction," *The New York Times*, 17 Mar. 2012, www.nytimes.com/2012/03/18/opinion/sunday/the-neuroscience-of-your-brain-on-fiction.html.

PART 2 INTRODUCTION

1. In 2018, for example, Angela helped lead the 6th-grade team at her school to 83% proficiency on the PARCC assessment. By comparison, New Jersey's non-economically-disadvantaged students were 68% proficient that year. Nationally, only 41% of children scored proficient. In 2017, Stanford's Center for Research on Education Outcomes reported the gains of the North Star Newark schools (where Angela was teaching) as being equivalent to around 4.5 months of additional literacy instruction. See Woodworth, James L., et al., *Charter Management Organizations 2017*, CREDO, 2017, credo.stanford.edu/sites/g/files/sbiybj6481/f/cmo_final.pdf.

CHAPTER THREE

1. Bambrick-Santoyo, Paul, and Stephen Chiger. "Until I Write It Down," *Educational Leadership*, vol 74. no. 5, Feb. 2017, pp. 46–50.
2. Saphier, Jon, et al., *The Skillfull Teacher: The Comprehensive Resource for Improving Teaching and Learning*, Research for Better Teaching, 2018, pp 255–257.
3. Bambrick-Santoyo, Paul, *Driven by Data 2.0: A Practical Guide to Improve Instruction*, Jossey-Bass, 2019, p. 22.
4. Please note, this is after reading and experiencing the poem itself, which—as we'll discuss later in this chapter—is always our first step with students.
5. See "Gaining Understanding on What Your Students Know," *Edutopia*, George Lucas Educational Foundation, 23 June 2015, www.edutopia.org/practice/exit-tickets-checking-understanding. See also Marzano, Robert J., "Art and Science of Teaching/The Many Uses of Exit Slips," *Educational Leadership*, vol 70. no. 2, Oct. 2012, pp. 80–81.
6. "Students will rise to the level of our expectations" was a favorite phrase of Linda Green, Steve's first mentor. For teachers, these are words to live by.
7. Alston, C. L. and M. T. Brown, "Differences in Intellectual Challenge of Writing Tasks Among Higher and Lower Value-Added English Language Arts Teachers." *Teachers College Record*, vol. 117, no. 5, 2015, pp. 1–24.

8. Just ask medieval monks, who would scribble anything from scatological pictures to phrases like "Now I've written the whole thing: for Christ's sake give me a drink." (So much for "illuminating" the manuscript.) See Dickey, Colin, "Living in the Margins," *Lapham's Quarterly*, American Agora Foundation, 22 Mar. 2012, www.laphamsquarterly.org/roundtable /living-margins.

9. Listing a variety of literacy benefits, Carol Porter O'Donnell concludes in a 2004 *The English Journal* article that, "Marking a text while reading is something that readers do outside of school; it is what we need to do with students in school, too." See Porter-O'Donnell, Carol, "Beyond the Yellow Highlighter: Teaching Annotation Skills to Improve Reading Comprehension," *The English Journal*, vol. 93, no. 5, 2004, p. 82., doi:10.2307/4128941. Doug Lemov and our colleagues on Uncommon's Teach Like a Champion team ascribe so much importance to annotation that they rebranded it "interactive reading." In *Reading Reconsidered,* they write, "It was clear to us that there was power in this system, that it should become as much a part of reading as turning the page or reading lines from left to right" (Lemov et al., p. 291). As our colleague Sarah Tantillo writes: "Annotation works. And although it may take a little extra time, it's time well spent. . ." (65). See "Annotation," *The Literacy Cookbook: A Practical Guide to Effective Reading, Writing, Speaking, and Listening Instruction*, by Sarah Tantillo, Jossey-Bass, 2013.

10. Consider the discovery scholars made in 2019: Milton's copy of Shakespeare. This didn't have marginalia, just underlines, but their response to this discovery is rather telling. As he began to realize what he'd uncovered, Cambridge fellow Jason Scott-Warren became "quite trembly. . . You're gathering evidence with your heart in your mouth." He noted that the underlines alone "give[s] you a sense of his sensitivity and alertness to Shakespeare. What's quite remarkable as well is that he's singled out for attention lots of the passages that have become incredibly famous—he goes through and marks out some of the most celebrated Shakespearean speeches." See Flood, Allison, "When Milton Met Shakespeare: Poet's Notes on Bard Appear to Have Been Found," *The Guardian*. 16 Sep 2019, https://www.theguardian .com/books/2019/sep/16/when-milton-met-shakespeare-poets-notes-on-bard-appear-to -have-been-found.

11. This was an adaptation of activist Emma Gonzalez's famous "We Call B.S." speech delivered after the mass shooting at Marjory Stoneman Douglas High School in 2018. Mallory located the adaptation on Newsela.com, a terrific website that provides texts at multiple complexity levels.

12. Hat tip to educator Dan Pereira, who shared this concise definition with Steve years ago.

13. "The Debt," by Paul Laurence Dunbar, is in the public domain and can be found in *The Project Gutenberg EBook of The Complete Poems of Paul Laurence Dunbar*, by Paul Laurence Dunbar, p. 213.

14. Amma has "zoomed in" on the falcon metaphor, an analytical move we introduced in Chapter 1.

CHAPTER FOUR

1. Lemov, Doug, *Teach like a Champion 2.0: 62 Techniques That Put Students on the Path to College*, Jossey-Bass, 2015.

2. There are other advantages to this setup. For example, Mallory can easily move the class to heterogeneous groups of four. Mallory can also say "Turn and talk—door-side first!" knowing that she is actually asking for students of a selected proficiency level to begin the turn and talk. Finally, notice that the proficiency difference between partners is never so great that it might create frustration for either student.

3. Lamott, Anne, *Bird by Bird: Some Instructions on Writing and Life*, Anchor Books, 2019.

4. It can be tempting to use independent work time as a chance to connect more deeply with individual students, but the biggest drawback is how few students you can reach in a given classroom. This keeps the remaining students from getting feedback and also keeps you from seeing the trend in struggle that the students are having that could be addressed in the moment. While you should still make time to conference with students, reserve these check-ins for longer moments when you can be fully present.

5. Kelly's approach really benefited students. In the 2017–2018 school year (the last year Kelly was principal before becoming an assistant superintendent), her middle school students outperformed the average for non-economically-disadvantaged students in every grade (5–8). From 6th grade on, they did this by double digits.

PART 3 INTRODUCTION

1. Picoult is a former 8th-grade English teacher. It's quite possible that this insight came from her classroom experience. Picoult, Jodie, *House Rules*, Atria Books, 2010, p. 453.

2. Whitman, Walt, *Leaves of Grass,* First Avenue Editions, 1892, n.p.

3. Hat tip to our colleague Aly Ross, who shared this neologism, coined by one of their high school teachers years ago.

4. This research "found that high academic demands and discussion-based approaches were significantly related to spring performance, with controls for initial literacy levels, gender, socioeconomic status, and race/ethnicity." See Applebee, Arthur N., et al., "Discussion-Based Approaches to Developing Understanding: Classroom Instruction and Student Performance in Middle and High School English." *American Educational Research Journal*, vol. 40, no. 3, 2003, pp. 685–730, doi:10.3102/00028312040003685.

CHAPTER FIVE

1. Britton, James N., *Writing and Reading in the Classroom*. Center for the Study of Writing, University of California-Berkley/Carnegie Mellon, 1988.

2. Wolf, Maryanne, *Proust and the Squid: the Story and Science of the Reading Brain*, Harper Perennial, 2008.

3. In its literature review, this study notes that discourse is often defined by what it isn't, rather than what it *is*. We think that's at the root of a gap in how it occurs in class. See Lawrence, Joshua F., et al., "Word Generation Randomized Trial: Discussion Mediates the Impact of Program Treatment on Academic Word Learning," University of California-Irvine, 09 Apr. 2015, doi.org/10.3102/0002831215579485. Accessed 31 Mar. 2017.

4. Davis, Viola, "Viola Davis on Acting," *YouTube*, uploaded by Bafta Guru, 1 Feb. 2017, www.youtube.com/watch?v=a-f4DDnGSBc.

5. We're indebted to mathematics researchers, who first coined this term. Its resonance allowed it to be quickly adopted in the world of literacy. See Fisher, Douglas, and Nancy Frey, "Show & Tell: A Video Column/The Importance of Struggle," *Educational Leadership*, ASCD, vol. 74, no.8, May 2017, www.ascd.org/publications/educational-leadership/may17/vol74/num08/The-Importance-of-Struggle.aspx.

6. Vygotsky, L. S., *Mind in Society: The Development of Higher Psychological Processes*, Harvard University Press, 1980.

7. Lemov, Doug, "Sadie McCleary's Guide to Making and Using Knowledge Organizers," *Teach Like a Champion: Doug Lemov's Field Notes*, Uncommon Schools/Wiley, 27 Aug. 2018, teach-likeachampion.com/blog/sadie-mcclearys-guide-making-using-knowledge-organizers/.

8. Hat tip to Steve's 12th-grade English teacher, Charlie Soriano, who must have spent hours perfecting it. Charlie's handbook is the inspiration for the one that's included with this book.

9. Smith, Michael W., et al., *Uncommon Core: Where the Authors of the Standards Go Wrong about Instruction—And How You Can Get It Right*, Corwin Literacy, 2014, p. 47.

10. When you do this, it's important to move quickly and correctly, because the start of class is the most important time to lock in new learning. If students forget a term or idea, that's the right moment to shift to a resource or provide a definition. To wit, educational neuroscience consultant David Sousa writes "I remember watching a teacher of English start a class with, 'Today, we are going to learn about a new literary form called *onomatopoeia*. Does anyone have any idea what that is?'" After several wrong guesses, the teacher finally defined it. Regrettably, those same wrong guesses appeared in the follow-up test. And why not? They were mentioned during the most powerful [opportunity for] retention. . ." See Sousa, David A., *How the Brain Learns*, SAGE Publications, 2016.

11. Writing at the Teach Like a Champion team's blog, Ashley LaGrassa reminds us of the value of making sure students know this opening prompt is not a test, but rather an invitation. Sometimes a shift as simple as adding the word "might" to your opening class prompt can do the trick. See LaGrassa, Ashley, "How Formative Writing Built Buy-In and Engagement," *Teach Like a Champion: Doug Lemov's Field Notes*, Uncommon Schools/Wiley, 6 Mar. 2018, teachlikeachampion.com/blog/ashley-la-grassa-formative-writing-improved-classes/.

12. A common metaphor for student discussion is that it should be volleyball (student-student) rather than ping-pong (student-teacher-student-teacher). We're not sure where this metaphor originated, but it's a handy way to conceptualize the difference between student-led conversation and a teacher-driven one.

13. One study estimated that for every hour of middle and high school instruction, fewer than two minutes were spent in classroom discussions. That's simply not enough time for our students to struggle with text, productively or otherwise. See Applebee, Arthur N., et al, "Discussion-Based Approaches to Developing Understanding: Classroom Instruction and Student Performance in Middle and High School English," *American Educational Research Journal*, vol. 40, no. 3, 2003, pp. 685–730.

CHAPTER SIX

1. Wray, John, "Haruki Murakami: The Art of Fiction CLXXXII," *Paris Review*, no. 170, Summer 2004, pp. 115–151.

2. Eric has been greatly influenced by our colleague Doug Lemov, who writes about the power of having a set of conversational habits and expectations. See Lemov, Doug, *Teach Like a Champion 2.0: 62 Techniques That Put Students on the Path to College*, Jossey-Bass, 2015. A tip of the hat, also, to our colleagues Matthew McCluskey, Sean Gavin, and Laura Palumbo, who assembled the foundations of this work as part of a fellowship with Stanford University.

3. While the term's precise meaning is still unsettled, Danny's definition matches a common one that can be found in the Merriam-Webster Dictionary.

4. To be clear, we didn't invent moves like "revoice" whole cloth. Researchers have identified this and many of the other moves you'll read about in this chapter as some of the most effective for student talk. These are time-tested moves, many of which you probably already use. See Sineath, Karl D., et al., "The Effect of Classroom Discourse on High School Students' Argumentative Writing Skills," Northeastern University, 2014, pp. 21–49, hdl. handle.net/2047/d20005052.

5. Herron, Frank, "It's a MUCH More Effective Quotation to Attribute It to Aristotle, Rather Than to Will Durant," *The Art of "Quotemanship" and "Misquotemanship,"* UMass Boston, 2012, blogs.umb.edu/quoteunquote/2012/05/08/its-a-much-more-effective-quotation -to-attribute-it-to-aristotle-rather-than-to-will-durant/.

6. Simply put, "retrieval practice" refers to the act of recalling facts and ideas. Consider, "Some people never seem to learn. One difference, perhaps, between those who do and don't is whether they have cultivated the habit of reflection. *Reflection is a form of retrieval practice.* (What happened? What did I do? How did it work out?), enhanced with elaboration (What would I do differently next time?)" (66). See Brown, Peter C., et al., *Make It Stick: The Science of Successful Learning*, The Belknap Press, 2014.

7. *Ferris Bueller's Day Off*, Directed by John Hughes, Paramount Pictures, 1986.

8. Used by permission of the author. You can find this poem online or in Jones's chapbook. See Jones, Saeed, *When the Only Light Is Fire*, Sibling Rivalry Press, 2011.

9. In the first years of his poetry career, Jones has already won the Pushcart Prize, Kirkus Prize, and was a finalist for the National Book Critics Circle Award. We highly recommend *Prelude to Bruise*, one of his poetry collections!

PART 4 INTRODUCTION

1. This vignette is based on a visit Steve did at Clinton Hill Middle School in 2018. He was there to observe instruction, but the discussion and spelling bee really did happen. It was a beautiful surprise.

CHAPTER SEVEN

1. Willingham, Daniel T., *Raising Kids Who Read: What Parents and Teachers Can Do*, Jossey-Bass, 2015.

2. Johnston, Peter H., *Choice Words: How Our Language Affects Children's Learning*, Stenhouse Publishers, 2004, p.79.

3. See, for example, Yoon, Jun-Chae, "Three Decades of Sustained Silent Reading: A Meta-analytic Review of the Effects of SSR on Attitude Toward Readin," *Reading Improvement*, vol. 39, no. 4, Winter 2002. *In Raising Kids Who Read* (Jossey Bass, 2015), cognitive scientist Daniel Willingham acknowledges that there isn't clear data that this practice will work, only that it "probably improves attitudes, vocabulary, and comprehension." Still, he endorses it, writing that, "I think the squishiness of the findings is attributable to the difficulty of the teaching method. I'm sure classroom pleasure reading is easy to implement poorly: stick some books in the room, allocate some class time and you're done" (173). He continues to suggest that educators and parents may not view independent reading time as legitimate in classrooms, sabotaging the practice as well.

4. While there are several great books on developing independent reading programs, the principles named in *No More Independent Reading Without Support* are clear and specific, and they make for a great starting point. They are reflected in this list. See Miller, Debbie and Barbara Moss, *No More Independent Reading Without Support*, Heinemann, 2013.

5. Research suggests that using text sets has real value for vocabulary development, suggesting that student word acquisition grows by as much as four times faster when texts are conceptually linked (versus when they jump between topics). See Liben, David, "The Importance of Vocabulary and Knowledge in Comprehension." *The SAT® Suite and Classroom Practice: English Language Arts/Literacy*, edited by Jim Patterson, College Board, 2020, pp. 53–69.

6. Resources for the Book Basket project can be found here: achievethecore.org/page/3081 /book-basket-project. For a discussion of grouping books by qualitative dimensions, see Lesesne, Teri S., *Reading Ladders: Leading Students from Where They Are to Where We'd Like Them to Be*, Heinemann, 2010.

7. Allington, Richard, and Rachel E. Gabriel, "Every Child, Every Day," *Educational Leadership*, ASCD, vol. 69, no. 6, Mar. 2012, http://www.ascd.org/publications/educational -leadership/mar12/vol69/num06/Every-Child,-Every-Day.aspx.

8. Alongside the earlier research in this chapter's endnotes, see Shanahan, Timothy, "Sorting Out the Arguments Over 'Independent' Reading," *Reading Rockets*, WETA, 17 Aug. 2015. Accessed 1 Apr. 2017.

9. Cron, Lisa, "Wired for Story: Lisa Cron at TEDxFurmanU." YouTube, TEDxTalks, 4 May 2014, www.youtube.com/watch?v=74uv0mJS0uM.

10. Heath, Chip and Dan Heath, *The Power of Moments: Why Certain Experiences Have Extraordinary Impact*, Simon & Schuster, 2017.

11. Michael Schlar, a celebrated principal at Brooklyn's William Alexander Middle School, lived next door to Steve's childhood home. As a new instructional leader, Steve asked him how to make change in a school. Schlar told him to create pockets of success with the most enthusiastic and risk-ready colleagues. It's easy to resist top-down initiatives, he told Steve, but once people see success, they get hungry to share it with their own students. Momentum doesn't need to come by fiat.

12. Sharma, Sharanya, "The Power of Reading Out Loud." BOOK RIOT, Riot New Media, 14 Sept. 2015, bookriot.com/2015/09/15/the-power-of-reading-out-loud/.

13. Our colleague, Doug Lemov, an indefatigable champion of reading out loud, reminds us that it's a moment to build fluency and comprehension in the face of challenging syntax, too. See Lemov, Doug, "TES Talks to. . . Education Guru Doug Lemov," *Tes Magazine*, 9 Sept. 2016, pp. 36–38, www.tes.com/news/tes-talks-education-guru-doug-lemov.

14. Muhammad, Gholdy, *Cultivating Genius: An Equity Framework for Culturally and Historically Responsive Literacy*, Scholastic, 2020, p. 78.

15. This question wasn't asked off-handedly—it was a deliberate part of her lesson plan. Credit goes to Sarah Schrag, who shared these plans with Julie and others to promote strong AP Language instruction across our high schools.

16. Arthur Shimamura, professor emeritus of psychology at the University of California, Berkeley, makes this case: "I believe that teachers should ask this question to students as often as possible: Did you like the novel? Who were your favorite characters? . . . By its very nature, the aesthetic question is open-ended as there is no right or wrong answer. The aesthetic question engages emotional brain circuits and forces us to attend to and organize our knowledge." See Shimamura, Arthur, *MARGE: A Whole-Brain Learning Approach for Students and Teachers*, CreateSpace Independent Publishing Platform, 2018. His comments recall the work of educational scholar Louise Rosenblatt, who wrote of two "stances" we take as readers—efferent and aesthetic. Rather than warring sides, these

work as a continuum, with efferent reading (reading to gather information) on one end and aesthetic reading (reading for our personal experience with the text) on the other. In their 2017 book *Disrupting Thinking*, Kylene Beers and Robert Probst remind readers of Rosenblatt's work, cautioning, "If efferent reading is all we teach kids, if we convince them that reading is only for extracting, then we will have failed to teach them that texts are not simply repositories of facts" (43). See Beers, Kylene, and Robert E. Probst, *Disrupting Thinking: Why How We Read Matters*, Scholastic, 2017.

17. Hat tip to Ayanna Taylor, clinical assistant professor of English education at NYU and Shana Pyatt, Uncommon's director of diversity, equity, and inclusion for making this initial suggestion.

18. Hammond, Zaretta, *Culturally Responsive Teaching and the Brain: Promoting Authentic Engagement and Rigor Among Culturally and Linguistically Diverse Students*, Corwin, 2015, p. 102.

19. Hammond cites Kleinfeld's work with indigenous peoples in Alaska. See Kleinfeld, Judith, "Effective Teachers of Eskimo and Indian Students," *The School Review*, vol. 83, no. 2, 1975, pp. 301–344. JSTOR, www.jstor.org/stable/1084645. Accessed 6 Nov. 2020.

20. Speaking about verbal feedback to young students, Peter Johnston argues that "Noticing first the part that is correct, or makes sense, is a perceptual bias we need to extend to students." This applies well to written feedback, too. See Johnston, Peter H., *Choice Words: How Our Language Affects Children's Learning*, Stenhouse Publishers, 2004, p.14.

21. Graham, Steve, and Dolores Perin, "Writing Next: Strategies to Improve Writing of Adolescents in Middle and High Schools," Carnegie Corporation of New York, Alliance for Excellent Education, 2007, www.carnegie.org/media/filer_public/3c/f5/3cf58727-34f4-4140-a014-723a00ac56f7/ccny_report_2007_writing.pdf.

22. Cummings, E. E., *E. E. Cummings Complete Poems, 1904-1962*, edited by George J. Firmage, Liveright Pub. Co., 1991.

23. This quotation is often attributed to management consultant Peter Drucker, but it does not appear that he said it. See O'Toole, Garson, "Culture Eats Strategy for Breakfast," Quote Investigator, 23 May 2017, quoteinvestigator.com/2017/05/23/culture-eats/.

CHAPTER EIGHT

1. Researcher Philip Jackson states that elementary teachers have 200 to 300 exchanges with students every hour—between 1,200 and 1,500 a day. Secondary school feels no less hectic. See Jackson, Philip Wesley, *Life in Classrooms*, Teachers College Press, 2009, p.149.

2. As you saw in Chapter 7, the way we speak to students signals to them who we think they are. In Vy's class, her language makes this clear.

CHAPTER NINE

1. Lorde, Audre, "The Master's Tools Will Never Dismantle the Master's House." *Sister Outsider: Essays and Speeches*, Crossing Press, 2007, pp. 110–114, http://s18.middlebury .edu/AMST0325A/Lorde_The_Masters_Tools.pdf.
2. Shanahan, Timothy. "Should We Teach Students at Their Reading Levels?: Consider the Research When Personalizing Your Lesson Plans," *Reading Today*, 2014, pp. 14–15.

CLOSING: THE CALL TO LOVE

1. Hayden, Robert, "Those Winter Sundays," *Poets,*1966, https://poets.org/poem/those -winter-sundays. Accessed 21 October 2020.

DISCUSSION GUIDE

1. The study of English, as we understand it today, didn't coalesce in the United States until the late 1800s. Before then, it was braided together from multiple traditions—ranging from grammar to rhetoric to literary history to prescriptive cultural indoctrination. Many of us want to imagine English as a concrete discipline with a tradition that stretches across centuries. In reality, our discipline was born of debate. Despite any pretense of pedigree, English instruction is undoubtedly a mutt. See Applebee, Arthur N., *Tradition and Reform in the Teaching of English: A History*, National Council of Teachers of English, 1976.
2. Popova, Maria, "Edgar Allan Poe on the Joy of Marginalia and What Handwriting Reveals About Character." Brain Pickings, 17 Sept. 2013, www.brainpickings.org/2013/09/17/edgar -allan-poe-marginalia/.
3. Burke, Kenneth, *The Philosophy of Literary Form*, University of California Press, 1974.
4. O'Connor, Flannery, *Mystery and Manners: Occasional Prose*, edited by Sally Fitzgerald and Robert Fitzgerald, Farrar, Straus & Giroux, 1969.

Index

productive struggle, finding, 154–167

questions, usage, 166–169

resource, supply/creation, 158–159

revoicing in, 181–184

schema, relationship, 157

sophisticate, 187–191

stamping,192–194

student leadership, 265

teacher planning template, 170–171, 196–197

Discourse habits, building, 177–192

#DisruptTexts, 23–24

Do Now, usage, 164

Douglass, Frederick, 30–33, 38, 164–165, 168

narrative, text (reordering), 42

Dowling, Kelly, 141–142

Doyle, Arthur Conan, 141

Driggs, Colleen, 39

Driven by Data 2.0 (Bambrick-Santoyo), 44, 113

Driveway moments, 225

Dunbar, Paul Lawrence, 124–125

Durant, Will, 184

Dutcher, Julia, 132

E

Ebarvia, Tricia, 23

End note, generation, 74–75, 77, 81

English

curricula, complexity, 30–46, 263–264

curricula, design, 23

instruction (execution), support (absence), 5

study, 4

English literary canon, biases, 32

Esperanza Rising (Muñoz Ryan), 178–179

Exemplar, 110–114, 236

analysis, 138

creation, 113

response, example, 170, 195

sparring, 112, 115, 241

Essential question, 30–31

Exemplar teacher annotation, 121f, 124f

Exit tickets, 114, 141

Explora Secondary Schools (EBSCO database), 60

F

Fariña, Richard, 7, 106, 115, 140

Feedback, 138–139

conferences, 235

targeted feedback, delivery, 234

written feedback, 233–234

Figurative language, 80, 88, 123

Fitzgerald, F. Scott, 49

Fitzgerald, Zelda Sayre, 52–53

Fluency, modeling, 226, 267

Forster, E.M., 109

Forward-looking feedback, usage, 233–235

Frame (rollout move), 250–252

Fun Home (Bechdel), 49, 50f, 78, 99

readings, 49, 51–53

G

Gabriel, Rachel, 215

Game of Thrones (Martin), 40

Gee, James, 214

Geographical knowledge, 27

Giver, The (Lowry), 226

class discussion, sample, 184–185

text complexity, 37

Gomez, Rebecca Lord, 221

Gonzalez, Emma, 117–118

Go Tell It on the Mountain (Baldwin), 99

Gradualism, 62

Graham, Vy, 162–163, 167–169, 249–250

Grapes of Wrath, The (quantitative complexity), 38

Great Depression, 62–63

Great Expectations (Dickens), 22

Great Gatsby, The (Fitzgerald), 49, 51–53

discussion, 161, 189

analysis, NEZZ (usage), 93–95
conferences, usage, 235
cycle, 172
opening prompt, absence, 169
power of ("Sonnet 65"), 112
skills, 44
Written feedback, 233–234
Written response, generation/usage,
127–128, 277

Z

Zelda (Milford), 52–53
Zone of proximal development, 156
Zooming in/out in analysis, 84–91,188
Zoom video conferencing software usage for
community and instruc-
tion, 266, 269